The Challenge of Religion

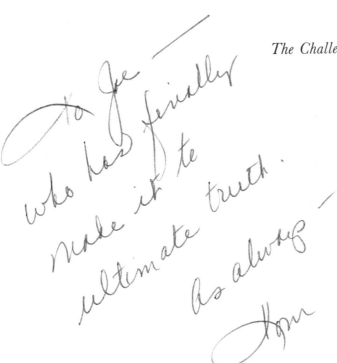

To Joe —
who has finally
made it to
ultimate truth.
As always
Tom

DATE DUE

GAYLORD PRINTED IN U.S.A.

The Challenge of Religion

A Philosophical Appraisal

by Thomas N. Munson

DUQUESNE UNIVERSITY PRESS
Pittsburgh, PA

Published in the United States of America
by Duquesne University Press
600 Forbes Avenue, Pittsburgh, PA 15282

Distributed by
Humanities Press, Inc.
Atlantic Highlands, NJ 07716

First Edition

Library of Congress Cataloging in Publication Data

Munson, Thomas N.
    The challenge of religion.

    Bibliography: p.
    Includes index.
    1. Religion—Philosophy.   I. Title.
BL51.M86   1985   200'.1   85-10297
ISBN 0-8207-0179-3
ISBN 0-8207-0181-5 (pbk.)

To the many friends who made the motto of
the University of Nijmegen appropriate:

In Dei Nomine Feliciter

Contents

Acknowledgements

IN ADDITION TO MY STUDENTS, I have been encouraged to write this book by friends who loyally struggled through my previous works on the subject: *Reflective Theology: Philosophical Orientations in Religion* (Yale University Press, New Haven, 1968) and *Religious Consciousness and Experience* (Martinus Nijhoff, The Hague, 1975). Most of these friends are years away from college philosophy and religion, but have been compelled by their children and grandchildren to question again the validity of a religious commitment. If this book offers them a portion of Socratic understanding and renewed hope, its purpose will have been attained.

I am grateful to the people whose supple minds and dexterous hands have contributed to this work's evolution. Many of its ideas have developed through conversations with Wilhelm Dupré, whose chair of philosophy of religion at Nijmegen I was privileged to occupy. Sometimes we wondered who it was that was enjoying a sabbatical· he officially, but I with an abundance of leisure and a congenial working atmosphere. For these advantages I am obliged to the philosophy and theology departments of the University of Nijmegen, in particular to their gracious secretaries and helpful librarians; to the Blessed Sacrament community at Brakkenstein, who provided life's necessities and an abundance of peace, quiet, and fraternal exchange in a mixture of French, German, English, and smidgen of *Nederlands*; and above all to Dietlind and Wilhelm Dupré who, in addition to their friendship and intellectual support, also appreciated the need for relaxing over a "Munson manhattan."

Introduction

HISTORICALLY, religion has always presented itself as a challenge to human thought and action. True, it may have become part of us along with our mother's milk, been re-enforced by familial and broader social ties or pressures, and deeply embedded in our patterns of thought through years of character training and formal education. Indeed, so natural is this formative process that, until comparatively recently in the history of humankind, the idea of humanity as "naturally religious" seemed not at all discordant. Yet however much a religious way of life may be the order of the day, the basic concepts of God and spirits, together with prescriptions and prohibitions regulating moral existence, emphasize the fact that religion is a call to action. It attests to our underlying disenchantment with the way things are, to the experience we all have at one time or another that we are all "cracked and live in a cracked world." We have to face up to human limitation and meet the frustrations of life with a measure of serenity that understanding may afford. Clearly, to invoke God and spirits is to locate the challenge of life on a personal plane. To regulate one's self so as to live in harmony with the world and with others becomes in religion a response: literally, a "promise back" or commitment that defines life's essentials in personal terms. Ecology—itself a

1

religious notion as has frequently been observed—would make us aware of the profound difference between looking upon nature as something to be exploited and regarding it as a gift, graciously accepted and respectfully treated. In this work we shall spell out further the meaning of religion as a personal challenge, that is, as a challenge to become a person.

It should be said at the outset that to write a work on religion, especially one from a philosophical angle, presents a peculiar sort of challenge. Religion, we are warned by the people who write about it, cannot be defined in universally acceptable terms. On the one hand, if we regard religion as a system of truths or beliefs concerning some kind of supernatural beings, we run the risk of intellectualizing religion, or making it simply into a certain set of facts of which we take cognizance. Methodists, for example, are such because they hold X, Y, and Z to be true, whereas Baptists believe A, B, and C, and Mormons L, M, and N. Some, therefore, have tried to define religion in terms of its origin: religion "grows out" of our sense of dependence or religion is the result of an effort to "overcome death," and so on. Such definitions prove unsatisfactory because we have no data regarding the origins of religion. There are those, on the other hand, who have essayed a functional definition of religion. In essence, they say that religions are sets of symbols that act as powerful motivational complexes. They aid us in facing up to death, in refusing to allow frustration and hostility to tear us or our human associations apart. In short, religion is our sanctuary of "ultimate concern."

That religion is motivational cannot be denied. But this kind of emphasis makes one wonder how religion is to be distinguished from any other "cause," whether political or humanitarian. Both Freud and Marx, who have influenced many contemporary writers on religion, illustrate some of the hazards of a restricted or slanted definition. Freud surmised that the origin of religion lay in the Oedipus complex, that is, in the particular difficulties of the socialization process in the human family. Religion, therefore, was to be envisaged as both the expression of a neurosis and its channeling in order to prevent the abnormality from interfering in our daily lives. In contrast, Marx—at least after a certain point in his career—saw the origin of religion in social inequality, and thus defined religion as a rationalization of an oppressive status quo. It is significant that in his earliest writings Marx had much to say about one's vocation in life and God's "inner call." It was with reluctance that he had to admit that the divine voice calling him to poetry was deceptive. At any rate, it is apparent that from either standpoint, Freudian or Marxist, religion is scarcely a necessary or inevitable aspect of being human.

The suggestion has been made that in our present circumstances, encumbered as we are with an unwieldy amount of information from anthropologists, sociologists, and other investigators into beliefs and practices, our real problem is not defining religion but finding it. What constitutes the religious meaning of a dance, a kiss, a building, a garment, a statue? For the moment let us simply answer *context*, and promise to elaborate the idea in the course of our study.

Within philosophy we are enjoying a period of relative calm, thanks to the truce between the warring factions of "analysts" and metaphysicians and between the devotees of Anglo-American and Continental philosophy. We have agreed to live and let live, either because the antagonists have exhausted themselves or because they have come to the recognition that their styles of philosophizing may indeed be complementary. And so, rather than tire the reader's patience by reliving those old battles, let me set forth the point of view espoused in this work.

I understand philosophy to be principally a reflective or critical activity. Naturally, when we criticize we do so to understand a position better. What is assumed in taking the position? Does it make sense of our experience and accord with the facts as we know them? Yet in the nature of the case our criticism cannot be wholly disinterested. Acknowledged or not, we start with our own presuppositions, which inevitably dictate how we evaluate responses to our queries. By ferreting out the various factors at work in a dialogue of this kind, philosophy would bring us to a deeper understanding of ourselves, that is, of the world of meaning in which we live. Hence a philosophical appraisal of religion means that accepting religion for the cultural phenomenon it is, we try to understand the kind of mentality or outlook it embodies. What, in fact, can we·learn about humanity, about, perhaps, an unexplored dimension of ourselves, from a closer look at some of the salient features of religious experience?

In this work "experience" is a crucial term, for one can account for the appeal of the Hare Krishnas, of The Way and similar cults, as well as for the attraction of the human potential movement, by their promise of the "experience" of an authentically religious or integral existence that fills the vacuum left by the mainline churches. The death of God during the fifties was followed by the counterculture of the sixties: youth's widespread experimentation with alternative styles of dress, living arrangements, social mores, politics and values. In religion many were looking for an "experience" of God, by which was meant something that would turn them on, give them, they believed, a permanent "high." As they had learned it, institutionalized religion frequently amounted to no more than a set of beliefs and moral norms; dutiful participation in stylized worship permitted one to ignore it as soon as one walked out the door of church or temple. Young people recognized this socially acceptable hypocrisy, not the least because their exposure to "counterculture" religions had taught them that religion calls for a radical conversion, a change of mind and heart. In their voluntary submission to the rigors of meditating and chanting, young enthusiasts have displayed a deep-seated hankering for discipline that the regimentation of the churches apparently did not kill. The cults have met this need with wholesale programming and the skillful enforcement of conformity, and have thus given purpose and direction to many lives that previously were feckless. The discipline of the cults is the training ground for "experience." Hence it is misleading to think of experience as some kind of inner occurrence, an ineffable interior happening that can never be captured by another. Rather, "to experience" is derived from the Latin *experior*, meaning "to try" or "to make an attempt." But its roots suggest that this attempt is related to a skill. One tries because he or she is experienced or on the way to becoming an expert (*peritus*). Consequently, having divorced our understanding of it from personal feeling, we must associate an "experience" with giving people standards or criteria of judgment, which, in turn, enable them to make sense out of things and so "have an experience." The cults illustrate my point. They offer an experience insofar as they provide norms for experiencing.

If I have belabored this point, it is because my impression is that many people have turned away from institutional churches or organized religion because of false expectations. They are looking for God, for the divine, they tell us: for an experience of the kind described by the mystics. Surely if the churches serve a purpose, this must be it. But the churches have become institutions. Their concern often appears to be theology, with religion as a by-product: correctness of dogmatic formulæ, not the exhilaration that stems from a living faith. Needless to say, these complaints are well-founded, but from my point of view wrongheaded. They attest the inadequacy of the churches as effective socializing agents. For patterns of thinking to be taught they must be verbalized. Yet however effectively inculcated, a program of any kind will fail to achieve lasting results if it is not sufficiently re-enforced both by the learner and by those who share his or her way of life. Until this socialization is accomplished, the shaping to a form of life can be restrictive, even repressive, if for no other reason than that knowledge makes a bloody entrance. As is the case with a language framework, German, French or whatever, we are restricted by grammatical rules, canonized modes of expression, and most seriously by a point of view, by the set of concepts that, albeit limiting, enables us to communicate and thus to expand. Church doctrine and discipline function in a similar way. By educating us to a form of life, they open us to "experience," to test that life by making use of norms and thus to come to a creative understanding of it and its possibilities. The emphasis here is upon *creative*, for more often than not, the expected socialization is not realized because of a failure to interiorize. Our education, quite literally a "leading out" of our capabilities, is defective because we are locked into the forms of understanding appropriate to children or beginners. Children require hard-and-fast answers not finely-nuanced moral distinctions. They become familiar with the spiritual world through stories and pictures. But creativity, especially if it is to remain faithful to the tradition thus learned, requires the grasp of principles, a level of understanding that enables us to be flexible. On this level we are principled, able, that is, to generate life and meaning.

This book began as an effort to meet the concerns of my undergraduate students at the University of Nijmegen, The Netherlands, where the philosophy of religion still retains a respected if unpretentious niche. Because many of them had taken up theology in order to find religion, all of their questions revolved around the basic issue: What kind of thinking, expressing, imagining goes on in religion? Can you explain to us how it functions so that we can determine its relevance? The terms I wanted to use, principally 'myth' and 'symbol', and the issues I had to engage, creation, for instance, and ritual enactment, necessitated my meandering about in our philosophical and theological history. Our language bears the scars of our controversial past, and a reliving of that past is indispensable to an understanding of religion because frequently only a hair's breadth separates orthodoxy from heterodoxy. Besides, it is not only in philosophy that our conceptions and models hold us captive. Too often religion is irrelevant because the images its language conjures up bamboozle us. Moreover, I have had to have recourse to our history because this book proposes an historical thesis that is essential to an understanding of the current religious situation. It was that thesis which necessitated a shift of emphasis from the structure of religion as such to its developments within our culture.

From a world-historical perspective, the deviant nature of these developments piques one's curiosity. Contrary to mankind's perennial apprehension as *homo religiosus*—an understanding attested by countless archæological finds from the Neolithic Age onwards, and thus a well-substantiated fact—we are, thanks to a group of thinkers and propagandists who flourished during the seventeenth and eighteenth centuries in that tiny segment of the globe known as Western Europe, to understand ourselves as *homo technicus*, as enlightened, rational beings whose science has liberated us from religion's superstitions.

Whether or not Voltaire and his followers were intent upon describing or dictating what comprises genuine human experience is arguable, since the answer is probably a little bit of both. But what is incontrovertible is that they inaugurated a trend of thought that appears to most Asians and Africans an ineradicable element of Western culture.

That trend of thought became dominant in the period of modern philosophy, roughly from Descartes (d. 1650) through Kant (d. 1804), which from its different emphases is known in the trade as the Age of Rationalism, of Immanence, of Enlightenment, of Subjectivism. Not all the thinkers of the period were infected by Voltaire's anti-ecclesiastical animus. On the contrary, many of them were personally committed to religious values. But in the aftermath of the Reformation and of the religious wars that ensued, philosophers heeded Descartes' proposal to established a "neutral" philosophy, one that in principle was untethered by religious constraints. If philosophers today, however, refuse to take religion seriously, it is in part because the process of freeing philosophy from the medieval theologies in which it had become embedded took an anti-religious turn. Voltaire, of course, had established the precedent. His hostility to the religion he found in the Church blinded him to the possible merits of religion as such. Yet this refusal stems also in part from Hume and Kant, who many contemporary philosophers believe sounded the death knell for "rational" religion. Interestingly, their premises and those of modern philosophers generally are being seriously challenged by some philosophers, as we shall see, and it is part of the purpose of this book to call attention to the derivation of some of those premises from religion. Whatever its preachments, modern philosophy, like Plato's, came to birth in religion—a fact of utmost importance not only for the reestablishment of a dialogue between philosophy and religion, but for the understanding of religion itself.

Were religion simply a set of concepts, a sort of intellectual game and not a way of life, a discussion of its issues would surely be less convoluted. As it is, an angle of vision that was at first sharply focused soon begins to blur and can no longer be clearly distinguished from others. It behooves my reader, therefore, to consider himself or herself as entering into a dialogue. As in any prolonged conversation, I have had to go back to pick up loose ends. Key ideas are such because they open many doors, and it has proved impossible to pass through more than one at a time. Insofar as our discussion is philosophical, it has been generated by the historical current we call modern philosophy: a history than can be read in a variety of ways and is rich in its suggestions. Perforce, I find myself assuming divergent standpoints in an effort to comprehend the impact of that history on religious thought. A measure of repetition is therefore unavoidable, and the book itself must be read as a whole if its parts are not to be taken as the final word. I apologize in advance for the limitations attendant upon a dialogue in written form. Face to face, we can express ourselves in diversified ways because we detect misunderstanding or note an obvious lacuna. In lieu of such an encounter, I have chosen topics for discussion that can both illuminate the structure of religion and highlight its conceptual evolution.

CHAPTER I

Religion as Framework

I am still intrigued by an episode that occurred a number of years ago at the end of a lecture given by Godfrey Lienhardt, the British social anthropologist, at the University of Chicago. Having discussed his travails among the Dinka while doing the fieldwork that was published in *Divinity and Experience: The Religion of the Dinka*,[1] he was asked by a member of the audience precisely what it was that he had investigated. "I really don't know," was the shrewd reply: from my point of view an answer that perceptively undercut the presupposition of the question. There was no single, readily identifiable, empirical item labelled "Dinka religion" that presented itself for scientific observation. Indeed, Lienhardt discovered what all other investigators of the religious phenomenon have come to accept: 1) that an investigation cannot be conducted on the basis of the investigator's predetermined concepts of what religion is or ought to be; and 2) that a religious system of beliefs, with its concrete expression in rites and objects, is a whole attitude toward life, and thus in most instances is interwoven with other aspects of a culture: a village layout, economic and social relations, political organization, etc. This makes for a great deal of vagueness in the whole undertaking.

1. Oxford: Clarendon Press, 1961.

9

Our penchant for clear-cut definitions and neatly determined objects is frustrated. Yet today we have come to accept in our academic research a situation taken for granted in everyday existence. We know that attitudes are important: in social relations, in job interviews, in political confrontations. The whole advertising business is built on the manipulation, or less pejoratively, the cultivation of attitudes. A winning product can owe its success to the right adjective: "smooth," "luxurious," "cool"; newspapers and magazines thrive on emotionally charged descriptions; many a jury has been persuaded by a passionate appeal. Is not part of the attraction of science the fact that "scientific" can insinuate the idea of an objective or value-free appraisal? Educators, accordingly, are more willing to accept themselves as engaged in a benevolent sort of brain-washing, in the development of structures of understanding. Facts have their place, but of themselves do not produce the cultured person. An education has been a success if it has engendered the right attitude, that is, has provided a framework and the motivation for the real task, self-education.

Religious education is this kind of undertaking. The development of religious perceptions and habits follows the same course we pursue in teaching a child language skills and social behavior. It would never enter into our minds to wait until a person is "old enough to choose for himself" before we equip him with the basic requirements of social existence. Learning to sit properly on a chair, to handle a knife and fork with dexterity, and to use the tongue and throat in ways suitable to our native language, is a formation, restrictive as any kind of training is. Yet we do not think this kind of education inhibiting. On the contrary, "the development of skills" has a positive ring about it. We regard ourselves truly as educators, as taking the necessary steps to "bring out" the real person. In like manner, religious people, through words and deeds, inculcate their vision of life. Whether religious or not, all parents and teachers just by living communicate a world of meaning: an outlook that is not simply intellectual but shot through with values, with a whole way of handling and feeling things. We readily forget that a language is more than a vocabulary, grammar and syntax. In learning French or

Italian, for example, we are taking on a way of life: intonations and gestures, of course, but likewise a mentality that expresses itself in distinctive works of art, music, literature, even in ways of driving a car. Because the emphasis in formal education is upon the word, we naturally think of teaching as simply a verbal communication, as providing children with a system of truths or beliefs, the set of facts, as it were, that in religion comprise the Word of God or religious "science." Yet our teaching belies this narrow conception. Along with a creed we instill attitudes of worship and prayer. Stories are told that embody moral principles: how one is to deal with the poor and unfortunate, to handle injustice, to cope with suffering. The lives of saints or heroes are narrated to concretize ideals and stimulate action. In liturgical celebration not only is the life of the community shared but the meaning of its creed specified.

That religions have functioned as this kind of comprehensive socializing is evident from both secular and religious history. Indeed, it is because people are aware of the power of education to shape lives that special interest groups have sought to control it. In the United States the public school was established as a nursery for democracy, with the result that sectarian education was branded divisive and anti-American. Nazi Germany concentrated on the Hitler Youth, and membership in the Konsomol in the Soviet Union has been necessary for any kind of further advancement. Would Plato's *Republic* have been complete without his program of education? The minds of the young must be captured if any form of ideology is to have a hold on the future. Yet, unlike the kind of framework we learn if we want to study biology or physics, a religious framework must be seen as a total scheme, as affording one a holistic sense of life: a reason to live and a reason to die. In this way it is truly comprehensive, holding within itself other, oftentimes overlapping horizons of meaning that can readily conflict. How do we unify the different viewpoints represented in the terms "nature" and "energy," or "technology" and "humanity"? If "religion" and "science" are in conflict, one cannot harmonize them simply by stating that they are different frameworks.

As I am using the word, a framework is not a once-and-for-all mold, an invariant structure that we impose on people. On the contrary, my earlier use of the word "attitude" and reference to language indicate that a framework is to be understood as a mode of understanding or knowledge structure that permits one to think. If I know nothing about chemistry, I do not think in chemical terms, and chemical data and techniques are beyond my ken. But once I am taught the rudiments and "get into the groove," I can live the life of chemistry. A whole world is open to me: an experience which further unfolds and in turn modifies my initial framework. Has not the basic problem in religion been that it appears to be a closed system, that it has provided someone with a bag of truths, the "God package," which is henceforth to be carried unsullied through life? Static molds have bred ignorance and intolerance; living frameworks enhance our understanding and our being. They are truly educative.

Although to the hostile critic religious people are imprisoned in an unreflected, archaic structure, the history of religions itself would contradict this judgment. A perusal of Marshall Hodgson's *The Venture of Islam: Conscience and History in a World Civilization*[2] affords but one example of how the framework triggered by the visions of Muhammed was accommodated to the development of Islam from a tribal, Arabian Peninsula religion to a world religion. Even before it adapted itself to the requirements of a missionary and imperial power, while Muhammed was still alive, the framework produced by the insight that man stands individually before God in total responsibility had to be fleshed out so that it could be an efffective pattern for daily life. A framework, I said, permits and stimulates thought, and that is why I have designated it a mode of understanding. We come to understanding, the Socratic *phronesis*, by developing the logic within our system. Growth requires this becoming aware of the entailments of our initial commitment so that we can adapt ourselves and our frameworks to our personal situations.

After the period of rapid conquest, the followers of Muhammed gradually settled, albeit as rulers, into a peaceful co-

2. Chicago and London: The University of Chicago Press, three volumes, 1974.

existence with their subjects, notably Christians and Jews. Inevitably there was some form of religious dialogue, which is the sort of thing that instigates reflection upon one's framework. This, in my terminology, is the critical moment in understanding, when one calls into question the validity of his standpoint. We all face questions concerning our frameworks: Why economics? Why history? One way of responding to the question is that ordinarily employed by economists and historians. They show us the logic of their systems: how their viewpoints enable them to make sense out of an accumulation of data. But the question actually demands more, for it is asking for a justification of the methods and the kind of knowledge offered by economics and history. This further critical moment is, properly speaking, philosophical. It turns the economist or historian, who normally takes notions of truth, proof and evidence for granted, into a philosopher of economics or history. In this kind of understanding we have passed beyond the logic within the system to the rationale of the system itself. The question: Why history? naturally leads to the next question: Why history rather than biology? In this perspective, religious understanding also involves us the further query: Why religion at all?

Before turning our attention to the question of how one goes about justifying a religious framework, which is to say, the question of what is specific about religion, let us consider briefly how we might use the conventional terms, 'faith' and 'reason', in a way consistent with our language thus far. The terms, to be sure, are freighted with theological controversy. Still, they are congenial to our viewpoint; and although my usage of them is in some respects indebted to Immanuel Kant, it is not my intention to embrace his philosophy.

In his book, *Personal Knowledge*, Michael Polanyi has noted:

Science is a system of beliefs to which we are committed. Such a system cannot be accounted for either from experience as seen within a different system, or by reason without any experience. Yet this does not signify that we are free to take it or leave it, but simply reflects the fact that it *is* a system of beliefs to which we are committed and which therefore cannot be represented in non-committal terms.[3]

Science, in our terminology, is a framework, an horizon of meaning that enables us to explore the world in a fruitful way. Anyone, therefore, who gears him or herself to do science begins with a *given*: a complex of techniques and meanings that have developed over time through trial and error. For most of us, that system works. It enables us to organize a certain amount of data, to work with these to produce useful results, and to predict: by adopting certain procedures we know what will happen. We are not seers, reading the future. We simply know what results are to be anticipated by making use of certain means. Given, therefore, implies not only givenness; it also means that there are limits to our knowledge. Our investigation is contextual, hemmed in by the framework to which we are committed. Kant called this counterpart to our knowledge "faith," for it is by our commitment to a limiting horizon that knowledge of any kind is possible. His distinction of Understanding from Reason marks the difference between what I have called a logic within a system, the rational development of a framework, and the rationale of the system itself.

Perhaps this distinction becomes clearer when we view it from another perspective. As humans we find ourselves in a world, caught up in a cultural environment because our bodies have situated us in a definite time and place. Such is our "existential" predicament: unavoidable because we are human, yet revealed to us as a predicament only because we have Reason, a thinking capacity that enables us to transcend the particularities of our existence. Over time and history we can reach out to those of other lands and cultures, for the power of Reason consists in abstraction, in drawing us out (*abs-trahere*) of those peculiarities arising from our bodily condition to a level of universal comprehension. The exactness or precision of Reason stems from its prescinding activity. Its universal or impersonal quality is manifested in perhaps its greatest triumph, mathematics. Once the

3. *Personal Knowledge: Toward a Post-Critical Philosophy*, London: Routledge & Kegan Paul, Ltd., 1973 (1958), 171.

numbers and signs are understood, there is no arguing about the fact that 2+2=4, an "eternal" or universal truth because it escapes the limits of perspective imposed by our bodies. If this is the nature of Reason, then "faith" is that total human or existential situation in which Reason is rooted and from which in reasoning we step back. Faith is thus the realm of the whole man, of the personal or inter-subjective environment, that gives birth to Reason which, in turn, appears impersonal or objective.

Polanyi spoke of a system of *beliefs*, an indispensable term in the language of commitment and one I find appropriate to the conception of faith presented here. To understand its religious usage, we have to reject our heritage of polemics, particularly the bandying about of Tertullian's unhappy phrase: *Credo quia absurdum* (I believe because it is absurd). Who would commit him or herself to what is patently irrational?

Two commonly used expressions provide an insight into 'believe' that are significant for us. In most cases when I say "I believe Smith," I mean that I can accept what Smith says because he is competent or knowledgeable. Smith may possess an expertise that I lack, or he may simply know something that at the moment I do not because I have had neither the time nor the inclination to learn it. In principle, his knowledge could be mine. But rather than spend the time or energy to acquire it, I assume that what he says is true. Believing him, therefore, rests upon Smith. Were Smith known to lie or to be ignorant, I would scarcely believe him.

The circumstances are obviously different when we tell someone: I believe in you. Knowledge is not the point except insofar as a special knowledge of the person elicits our trust. In fact, our belief may fly in the face of common knowledge, as when we tell someone that we believe in him despite what others say. Our belief voices personal commitment, which has made this kind of language particularly suited to person- or God-focused religions. In these, faith or the givenness of the framework has its origin in a special occurrence. Something happened to Abraham, for example, or to Moses or Muhammed, that triggered an horizon of meaning. God, we are told, revealed himself, so that the framework is not simply a given but a gift. The attitude that it inculcates is personal: a respect for everything in creation as a gift and a love of gratitude for the person who is the giver, the ultimate source of the meaning of things. Religion thus begins in that response to a challenge in which one, in gratitude, promises back. Even in Buddhism where the role of a personal god and the language of belief are muted, the basic pattern is similar. Something happened to Gotama under the bodhi tree. He was enlightened, favored with a vision in which he saw the unity of all things, an insight that translated itself into an attitude of profound respect. Love, therefore, has in all these traditions been the unique criterion of the religious person. Both in Hinduism, in which personal gods like Vishnu and Shiva are conspicuous and the bhakti (love of God) movement has had its impact, and in Buddhism, the freedom of the enlightened person manifests itself in a profound peace and graciousness that one does not hesitate to call a love for all things. In Judaism, Christianity and Islam, the precept to love God and one's neighbor is clearly formulated and hailed as the true mark of the believer.

When Polanyi claims that although science is a system of beliefs, we are not free to take it or leave it, I understand him to mean that science is so much a part of our notion of reality that it would be foolish to suppose that we can say: it is just another system, an hypothesis with which we can readily dispense. An example of what I have in mind is our use of terms like manic-depressive and schizophrenic. By organizing disparate forms of behavior into a comprehensive pattern, it affords us understanding. But because there is no simple, easily identifiable, empirical object called "schizophrenia," are we to say that it is "just a word," only a "way of thinking"? Whatever this kind of faulty epistemology may lead us to suppose, if a person shows the signs, we had better treat him as he *really* is. Thus we might suggest that the commitment to science is twofold. We are free to embrace it on the level of interest, preferring either sociology or psychology as a subject of personal concern. But we are not free at this stage of thought in our culture to accept or reject the methods and discoveries that constitute our science. For better or for worse, we are part of the technological age.

For many years religion enjoyed the same privileged position

in our culture as science does now. People were free to pursue it
or not as an item of academic or other interest; they were not free
to take it or leave it. It was too much a part of the culture, too
built into the whole pattern of thought and action to be jettisoned. Theoretically, of course, it always remained a choice, the
fundamental moral act of one's existence. But practically the
social pressures were too great, and political pressure was there
to enforce these. Now, however, in our changed situation, the
question of the justification of the religious framework is paramount. Like any other system, it must present itself as consistent. Its rationale must be developed so as to display its
entailments. To what, in other words, are we committed by the
system? But because religion, unlike other frameworks, is not
limited to a determinate field of data but offers a total view of
life's meaning, we cannot organize and predict in the abstract or
piecemeal way we do when operating within more limited frameworks. The extent and duration of its existence can prevent us
from dismissing religion out of hand as useless, for it has offered
"folk like ourselves" a meaningful way to live and to die. Yet an
attention to the diversity of viewpoints within that general
framework and the historical accidents that have created division and hostility can deter us from the critical question: Does
religion as such have a criterion or criteria whereby we can judge
it as a satisfactory or fruitful outlook?

Although this question presupposes a pluralistic milieu —
religions are classified as "higher," i.e., no longer tribal, when
expansion beyond their original geographical limits has necessitated a theological and apologetic development that other mentalities can assimilate — such a criterion, I believe, is suggested
for religion in my proposal that faith be thought as functioning
like a language. When we distinguish our language from another, we presuppose a totality of meaning — all the words of the
Oxford English Dictionary, for instance — that none of us ever
grasps in its entirety. English is a given, but our proficiency in it
requires the development of skills: the ability to form proper
sentences and to use the elements of the language in a constructive way. We are formed by our language. But we, in turn, form
it, shape it to the exigencies of daily living. We act, Martin

Heidegger noted, as if we were the shapers and masters of language, whereas it is language which remains our mistress. It is a creative art insofar as with it we forge new or striking modes of expression. Yet it likewise creates us by providing us with rich and variegated ways of communicating. Through communication we commune, we enter into unity with other people. If, therefore, we are to become persons, we must open ourselves to this kind of *comm-union*, to a genuine "becoming one with" others that conversational chitchat or a superficial talking *to* or listening *to* others does not achieve. It is this formative character of language that has led religious people to use the expression, "the Word of God," a Word that is effective, creative: "by His Word all things came to be."

The point can be illustrated from a rather dismal episode in our history. In the medical, psychiatric report issued on the prisoners of war during the Korean conflict, there was a description of the process by which a group of prisoners were effectively "brainwashed." After a careful screening, the group consisted mainly of "followers"; the more forceful, thoroughly principled types had been sent elsewhere. First, an appeal was made to a sense of fair play. "Hear our side of the story. . ." Unwittingly, the group found itself in a course of indoctrination in which psychological, not physical, techniques were used with the utmost skill. After a time the group was invited to participate in criticism sessions. These were responded to with some hesitation, but scruples were gradually overcome by the rationalization: "We're all Americans. Who is going to take it seriously? It's just a game."

The sessions began innocently enough. It was a joke; people had a chance to communicate and thus get to know one another. But that was the problem. They did get to know one another, for they soon discovered that they could not forever engage in trivialities. People were soon returning from these sessions upset because they had said too much. Others *were* listening, taking seriously what had been meant in jest, and, so it was believed, judging.

The outcome, to be sure, was psychologically devastating. When the group had been liberated and disembarked in Tokyo for treatment and rest before returning home, they were told that they could call anyone in the United States at government expense. Over fifty percent refused to talk to anyone. In the hospital these ex-prisoners were loners. In contrast to the gregariousness that one usually finds in such circumstances, the people did not talk to one another. When they went to town, they went alone.

The point is ovbious. The "brain washers" had succeeded in destroying communication because they had undercut the normal confidence we have in people. Generally, we take our reliance on others for granted. It never enters into our minds that the communication of "intellectual" truth rests upon veracity, upon the "truth" or openness of people to meaning. Most of us, at least unconsciously, choose "coherence," repudiating the "violence," the nonsense that ensues when 'yes' means 'no'. What these prisoners taught us was that the refusal of communication spelt personal death. Because they were not personable, they lost their own personalities: their identities before others and before themselves.

All the world, we say, loves a lover. Yes, we all appreciate the kindness, the compassion, the humanity that characterizes the truly humane or loving person. But as the Korean episode indicates, our love is a matter of life and death. By it we live or die precisely because it is the only thing that we truly own. Most other facets of our lives lie beyond our complete control, especially vital concerns like jobs and health. Our love is completely ours: ours to give or not for no one else can command it. Its very spontaneity makes love a treasure, for its unwarranted bestowal is the gift of a person, his or her quality as a human being. For every civilization love has thus been sacred. It consecrates us, literally, makes us holy: in religion by making us whole, capable, that is, of giving and receiving such a gift.

Throughout the rest of this work we will, in considering different aspects of the religious framework, be putting this criterion to the test. Why, we want to know, is religion necessary for our humanity? For the moment, however, I hope that the general picture is clear: that religion functions as a horizon of meaning; that unlike most other frameworks, it is a comprehensive view of life, affording us a reason to live and a reason to die; that unlike even other total views such as Marxism, if compelled to discuss provenance, it has recourse to events or occurrences "in illo tempore," either in that faraway time of tribal fathers and heroes or in that of the prophet whose encounter with God or the sacred inaugurated a religious pattern of thought; that its criterion as a meaningful way of life is love, its capacity to develop integral persons.

Since the purpose of this work is not polemical, I shall not attempt an extensive refutation of competing world views. Perhaps I can point out what I consider to be the inadequacies of some of them as we pursue specific topics. At this point let us give closer attention to that pervasive personalism which I have singled out as characteristic of the religious viewpoint. No doubt it is the failure of religion to fulfill this expectation that has given rise to its competitors. Theism has always been the generator of atheism.

The word "person" hides within itself the basic tension of the human situation: being individual yet social. I like the word "individual." Its Latin root, *individuum*, expresses our individuality as something undivided: integral, no doubt, but likewise undivided from others. Our use of the word "person" has, to a degree, gotten away from its original meaning. The *persona* was the mask worn by actors, concealing the individual behind a role, the comic or tragic appearance displayed to the public. In our use of the word with its stress on the uniqueness of the individual, we have retained the idea that one's person(ality) is what is displayed to others. What we have added to the original usage, comic or tragic, is the idea of development. We manifest to others what we have become. We are born human; we become persons.

I mention these nuances of terminology because, as we know, not every age has been as self-conscious as our own. In cities of the classical Greek period, a person's worth was adjudged by his conduct in public affairs. A private, family life was regarded as restrictive. The full life was that lived in the presence of one's fellow citizens; its principal measuring stick was, accordingly, oratorical ability. This primacy of the civic or public is apparent in Greek biography and history. The lives of heroes were written as paradigms, and the purpose of historical narrative was, in Thucydides' words, that the memory of great deeds not be forgotten. Greek biographers and historians were moralists. They proffered examples of virtuous conduct principally for edification. Because virtue was civic, Socrates, not to mention other Greek philosophers, was accused of impiety. By disturbing the life of the city, he was an affront to the gods.

The dominant religions of the West, Judaism, Christianity and Islam, are rooted in this world which accorded primacy to the group. The bringing of the Hebrew nomadic tribes together as a people was attributed to Moses. The covenant they made with Yahweh not only made them *his* people but *a* people, so that even today the question is raised whether being Jewish is religious or racial. Salvation, therefore, was to be sought by becoming part of the people: a conviction that forms the background of several New Testament narratives of Jesus in debate with his opponents. Because his followers accepted Jesus as the foretold Messiah, they naturally regarded themselves as constituting the "new Israel." To follow him entailed incorporation into the people of God, "his body," just as his specially selected disciples formed a group known as "the twelve."

Along with this communal emphasis, both Judaism and Christianity as religions address us as moral beings. The call to repentance is above all a challenge to the individual conscience. Inevitably, then, one who responds to this challenge is drawn into the dialectic of person, into becoming through interaction with others. A similar structure is to be found in Islam. The individual's submission to God incorporates the believer into the group, the Ummah, for which he, in turn, takes total, personal responsibility. Only in the great traditions of the Far East, Hinduism and Buddhism, is an adherence to a group deemed unessential. Salvation, in these traditions, comes through the achievement of enlightenment, not through the gift of divine redemption. *Nirvana* and *satori* are of their nature individual accomplishments. One makes use of the techniques of meditation and/or Yoga that will bring freedom: the stilling of disruptive desires that destroy inner harmony and one's fundamental unity with the cosmos. Still, the criterion remains, as for the redemptive religions, the person: the integrated human being who expresses oneself in "works of charity." Because things are weighted differently here, we must not overlook the identity of religious impulse. The manifestation or becoming of person — the drama in Greece which introduced the concept had religious origins — arises from the challenge to become human. The moment of religion, therefore, is likewise the moment of humanity.

To understand what is happening to or in religion in the area that we commonly call "the West," — I have accepted common parlance even though specialists rightfully quibble about our territorial designations; culturally, a significant part of the "Middle East" is "Western" — we might ponder some of the events of our history which have borne heavily upon the dialectic of person. What, we may wonder, do young people find in the religions of the East that they have not found in the West? What is the attraction of Zen? The magic of a Maharishi or a Maharaj Ji? Is it simply that they cast the spell of a person in a way that it is impossible for the "mainline" or "institutionalized" churches?

Western religion, I remarked, is community oriented. By noting the verbal relationships: "community," "commune," "communion," etc., I have intended to stress that feeling of belonging which is the essential ingredient of the experience of community. The early Christian community was tightly knit together by persecution. Followers of "the Way" found fulfillment in bearing witness to their master. The personal awareness of being in and with Christ had cosmic repercussions: it signalled the redemption of the world, the bringing of all mankind into the unity of God. The Jewish sense of belonging was put to the test once again in the year 70 A.D., when the Romans under Titus destroyed their temple. From that time the Torah was, perhaps more than ever, the rallying point for the Jews. It sustained them through centuries of persecution: a repression never so persistently visited upon Christians or Muslims, with the result that if the sense of community has diminished among young Jews, one tends to account for it by excessive legalism. In Judaism, as in all religion, the zeal for minute observance can extinguish the spirit of the law. The experience of Islam runs parallel to the Christian. Persecution in Mecca brought a unified community to Medina. In its period of early expansion, cohesiveness was maintained because it spread among the Bedouin: people, like the Jews who were the first Christians, with a strong sense of tribal loyalty. But as Islam spread beyond the confines of the Arabian peninsula and rapidly became an empire stretching at first from Nile to Oxus, how was the experience of community to be kept alive? Someone modestly conversant with Islam can read into the disputes regarding succession, into the collecting and sorting of reports concerning Muhammed and his early followers, into the arguments over the interpretation of the Qur'an, as well as over the role to be played by Medina and its first families, an effort to keep alive that initial, deeply felt Islamic unity and the experience of the Prophet that originated it. Within Christianity the situation was no different. How does one sustain community in an empire?

The experience of the American Catholic Church illustrates the problem. The periods of greatest immigration brought Catholics from Europe who, by and large, settled in cities where jobs were available. Poles, Germans, Slovaks, Italians: all naturally gravitated to sections of a city where they were among their own. The tedium of work could be relieved by old country celebrations; the foreignness of the new ways could be diluted with a mixture of traditional customs. In these circumstances, the Church proved a bastion of security. Above all, it represented continuity: the universal succession of feasts, the time honored services conducted in the universal language, Latin. But in addition it offered status to the menial laborer; its schools gave one's children opportunities for economic and social betterment; the hostility it invoked among one's non-Catholic neighbors only enhanced it as a focal point for one's loyalties. We can envisage the situation as a replica of the pictures we have seen of late medieval towns, which grew up around churches and monasteries. Not only a religious life but practically one's whole social existence has a single focus. In this way religion served as a social cement. The history of socially marginal groups confirms the picture. For confirmation today, we need only look to the experiences of minorities: the French in British Canada, Catholics in Northern Ireland, Kurds or Assyrians in Khomeini's Iran.

The search for community evidently cannot be a return to the sources in the sense that in a history defying mood one can successfully turn back the clock. It is folly to suppose that we can revert to the days of the primitive Christian community, under the delusion that its experience was one of uninterrupted internal harmony and peace. But the problem that prompts the dream of a return is acute. The turn toward the East is symptomatic of it. Unlike the present generation of middle-aged and older people, contemporary American youth have not grown up in neighborhoods. A grouping may be sociologically and economically homogeneous, but in general the sense of community is lacking. We can laugh at the busybodies of Sinclair Lewis' *Main Street*. But in doing so, have we turned "minding one's business" into a vice? Have polite greetings been made to mask a pervasive indifference? Indeed, it appears that the ethics of the marketplace have infiltrated the home. Because the Church no longer plays its cementing role, it is relegated further into social irrelevancy. Since Vatican II, the division caused by liturgical changes and shifts of emphases has deepened alienation.

Can we not interpret the winds of change sweeping through the Islamic world as symptomatic of a similar malaise? The experience that brought Muhammed to a complete submission of himself to Allah transformed him into a prophet: into one called to announce to all mankind its duty of obedience. The response to that obligation, of its nature an act of mind and heart, had to be like dropping a stone into a placid lake. The ripples of one's internal change were to extend out even beyond household and village to the farthest reaches of humanity. All the world must be brought to this divine submission. Islam was essentially a missionary enterprise, in duty bound to shape the world according to its own ideal. For the true believer, there could never be a divorce of inner from outer.

Bearing this in mind, we can appreciate the attraction of Islamic "fundamentalism," essentially, as is in the West, a call to return to beliefs and practices that created and flourished in Islam's golden age. Today the governments of the Islamic world are, for the most part, secular institutions, committed to Islam in theory, if at all, yet compelled by force of circumstances to curtail a missionary zeal that would change the social order. In fact, government under Islam has always been some kind of compromise. There were those willing to surrender power and grant authority to the caliphate in the name of Ummah unity. But there were also those who prized the religion's Bedouin traditions, notably an uncompromisingly equal standing of all men. The absolutist tendency in a central government was abhorrent to them: a disposition that has perdured down through the centuries and turned itself into a cause in our own times. Instead of consisting of a people, an Ummah, the Islamic world has been divided by Western colonialist powers whose values, principally secularist and materialist, have prevailed. As a result, the world of Islamic culture is endangered, for the experience that brought it into being is almost impossible to realize. The remedy, of course, has been tried countless times before: change the world by turning back the clock.

Clearly this study is not sociological, but these commonplaces serve to remind us that religion is inescapably a cultural phenomenon, deeply rooted in and formative of a spiritual, intellectual and social milieu. At the time when Christians and Muslims came to realize this fact, first, no doubt, when their missionary enthusiasm necessitated a translation of their conversion into verbal, intellectually comprehensible form — the encounter with Jesus or following of "the way" and the wholehearted submission of oneself to God surely entail certain committals that must be articulated if another is to be convinced — and later when their political ascendancy enabled them to alter prevailing social arrangements, definite decisions were made which, I believe, are pertinent to our situation. To repeat: the problem is that religions which are meant to teach us norms of experiencing to facilitate an encounter with God, and which in their beginnings could do so more readily because they fostered communities in which like-minded people, through close personal contact, could mutually re-enforce one another, gradually found themselves developing into institutions. If converts were to be made and the intellectually curious were to be satisfied, the experience had to be crystallized. As we shall see, many things reverberate from the missionary vocation that rapidly changes a personal conversion into a commitment with extensive societal ramifications.

Although I have used the word "decision" in reference to the inevitable process of adaptation, we should not suppose that in every case a conscious determination was made. That Christianity became a religion of the book was not a consequence of a general weighing of the matter, as if the early Christians felt the need for their own scriptures after they had made the final break with the synagogue. Quite the contrary. Luke wrote his book of *Acts* so that some kind of historical record might be available. The Pauline letters are exhortations and admonitions, principally to the churches founded by Paul. Evangelists assembled the traditions of the various churches into written form because the older generation was dying out and the memories of the life and deeds of Jesus of Nazareth must be kept afresh if one is to follow him. The Qur'an, on the other hand, represents itself for most Muslims as the direct revelation of God: revelations accorded Muhammed that provided guidance for the changing circumstances of his life. In comparison with the sacred books of the Eastern traditions, the *Mahabharata*, the *Bhagavad Gita* and the like, Western scriptures, as we know, became normative. It is this fact that accounts for periodic bursts of fundamentalism: a return to "Scripture alone" without the embellishments that the course of history inevitably adds.

It is not to our purpose to argue theological issues, nor to engage in a philosophical discussion of hermeneutics, the "science of interpretation." The point is that once traditions are written down, we can judge the distance we have traversed from their originating events. In the book of *Acts*, for example, we read of the circumstances that precipitated the Council of Jerusalem, in which the major question was what was to be done about the gentile converts to "the way." Were they to be obliged to obey the precepts of the Mosaic Law? Jesus had evidently said nothing about the matter, although there are several stories which indicate his attitude toward legal observance. A decision had to be made; the process of invention and adaptation had begun. This, of course, is an instance of conscious improvisation. In the ordinary run of events, we accommodate ourselves without fuss, doing what we do as believers with the conviction that we are acting in accord with the principles and examples of Jesus and Muhammed. Only, as I say, when someone accosts us with our working out of things do we become aware of our developments or changes. And that, understandably, is a source of difficulties. Did the prophet, whether Jesus or Muhammed, intend a once-and-for-all framework, a trans-historical point of reference, so that anything we decide is an aberration, a betrayal that is nothing less than a compromise with the secular world? Is the Word of God to be contaminated by human accommodation as if God's ways were our ways?

The problem here is an important one, both philosophically and theologically. I say *problem* in the singular: 'problem' because of the adage that problems have no solutions; we learn to live (or without?) them. In the singular, too, because although several issues are involved — for the theologian, the meaning of revelation, for instance, or the normative role of Scripture; for the philosopher, the place of Reason in religion — I think that we can bring all the issues together under the umbrella of "development." This, it has been said, was actually the underlying issue of all debates in the Roman Church's Vatican II. As an issue, we shall encounter it throughout this study in different guises. But this raises the basic question which eventually comes to the surface. Is development really a problem? Or has our mode of thinking, our conceptualization, created it?

To provide ourselves with some bearings, we might begin by taking note of a significant terminological shift. The word commonly used in the New Testament which we translate as "faith" is *pistis*: more properly, "loving trust." The word indicates a personal commitment, an encounter with Jesus that leads one to follow him "wherever he goes." Might it not be the case that the switch to "faith" or "belief" seemed more natural when Christianity moved from its world of origin into an alien intellectual and religious milieu? It then became necessary to identify the believer by something more tangible, by a more precise criterion than love or trust. The point has been made with respect to the Muslims.

The Mu'tazilis were among the first Muslims to push strongly a point of view which was already represented in the Qur'an, though it did not have so exclusive a place there: that *belief*, in the sense of acknowledgement of certain propositions, was crucial to salvation. The monotheistic conception of faith implies, initially, an act of will more than one of intellect: at once trusting God and being faithful to what He requires of one. But in all the monotheistic traditions, the notion of *trusting* God — not a convenient basis for identifying adherents — has tended to be replaced with that of believing that one should be faithful. The notion of *belief* allowed a reasonably objective criterion of community allegiance. Hence the very words that conveyed the more voluntary notion of 'faith' have come to be understood as meaning 'belief'. (Such a rendering of the words makes nonsense of many passages in the Qur'an, though it fits some fairly well.) The Mu'tazilis emphasized works as well as belief, but it was insistence on intellectual belief that led them to develop their elaborate systems of doctrine, defining and defending the proper belief. This point of view was never lost among Muslims afterwards.[4]

This brings back into focus the problem with which we began. Are we to account for the turn toward the East on the grounds that our Western traditions have developed into systems of belief, and have thereby become so institutionalized that they filter out the experience that the beliefs were intended to mediate? We are all familiar with the image of the imprisoned believer, so locked into a framework and the group it has spawned that he or she has forgotten the crucial point: the purpose of joining a group is to see beyond it. If a framework curtails development and is thus at odds with the becoming of person which is religion's own criterion, ought we not in our own way turn back the clock? Should we not cut through this strangling tissue of beliefs in order to experience, to try for ourselves a liberating contact with God?

The sentiment is not only understandable; it is painful in its urgent actuality. It continues to galvanize the fundamentalist movements that periodically burst upon the historical scene. But it is basically unreal. It supposes that language, history, the

4. *The Venture of Islam*, Vol. I, 385.

whole ensemble that we call "culture" is something to be donned or doffed like a suit of clothes. Underneath the trappings of culture, supposedly, lies an atemporal, ahistorical "pure Ego": a consciousness that as it unfolds in history must somehow catch itself in its pristine state so that it realizes that its development is necessarily piecemeal, biassed or faulty. Similarly, the effort to stand outside of our language in order to appreciate how it had programmed us to apprehend reality is "an attempt to step outside one's own skin of consciousness . . . [Language is] a vital cover more intimately enfolding, more close-woven to human identity than is the skin of our body."[5] We must recognize that efforts or attempts of this kind are thought experiments. They are necessary if we are to take cognizance of the limitations of thought. But they are exercises in futility if we try to realize them: if they lead us to suppose, as Rudolf Bultmann at times does in his project of 'de-mythologizing," that we can get behind the mentalities and language of the first century Gospel writers and discover the "real," historically unadulterated message of Jesus.

The problem of development does not afflict the Eastern traditions because these are not tied to an historical revelation. Like that of Moses or Muhammed, the teaching of the Buddha was an articulation of the framework triggered by his conversion experience. Its precepts enjoin right ways of living, not the kind of personal commitment that entails specific doctrinal formulations concerning Allah and his prophet, the person of Jesus, etc. That formulations of this kind, whether through the decrees of Church Councils or, as in the case of the role of blacks in the Mormon Church, through a new revelation, have been promulgated throughout history is incontestable. The churches and the Islamic Ummah have of necessity adapted their initial forms of order to meet present-day conditions. These are *de facto* acknowledgements of our inescapable temporality. Theoretical difficulties notwithstanding, the day-to-day living of religion has always entailed improvisation.

5. George Steiner, *After Babel: Aspects of Language and Translation*, New York and London: Oxford University Press, 1975, 110.

It is these theoretical difficulties, of course, that have provided a foothold for fundamentalists. Revelation religions must be concerned about fidelity to a revelation accorded in specific historical circumstances. The event, as historical, is a once-and-for-all occurrence. But no single description of it (the New Testament writers offer different "theologies" or viewpoints) nor subsequent elaboration of its meaning is timeless, *pace* theologians who relish the phrase, "the event of Jesus Christ," because the Latin *eventum* might suggest a once-and-for-all coming that makes a mockery of the temporal process of history. Only extremists would contend that we are tied to words that partake of divine eternity, God's verbatim utterances. I say "extremists" because they propose a radical solution to a difficult problem. Words are not simply the husks of meaning: external expressions, as it were, that we shuffle around while an interior meaning stays the same. It has been said, for example, that the faith is unchanging; only its expression changes. This, apparently, was the program of *aggiornamento* Pope John XXIII outlined for the second Vatican Council: to clothe the ancient truths in up-to-date language. His intent is clear. Being a Christian supposes an adherence to the "event" of Jesus Christ. But Pope John's proposal entails more than the adoption of a new vocabulary. Adherence for us is a human act, rooted in our contemporary world of meaning. In addition, the interpretation of the historical documents of Scripture is dauntingly complex.

> Thus the elucidation of what was meant, implied, concealed, inferentially omitted, equivocated on 'in these circumstances, to this audience, for these purposes and with these intentions' . . . can never be reduced to a single, stringently verifiable method. It must remain a selective, highly intuitive proceeding, at the very best self-conscious of its restricted and, in certain regards, fictional status. It hinges, in Schleiermacher's phrase, on the 'art of hearing'.[6]

Christianity, more so than Islam, became a world religion in a

---

6. *Ibid.*, 137. The quotation, J. L. Austin's rubric for defining the truth or falsity of an utterance, is taken from his *How To Do Things with Words*, Oxford, 1962, 104.

milieu in which Greek patterns of thought were predominant. That is to say, at the time when belief as an adherence to a certain number of propositions became the touchstone of the believer, the Greek theory of knowledge was taken for granted. The important points of that theory are these: 1) The model for knowledge was sight, evidenced in our use of "theory," from the Greek "to look at." Knowing something meant seeing it (do you *see* what I mean), even though for Plato this seeing was with the eye of the mind in an intellectual grasp of Forms, not with the eye of the body. The attractiveness of this model was its definiteness, its certainty. Either one sees the moon or he does not. 2) This seeing was a once-and-for-all grasp of what something is. I know a tree whether with leaves or without, whether an oak or a maple. Thus knowledge must be thought of as a taking hold of an essence, divorced from the accidental properties that are its historical or temporal encrustations. Such knowledge, immaterial and transtemporal, is eternal. Mathematics, accordingly, and perhaps formal logic present the ideal of truth.

That this conception of knowledge and truth was basically at odds with the deep historical commitments of religious people apparently made no difference. It satisfied their demand for an unalterable system of beliefs, as well as launched them on diverse theological justifications for historical improvisation. Significantly, both Christianity and Islam emphasize community, so that each religion has in its own way weathered the changes of time by recourse to the community, whether its consensus, its guidance by the Holy Spirit, or, in later developments, its charismatic or "divinely-appointed" leadership. For our purposes these later developments are interesting because they illustrate a method of coping with our problem. Initially, and with the encouragement of the Greek pattern of thought we have briefly described, holding onto the faith meant preserving those "eternal truths," handing them down intact from generation to generation. Thus the important component in the *traditio* ("handing on") was what was handed on, the *traditum*. But as the realization dawned that this *traditum* comprised all sorts of historical developments — in the Roman Church, for example, declarations about Mary, about the Papacy, etc. — the emphasis switched over to the *traditio*, the act of teaching or handing on which, because it was the prerogative of a select ("divinely-appointed") group, guaranteed fidelity to its original inspiration.

To sum up: we have noted that the geographical extension of both Islam and Christianity turned them into political entities, caliphates and Christendom, which in itself is problem enough for any religion but more so for these historically-oriented religions. The Eastern traditions, we observed, because they are neither historical nor communitarian, were not faced with this kind of development. The Western experience of empire has deeply affected religion: on the one hand, turned it into a system of belief which can readily identify the believer or political loyalist, and on the other, gave religion its political arrangements, its institutionalized authorities of caliphs, imams, popes, bishops, etc., who would safeguard development. Religious developments, clearly, have not been simply rational deductions. They have been responses to the pushes and shoves of history, and thus called forth repeated efforts to justify them as "traditional," as faithful or appropriate responses.

There is another side to development that merits attention. Having emphasized religion as a system of beliefs and cultural adaptations, are we still entitled to call it a vital framework, to think it in terms of a formative language that creates us as persons? We have remarked, if some of the reasons given for the widespread disenchantment with traditional religion are valid, that it is these developments which constitute the major obstacle to the experience of Allah or God that elicits commitment. Religion, we said, is like a language, but unlike it insofar as language is not a choice. Someone can live without religion; one cannot think without language. The point of the objection here is neither to deny our temporality nor to suggest that authentic religion be unhinged from culture. Rather, if religion is like language and our modes of inculcating it presume it to be such, why do we so often fail to educate? Have we measured our success so much in terms of conformity that, until recently, we were not aware that the socialization or acculturation never took place? Exposure to religious education has in many instances educed nothing, at least not the freely responding person it supposedly develops.

We have no ready answer for this lack of effectiveness, not the least because our psychology has yet to tell us how it is that an institution (a framework and its articulations) develops attitudes of mind and heart, can provide motivation, and eventually lead one to an "experience" that validates the institution. The studies of Jean Piaget and his associates have been directed toward that end. Why is it, for example, that a child of seven and a half years understands the idea of causal sequence whereas one of five does not? Both are subjected to our patterns of speech. How do we know, Wittgenstein asked, that a child has grasped a principle of counting: 1,3,5,7,. . .? Must the youngster run through the whole series of odd numbers? Or do we suppose that running through thirty of them correctly means that the child understands? We forget, at times, that we are limited to educational techniques; we are not programming computers. More realistically, we acknowledge the importance of example. Will a child pick up the habit of reading if his or her parents are forever in front of the TV? Even if they are not, why is it that one child in a family will follow the example and another will not? In a similar vein, philosophers have puzzled over our use of the word "good." To tell someone that an action is good does not necessarily guarantee performance. Yet what is it about the human psyche that leads us to expect that the factual statement, "Spinach is good for you," will prompt action?

To suggest, therefore, that religion functions like a language or framework of meaning, and that in a peculiar way because its criterion, love, is an estimate of the believer as a person, is not without difficulties. But because history presents us with a record of the failure of religion, are we to conclude that this perspective is false? Indeed, much of the history of religion has been an eloquent testimony to its failure: a grim reminder that religion, as the Western traditions have understood it, has been mainly a narrative of mankind's rebellion against God. In religion, as in all other facets of human life, we are up against perversity. Made to love and to communicate, we spend our days in petty hatreds and misunderstandings. For all of its failures, religion, East and West, is meant to deliver us from this situation. If it has not succeeded in its task, it can at least bring us face to face with the mystery of ourselves.

By describing religion as a structure or framework of meaning that seeks to develop us as lovers, I have presented in this chapter a rationalization that, as the philosophers would complain, provokes more questions than answers. Precisely. For as I see its role, and will unfold it as we proceed, religion is mankind's testimony to itself as an enigma. We have already seen that we must be constrained in order to expand, our being rooted in a culture is a *sine qua non* of our creativity, and that we manipulate history in the name of fidelity to the past. Indeed, I shall argue that it is because religion has preserved our mysteriousness that it has given birth to a philosophy that would, by dissolving that mystery in Absolute Knowledge, put an end to thought itself. We can be grateful, therefore, to religion for keeping alive the challenge of our being.

CHAPTER II

Strategies of Expression

ALTHOUGH Aristotle formulated the definition that man is a rational animal, he is scarcely responsible for all that has been made over the centuries of that declaration. The rationalists of Western philosophy beginning with Descartes understood his "animal" or "living thing having *logon*" within their context. The human being not only "has reason", he or she is Mind. *Logos* as speech or word was simply a sign of reason. By comparison, little was said about humans as animals, and nothing about "having *logon*" in the other sense of that word, "definition." Personally, I think the idea that we define because we alone, according to the strict canons of Aristotelian definition, are definable, merits attention. Be that as it may, it is remarkable that the rationalists who delight in Aristotle's definition have ignored his statement in the *Metaphysics* (1072b 14) that no one can sustain the life of pure reason for more than brief periods, and consequently they were not inclined to study the irrational factors of behavior to achieve a more realistic understanding of human nature. Our prejudice is to translate *logos* as "word." In philosophy we are language or communication oriented, and so it is from this perspective that I wish to develop the concept of religion as framework. I have avoided the word "language" in the title of this chapter because I am not taking the conventional philosophical approach.

It is not to our purpose to argue the difference of human language from animal systems of communication. Humans, in my viewpoint, are unique in that they, unlike porpoises and bees, have developed a set of symbols (letters of an alphabet, ideograms, numbers) that not only stands for, or communicates the meaning of, another set, but also includes the counterfactual, the potentials of fiction, the unpredictability of futurity. Moreover, by characterizing religion as a framework that functions like language, I have obviously intended the reader to understand language more broadly. It is not limited to speech acts, that is, to verbal utterances. The point of comparison with language is twofold: to show that religion affords us a comprehensive horizon of meaning and how it is acquired through both verbal and other kinds of signs. Learning Italian, for example, is in its fullest sense the acquisition of categories, modes of assertion. Clearly a mode as a manner of expressing oneself is not limited to vocables. It comprises all the gestures and tones that exhibit a pattern of speech.

I have, as noted, avoided "language" in the chapter title because for many, especially those educated in the Anglo-American tradition of philosophy, the expression "religious language" can suggest a stringent investigation into its logic. There are any number of books written from this point of view: *Reason and Religion*, edited by Stuart C. Brown[1] is one such that readily comes to mind. It exemplifies a fruitful way in which philosophers have explored religion. More akin to our approach would be something bearing Heidegger's title, *Unterwegs zur Sprache*. We are "underway": exploring some of the bypaths and points of interest, without following his detour into Being, that alert us to the real complexity of language. We take our expressions in their apparent simplicity for granted, failing to notice the underbrush that a stranger to our speech must hack through. "Strategies," which in common parlance means ways of going about or getting around things, underscores the ambiguity that has always characterized the language of religion: affirmations that undergo the death of a thousand qualifications, it has been said,

---

1. Ithaca and London: Cornell University Press, 1977.

in order to avoid grosser forms of anthropomorphism. Thus there are prescribed tactics in religious discourse. But a strategy as a way of "getting around" connotes something sinister, a certain deviousness. It is this aspect of language that deserves further attention. In our concern with expression, the "pressing out" of meaning into a system of communication, we have forgotten language as concealment. It has been designated "the main instrument of man's refusal to accept the world as it is,"[2] and so attests as much our genius for lies as for communication. The problem, therefore, is not just religious language; it is language as such.

It is for this reason that the word "mystery" stressed at the end of the preceding chapter, anathema though it may be to philosophers who damn its obfuscation, is peculiarly appropriate. Little, really, do we understand of ourselves. We may avoid referring to ourselves as half-angel and half-beast. But has our philosophy gotten us much farther? Plato's immortal soul, the principle of ontological continuity with the Forms that he postulated in order to explain knowledge, remained discontinuous with the body which imprisoned it. Joined together metaphorically like a pilot in a ship, these components have hounded philosophers ever since. Aristotle softened the abruptness of their union: the soul was the form of the body. But he bequeathed to his followers the difficulty of explaining how such a soul, indivisible because it was immaterial, could have an intellectual 'part' (the *nous*) that could be both form of the body (as form, the *psyche*) and still, as immortal, operate independently of it. Descartes' mentalism merely gave new breath to the debaters. For all of our efforts to overcome this "Cartesian dualism," we understand *that* we know but are still ignorant of *how*. When Kant came to the crucial issue in his *Critique of Pure Reason* — the move from the material world of sensation to the immaterial sphere of intellection that had led Plato into his doctrine of reminiscence — he brushed over the "schematizing of the categories" as too tedious a matter to hold the interest of his readers. Not one to confess his ignorance, he was sure that we were eager to press on to

2. *After Babel*, 217–18.

weightier matters. Today, at any rate, there are philosophers who are willing to admit that it is not only in our moral lives that the human being remains a mystery.

When I was a very small child, my father read to us from his "Short Stories for Small Boys": narratives that fleshed out episodes taken from the Bible or the lives of the saints. The stories were rich in descriptive detail; the dialogue was period mid-American; a moral was always drawn, pointedly but not heavy-handedly. They were intended to entertain, which they did, but they were also formative. Only in later years did I realize what had occurred. We had been drawn into a family life. Subtly introduced to a system of values, we gradually assimilated them. Now, of course, I appreciate the finesse with which this was accomplished, as well as the sense of responsibility that prompted it. My parents realized that we would need principles of judgment: ideals that we in turn would tailor to fit our circumstances in life. Specific do's and don'ts, because they are *ad hoc*, are rarely so effective in instilling general norms. It is these that a truly moral life requires: one befitting our dignity as free, responsible human beings.

It was this bit of personal history that led me to think in a different way about the stories that abound in religious literature. If we peruse some of the creation myths, for instance, which Mircea Eliade has gathered together in his collection, *From Primitives to Zen*,[3] we can easily be overwhelmed and repulsed by their fantastic detail. What could be the purpose of these bizarre accounts of water snakes and earth divers, of the primordial struggles of Titans or of Zeus and Chronos? Closer to home, what are we to make of the first chapters of *Genesis*, specifically of the story of Adam and Eve and the dire consequences visited upon the human race because they ate forbidden fruit? All religions, it is said, provide us with a myth of origins. Later we shall concentrate on these stories of origins. Here our concern is to clarify, and so emphasize the intellectual importance of, myth.

The notion that a myth is a fiction, a primitive kind of

3. *From Primitives to Zen: A Thematic Sourcebook of the History of Religion*, New York: Harper & Row, 1967.

explanation resorted to by people who lack scientific or intellectual sophistication, is still commonplace. Philosophy, supposedly, is rooted in the endeavor to overcome this bewitchment of intelligence. Through the discipline of rational thought we will overcome, purportedly, the naivety of the mythical imagination. "Myth," David Bidney declared,

> must be taken seriously as a cultural force but it must be taken seriously precisely in order that it may be gradually superseded in the interests of the advancement of truth and the growth of human intelligence. Normative, critical, and scientific thought provides the only self-correcting means of combating the diffusion of myth, but it may do so only on condition that we retain a firm and uncompromising faith in the integrity of reason and in the transcultural validity of the scientific enterprise.[4]

Statements of this kind readily provoke an immediate rise to the bait because its author never spells out his understanding of "reason" or "science." In spite of the efforts of Eliade, Lévi-Strauss and countless others to understand the nature and function of mythical thought (I use 'thought' designedly), are we condemned always to begin a presentation of myth by calling attention to the prejudice against it? In this work my point of view is that without myth neither the "advancement of truth" nor the "growth of human intelligence" is possible. It is within this perspective that the statement that religion is a myth should be understood.

That myth is a fiction owes as much in our culture to the narrative of creation and fall in the first part of *Genesis* as to anything else. We take the myth to be the highly imaginative story. But what if we were to see the story as the articulation of a myth? To effect this kind of reversal of thought, we might begin from the common human experience of universal transience. If all the world is a stage and we are the actors (or stagehands) who, after a brief appearance, vanish into the wings, why can we not think of human life in terms of a play so that it and its

---

4. David Bidney, "Myth, Symbolism and Truth," in Thomas A. Sebeok, ed., *Myth: A Symposium,*, Bloomington: Indiana University Press, 1965, 23.

settings compose a drama with beginning, middle and end? Birth and death are, surely, the most poignant facts of our experience. And so, even if we find the prospect of billions of light years mind-boggling, we find it necessary to postulate a "big bang" or similar cosmic happening to inaugurate the universe and a comparable "death" that will terminate it. Our experience, therefore, enables us to approach life with an anticipatory scheme, and it is this thought pattern that enables us to hypothesize and so account for what is happening now in our universe. This is the kind of pattern I have called a framework. Accordingly, religion is the myth that enables us to understand our lives here and now and to make decisions about them because it has provided us with life's meaning, the encompassing horizon for those fundamental questions: Why am I here? What is my life all about? Some of the Hollywood movie productions of recent years, particularly the rash of star-produced, polemical films like Robert Redford's *The Candidate* and *Three Days of the Condor*, or Jane Fonda's *The China Syndrome* or *Coming Home*, are mythic in the sense in which I am using the term. These films not only convey a framework of meaning in their authors' social and political messages. They exhibit the definite kind of religious persuasion which we usually call puritanical. Their authors are convinced of their absolute righteousness; what they oppose is unadulterated evil. There is no middle ground of morality, no shading of gray between the stark black and white. Can it be that much of the attraction of these films is their appeal to the simpler religious world of early America, to the more homogeneous society evoked by much of our political rhetoric?

That thought of any kind requires a context is, I believe, indisputable. Someone can hold up before us the queen piece from a chess set and announce: "This is the queen." But unless we understand chess the statement is not clear. Is this a new idol? A piece of art? When Godfrey Lienhardt was asked what it was that he had investigated among the Dinka, he could have said: what the Dinka consider to be religion. Gestures, words, ceremonies are religious because of their context, which explains why most attempts to return to a traditional, tribal religion have misfired. All religions become embedded in a milieu. In a tribal society it is so much a part of a group's life that the religion becomes unthinkable without its socio-economic support. For this reason it is sometimes remarked that an advantage of our civilization is that it has been formed by the interaction of many groups. Unlike members of a tribal society who have grown up either in isolation or with minimal contacts with people of different minds, we are accustomed to divergent or contradictory points of view. We are blessed, therefore, with a certain flexibility. Even if we discard the myth of religion, we find another myth to replace it, whether "science" or "progress" or the "dictatorship of the proletariat." The important point, to be sure, is that we do replace it. We have to have something that rescues life from a meaningless succession of "one damned thing after another." As Steinbeck put it so well at the beginning of *East of Eden*: when we come to the crunch, when something happens that affects us deeply or mortally, we have to face the hard, clean questions: Is it right or wrong? Did I do evil or good? The myths of *Genesis* and similar books furnish us with a general structure within which to situate these questions and answer them satisfactorily.

The difficulty, no doubt, is that *Genesis* presents a story: a highly imaginative and concrete account that has all the appearances of an accounting. Would there have been a science-religion conflict, the enduring debacle over creationism versus evolutionism, if people were not literal-minded? The question of who is right in the form of a simple either-or does not arise when one is prepared to admit that these are different kinds or levels of explanation. "Genuine mythic cognition," Adolf Jensen remarked,

> makes statements about the nature of reality for which there cannot be any comparable scientific statements; the methods of science are oriented toward a different nature of reality, toward the quantitative and measureable which is never understood through direct impression but only by the detour of de-anthropomorphization.[5]

5. *Myth and Cult among Primitive Peoples*, Eng. trans., Marianna Tax Choldin and Wolfgang Weissleder, Chicago: University of Chicago Press, 1963, 324.

If we are prepared to acknowledge, as surely we must be, the legitimacy of different kinds of explanation — that given by a biologist who de-anthropomorphizes by giving us anatomical "facts," purified of their human and emotional components, is evidently quite different from that given by a parent to a seven year old who has become aware of sex — then the problem is to clarify the strategy at work in this religious use of story. Offhand it can be pointed out that scientific statements, as we usually encounter them, are concerned with specific questions, not with the myth or overall framework of science but with its internal logic or its developed mythology. Religious statements are also of both kinds. Hence a scientific parallel to our immediate concern would be something like the TV series, *Cosmos*: a program packed with detail but, I would presume, designed to interest the general listener in the kinds of questions and answers that agitate the astrophysicist. In this sense, the program — replete with pictures, drawings, charts: all the concrete fillips to one's imagination — was aimed at inculcating a myth: a general pattern for thinking about the beginning and end of our universe. Science, as the big bang theory reminds us, is also geared to telling a story in terms that owe as much, of course, to speculation as to empirical phenomena. Yet the storied elements of religious myths have been a constant source of uneasiness and so merit special consideration.

The sacred books of East and West are in their ancient parts narratives that date back not to the "pre-logical childhood" of mankind that some would suggest, but to the period prior to the written record. Neither historians in our sense nor tape-recorders were available to transmit accurate reports of events like those depicted at the beginning of *Genesis* which defy human witness. The "events" narrated in the *Iliad* and the *Odyssey* took place long before the time of Homer. Their handing-on was a feat of prodigious memory, successive embellishment, creative imagination. Of the Indian epic, *The Mahabharata*, we are told:

> The text of *The Mahabharata* itself gives us some idea how we should picture its authorship. In its present form it is recited by the bard Ugraśravas, who recites after Vaiśampāyana, who was one of the pupils of Kṛṣṇa Dvaipāyana. In other words, we have

right here three generations of reciters through whom the text had been transmitted. One cannot expect·that this transmisson was a literal one, as it has been in the case of the Veda. A reciter's reputation was based on his skill in bringing the old stories to life again. Successive generations would add, embellish, digress: but also understate what might have been emphasized before . . . All this creates the impression that what would come down from generation to generation were, first, the summaries, and, second, the technique of spinning out a tale to please the listeners. The reciter was thus also a creative poet, within the idiom of his craft.[6]

Stories, besides, are effective educational techniques not only because their concreteness engages us holistically as beings of imagination and feeling, but also because that very concreteness leads us to the further goal of criticism. The details of a story are embedded in a history. An understanding of the lives of Jesus and Muhammed demands the ability to retrospect, for their worlds were different from ours and the authors who wrote about them addressed themselves to audiences with presuppositions and needs unlike or even contrary to our own. When we read the Adam and Eve story, for example, its fantastic elements force us to look for the point. What was the author telling his audience and how is it relevant to us? The importance of this question must not blind us to its pitfalls. These merit some consideration, even if we must digress somewhat to discuss them. For only if we are alert to what is at stake will we appreciate why Mircea Eliade and Claude Lévi-Strauss, as I understand them, have devoted so much of their energy to the clarification of myths.

To these men we are indebted for a wealth of historical research into myths. Yet ironically, both have been accused of being anti-historical: Lévi-Strauss insofar as he accepts all interpretations of a myth throughout its history as equally valid; Eliade insofar as he emphasizes the importance in religious ritual of a return to the mythic past, to the event(s) "in illo tempore" that inaugurated a particular way of life. The former is censured for minimizing the importance of a myth's original

6. *The Mahabharata, I, The Book of the Beginning,* Translated and Edited by J. A. B. van Buitenen, Chicago and London: The University of Chicago Press, 1973, xxiii–iv.

version, the latter for maximizing it by ignoring its historical developments. Eliade's "return" is illustrated by the fact that when God wanted to call the Hebrews back to fidelity, he reminded them through his prophets of the two great events in their history that established them as his people: I am the Lord, your God, Who brought you forth out of the land of Egypt; I fed your fathers with manna in the desert. Similarly, Christians recall or re-enact the event of Jesus (his sacrificial death and resurrection): "Do this in memory of Me." From our standpoint the irony of branding these positions anti-historical is that it misses the real point. In one case, we revert to the events "in illo tempore" to celebrate them and thus *assess* the ways in which that inaugurating myth has been historically articulated in mythologies. We thus go back through history in order to recover that history in its entirety, that is to say, in its source and unfolding. In the other, the acceptance of various mythologies as equally valid is itself a criticism of the unhistorical notion that a myth must be translated into a single mythology, which, of course, is tantamount to wrapping the myth in mothballs to guarantee its irrelevance to subsequent generations. Such a process of univocal interpretation is what Paul Ricoeur, if I understand him correctly, has called *gnosis*: a pretense to a secret knowledge that is destructive of myth as myth.[7] Does this mean that we should never look for *the* point of a story? Do our efforts at explanation spell the death of further disclosure? Because Ricoeur appears to say "yes" to both of these questions, I shall spell out the issue that his terminology can obscure.

What Ricoeur had in mind are myths like the Adam and Eve story: a narrative that offers us an orientation to life. The story opens up possibilities for thought, inviting our reflection upon the meaning of suffering and death, upon rebellion and our estrangement from God, upon the role of work in our lives, upon our sexuality, etc. It lacks the definiteness of an explanation which is possible, for example, in the case of the New Testament parable of the Good Samaritan. This story, as part of the

7. See his *The Symbolism of Evil*, translated from the French by Emerson Buchanan, Boston: Beacon Press, 1969, 164–5.

mythology of the overarching Christian myth of salvation, presents in concentrated form a single aspect of Christian living. It
is, to revert to our previous terminology, a development of the
logic within the Christian framework, whereas the Adam and
Eve story is formative of the rationale of the framework itself.
But if Ricoeur were making simply this logical point, why would
he use the term *gnosis*: a word whose root is "knowledge" but
which came to mean in the early Christian era an esoteric
knowledge? He insinuates, of course, that just as the Gnostics
claimed to possess the true knowledge that others lack, so those
who would tell us *the* meaning of this myth are modern-day
heretics. "Between gnosis and reason a choice must be made."
Gnostics are those who do not regard the *Genesis* story as a sea of
interpretative possibilites, one of which might be a theory of
Original Sin. Rather, they give us *the* meaning, a doctrine which
closes off other avenues of reasonable inquiry. In short, dogma,
the source of endless contention and intolerance, has triumphed
over reason. To avoid this pitfall, we must recover "the myth as
myth, before it slipped into *gnosis*."

I suspect here in Ricoeur's advocacy of recovering myth more
than simply an airing of the Calvinist's difficulties with Catholic
dogma. What does it mean to recover myth as myth? The project
strikes me as both similar to, and yet dissimilar from, Bultmann's de-mythologizing. Bultmann would have us ask what
the point of a story is so that we can see through its historically
conditioned elements to ascertain what prompted them. Ricoeur, on the contrary, seems to be wary of asking the point of a
story because the point is its explanation. In telling you what it is
about, I have specified its meaning. Yet to recover myth as myth
would appear to mean that we must keep all of our options open.
All derivative mythologies, all versions as Lévi-Strauss would
say, are equally valid. We entertain myths, therefore, to stimulate thought. They are to be judged by their fruitfulness, not by a
gnostic standard of truth.

Looked at from a philosophical point of view, Ricoeur's difficulty seems to lie in the very nature of reason. If we ask someone
why he is shaking his hand, we are not satisfied when he offers us
six or seven different reasons running from birth trauma to his

current bout with arthritis. We want to know *the* reason, *the* cause. Reason, we say, is determinative. It begins its work by defining. By setting the limits determinative of what things are, it lays down guidelines for a logical or rationally consistent investigation. Yet how are we to reconcile this intentional constriction or closing off which is what makes rational explanation cogent with that openness which is the very spirit of rational inquiry? We have already mentioned this problem in connection with language. The paradox or mystery of our human condition is that on the one hand we must have structure, be confined within the categories of our language, in order for us to develop through communication. Yet on the other hand, reason, though it progresses through successive determinations, dies if these determinations put an end to thought. If being reasonable means continued openness, why did Ricoeur entitle his book: *The*, not *A*, *Symbolism of Evil?*

To make his point Ricoeur juxtaposed gnosis to reason, but he has not developed some suggestions that are latent in his choice of 'gnosis'. Secret knowledge by definition cannot be brought into the marketplace. It is doubly suspect: as belonging outside the realm of community control in which even prophetic inspiration operates (charisms are always "in" a community because they are "for" a community; they do not fall outside of a group's traditions) and as being impervious to rational debate (the rational is always universal; it is beyond the arena of personal whim and thus open to the inspection of others). Thus the heresy of gnosis is not the unbridled desire for *the* meaning or *the* explanation but the decision, written into the meaning of heresy, to emancipate reasoning from the constraints of a community tradition. I have already remarked concerning development that both Christianity and Islam rely upon the community to guarantee fidelity to their inaugurating revelations. The principle of this reliance is theological, not sociological. We are not dealing with pressure groups nor with "nose counting." Since the revelation has been formative of a group, that group's continued existence remains so tied to the revelation that the revealer's fidelity will not permit a development that would destroy the group as a faithful witness. Needless to say, my emphasis upon the role of the community in this development of meaning does not resolve the problem which may have been in Ricoeur's mind: which articulation of the Christian myth is correct, the Catholic dogma or Protestant theory? But it does underscore the inappropriateness of the word *gnosis*. For even in the Middle Eastern myths with which Ricoeur has worked, there is no hint of a secret explanation: something arrived at by a kind of gnostic navelgazing. An example can clarify this point.

We have noted of the transmission of *The Mahabharata*: "A reciter's reputation was based on his skill in bringing the old stories to life again." Of course, "successive generations would add, embellish, digress . . ." but within those limits set by the old stories. The Homeric bards, we are told, were similarly constrained. They recited to entertain, and so their presentations had to attract by their novelty. But how they fashioned their narratives was determined by their hearers' expectations. New ventures, new episodes were enthusiastically received so long as they were in harmony with the older traditions. This kind of community control is in evidence among early Christians who determined what stories about Jesus were retained, and later, what books were acceptable as canonical scripture.

Ricoeur's *bête noire*, I mentioned, is the doctrine of Original Sin: a determination of the meaning of *Genesis* that indeed would be a feat of gnostic ingenuity were the dogma solely read off from that story. It has been said that in the original version of the myth utilized by the Old Testament redactor, Eve, the Mother Goddess who is a multiform of the snake and the tree, offered the apple to the shaman who successfully climbed the tree at the center of the world. The apple was a positive boon, embodying the elixir of life and the knowledge of good and evil. In our version, Eve has been made into the villain of the piece, and the shamanistic goal of the "opening of the eyes" has become a sin. Obviously, the redactor reworked the story in this way for theological reasons: which is to say, to fit in with the religious expectations and needs of his readers. Ricoeur's *gnosis* was already at work, not giving us a full-blown doctrine of Original Sin but providing materials whence such a doctrine could be derived. Certainly Christians thought about *Genesis* in the light of St. Paul's declaration that through a man sin entered into the world, and thus through a man it was overcome. In brief, Paul enriched the myth of *Genesis* by one that affirms the hope and dignity of our race. In "gnostic" fashion he specified the meaning of Adam and Eve: the ineffable sense of guilt borne by each individual can be lifted through an imitation of Christ.

I have brought Ricoeur's *gnosis* into focus because, although its nuances and his juxtaposition of it to reason muddy the waters of discussion, it permits us to clarify some important features of myth. A myth, we said, is a framework of meaning offered to us in a mythology, in the storied form which reason itself elaborates. Mythologizing, therefore, is not the irresponsible play of an unbridled imagination. Rather, it is an indispensable human activity that, because it takes place in a concrete historical, social situation, inevitably calls for subsequent demythologizing. Each age or generation must articulate for itself its horizon(s) of meaning. Besides, since mythologies oftentimes represent a point of view or are fashioned to drive home a particular message, we find ourselves engaged in criticizing these reasoned elaborations in the light of the myth as we understand it. The retrieval of "myth as myth" which Ricoeur has recommended is not a return to a skeletal framework devoid of any mythological interpretation. Rather, it is simply the stipulation that we have to bear in mind the story-character of myths. As such, they open before us any number of paths for speculation, without compelling us to choose one as *the* meaningful or fruitful one. Our historical circumstances will dictate our preferences.

I have suggested that the gnostic tendency deplored by Ricoeur is to be found already at work in the Old Testament redactor's fashioning of an ancient myth into the *Genesis* account of Adam and Eve. He has reconstructed a story in order to make his point and thus provided us with a new myth. In like manner, St. Paul embellished the story of the Fall and its promise of redemption with Christian materials in order to form the specifically Christian myth. If I understand it correctly, the doctrine of Original Sin is not the elevation of a particular version of this myth to canonical status. Rather, it is a declaration made in the light of *Genesis*, of the Old Testament history of rebellion against God, and of the Christian interpretation of the mission of Jesus, that primordial evil, because it is essential to the myth itself, must feature in all of that myth's articulations. In the course of this study, we shall pursue some of the ramifications of this statement. For the moment, its importance for us is this: myths, mediated by mythologies, suggest ways of coping with the mystery of existence by presenting us with interpretations of life. All of the great religious traditions: Buddhism, Hinduism, Judaism, Christianity, Islam, are concerned with evil, with the suffering that figures so prominently in our experience. They offer us myths that enable us to make whatever sense we can out of this situation. Through understanding, it is hoped, at least the door to liberation is opened.

This understanding is concretized for us in the great religious symbols: in the mien and gestures of the contemplating Buddha, in the figure of Jesus suspended between heaven and earth, in the tablets of the Law: God's gift of wisdom to mankind. But our everyday lives are hemmed in by the ordinary: food in all of its forms, water and fire, the cycles of sun and moon, the patterns traced out by East and West, by up and down. Assuredly, no detail of life is too minuscule, too humdrum, that it cannot be pressed into service to convey a wealth of religious meaning. "God," I should also like to say, is a symbol: a term that likewise condenses for its users a world of meaning. Yet for many people this would be tantamount to the statement that God is not real; just as when I classified religion as a myth, I have supposedly said that it is unreal, a figment of one's imagination. I hope that I have dispelled this latter misunderstanding. I must now try to dispel the former.

What do we mean by a symbol? A *symbolē* meant to the Greek who used the word some kind of identifying badge, a chit of recognition. Two people, let us suppose, are going on journeys and want to be sure that they recognize each other when they return. They tear a card in two so that when they meet again, one can piece together his *symbolē* with the other's. This usage may be derived from the verb *sym-ballein*, to throw or hurl together. Hence the term suggests a meeting place, an encounter in which people recognize one another because of identifying signs. Appropriately, early Christian Church councils summarized their decisions in what they called an "apostolic symbolon." By profession of certain articles of faith, Christians identified themselves as such. A profession, moreover, was more than mere verbalization, for through this act of faith one entered the meeting place, the temple, the place "cut off" for an encounter with God.

The word 'symbol', therefore, has connotations that have vanished from most current usage. We still think of a national flag as a symbol in its fuller meaning because in it a country's ideals, its national spirit, are condensed, and those who respect it are marked as that country's citizens. Yet the coinage is debased when we say that our language is symbolic, for that has come to mean no more than the fact that we use certain signs to convey meaning. Symbols, of course, are signs, but they have a density of meaning not to be found in the spare, unambiguous "Slow," "Bank," or "No Hunting." Symbols I think of as fuller indications of our human situation. The common assumption — let us prescind from the arguments of philosophers regarding 'body' and 'soul' — is that we are a strange combination, capable of soaring intellectual and mystical flights while tied down to the earthly needs of material bodies. Indeed, we are the symbol *par excellence*, the encounter of matter and spirit, the meeting place of heaven and earth. No wonder that we use symbolic language: one that grows out of our bodily condition within a specified historical-temporal situation. Our language, that is, however capable of conveying thought or spiritual meaning, bears undeniable traces of its material roots. We communicate using the material resources of our milieus: signs suffused with a tonus and imagery redolent of daily existence. Even a gesture, as we know, which may appear perfectly innocent to us can in another culture or language group cause embarrassment, or sometimes uncontrollable anger. In short, symbols are a product of, and thus lead us into, an environment, a whole world of imagination that engulfs us. Symbols evince a people's way of life, their modes of perception, their entire feel of things which it is the genius of their language to capture. Accordingly, Eliade has suggested that symbolism appears to be a "language" understood by all members of the community and meaningless to outsiders, but certainly a "language" expressing at once and equally clearly the social, "historic," and psychic condition of the symbol's wearer, and his relation with society and the cosmos.[8]

Symbols, then, are cultural expressions, with all the richness that the word 'culture' suggests. Derived from the Latin verb *colere* (past participle, *cultus*), the word signifies "to dwell with" or "inhabit," and also "to cherish." This connection is significant, for it is those with whom we dwell, those who are like us, that attract our concern and affection. From the past participle comes our 'culture', which, intellectually speaking, characterizes someone as cultivated. Finally, 'cult' is a cultural celebration. Members of a culture make use of symbols to celebrate their meaning and thereby to re-enforce their identity. In their origins this was the purpose of Bastille Day, Independence Day, Dominion Day, etc. These festivals not only afforded a welcome rest; they were also effective means of socialization. They acculturated. Even the political speeches that have come to be their bane were initially reminders of a heritage and thus devices for inculcating civic virtue. Obviously, by celebrating together we become of one mind since we are emphasizing the bonds that unite us. Religious rituals serve an identical function. Their current lack of appeal suggests their failure to socialize, for how can we be expected to celebrate with people with whom allegedly we have little or nothing in common?

Having stressed the intimate connection of symbol and ritual, together they constitute "symbolic expression." I must defer further consideration of ritual until later in this work, after I have called attention to some other aspects of symbolism as a language. Symbols, I said, are differentiated from signs by their density. Their meaning is multi-faceted because they give full weight to our bodily condition, to our being situated in particular historical circumstances. The play on words in a Bob Hope story, for instance, or the local color of a Chicago joke are lost on

8. Mircea Eliade, *Patterns in Comparative Religion*, Translated by Rosemary Sheed, Cleveland and New York: The World Publishing Co., A Meridian Book, 1963, 451.

Dutch students. But there is more to symbolic density, I believe, than our material rootedness.

Heretofore I have espoused the conventional idea that language is a system of communication, though I have been at pains to emphasize its living, formative quality. It involves us in a history, in a web of significance (an *histos* in Greek is a "sail" or "web") for meaning is a "function of a group's social-historical antecedents and shared responses."[9] Were this not the case, we might attribute the "death" of the English language simply to the failure of our grade schools to teach grammar, syntax and reading, and to the deleterious influence of the media: newspapers, television, radio, etc. Undoubtedly these are partially responsible for the widespread functional illiteracy in America. But to appreciate the general debasement of English, we have to cast our net wider. The language, for good or ill, has become the primary medium of global communication, whether in its proper spoken form or in its diverse pidgins. An impoverishment has been inevitable, for in its expansion the language has been severed from the culture, the historical roots, that have nourished it. Even native speakers are all too often content with the basic or minimal communication that results from an ignorance of the biblical and classical sources that were the inspiration and lifeblood of its literature.

But is this linguistic insensitivity the only grounds for a language's diminishing communicative power? Is there a point to suspecting a deeper density to language; that it is as much the device for concealment, as I remarked at the beginning of the chapter, as for communication?

> Linguists and psychologists (Nietzsche excepted) have done little to explore the ubiquitous, many-branched genus of lies. We have only a few preliminary surveys of the vocabulary of falsehood in different languages and cultures. Constrained as they are by moral disapproval or psychological malaise, these inquiries have remained thin. We will see deeper only when we break free of a purely negative classification of 'un-truth', only when we recognize the compulsion to say 'the thing which is not' as being

9. *After Babel*, 465.

central to language and mind. We must come to grasp what Nietzsche meant when he proclaimed that 'the Lie — and *not* the Truth — is divine!' Swift was nearer the heart of anthropology than he may have intended when he related 'lying' to the 'Nature of Manhood' and saw in 'false representation' the critical difference between man and horse.[10]

Among contemporary philosophers, Heidegger has followed Hegel in equating Being with Nothingness, light with darkness. Most significantly, this 'concealing' Being or ambivalent Meaning is said to be *Logos*: the disclosure of expression that is simultaneously a closure. What do these oracular pronouncements tell us about symbols?

Instead of the word "language" we sometimes refer to our 'linguistic categories'. Undoubtedly this is a more pretentious expression but not simply that. We have already noted the derivation of category from the Greek, "to assert." It was this fact that prompted Hegel to ask of Kant's categories: Why these modes of assertion rather than some others? Are we limited solely to the Aristotelian, determinate forms of judgment? It is important for us to know, as Robert Frost was later to put it in his little poem, *On Mending Wall*, what we are fencing out as well as what we are fencing in. The emphasis in philosophy, naturally enough, has been on Being, on the expression of meaning or the "facts" of the case. What we have ignored is its counterpart and consequently discounted a considerable segment of our linguistic behavior: our penchant for spinning out fictions, for dreaming up possible futures, for imagining counter-factual situations. We have been content with half of ourselves.

This darkness, the opaqueness of symbols, has several phases. We speak to communicate all right, but we know that words fail us, that a full disclosure would be almost endless, and that an utterance is as likely as not to fall on deaf, or partially deaf, ears. Does anyone really understand everything we mean? Is it possible to translate perfectly Japanese haiku into English? As Vladimir Nabokov remarked in his poem, "On Translating 'Eugene Onegin' ":

10. *Ibid.*, 220–21, with appropriate bibliography for points mentioned in the text.

What is translation? On a platter
A poet's pale and glaring head,
A parrot's speech, a monkey's chatter,
And profanation of the dead.[11]

Our incomprehension of others and theirs of us stems from the density of our symbols. Symbols are impenetrable in the sense that, as material, they fail to let the pure light of meaning through. Words, we say, are inadequate to thought. But they also have an impenetrable density in the already mentioned sense: their materiality harbors a multitude of possible meanings. "The Lord," sang the psalmist, "is my shepherd." Because no single meaning is apparent, the statement evokes a multiple response: the Lord, however one responds to this title, as caring, as leading, as gentle, etc.

Because we are aware of the fundamental ambiguity of our words, we can exploit them with an air of sincerity that masks our talent for deception. Lying, I noted, attests our refusal to accept the world as it is. Our language, our education, our culture, not to mention our social, economic and political involvements: all conspire to make us the proverbial Wittgensteinian fly in the fly-bottle. A lie, therefore, is not an act of self-deception. It is at its deepest level an ontological commitment to a different world of meaning, the possibility of which underscores the radical contingency of our own. The lie is a protest against our limitation. It manifests a resentment, conscious or unconscious, against the constraints imposed upon us as finite beings. We want, in Wittgenstein's graphic expression, to show the fly the way out of the fly-bottle.

The modern philosophy that began with Descartes culminated in Kant's metaphysics of finitude: a description of the limits within which thought takes shape. The crowning, guiding ideal of conscious activity is, Kant said, a postulate of God: a totally unifying concept, the standpoint of complete intelligibility. We can imagine that a theoretical physicist dreams of presenting us with *the* formula: "This, ladies and gentlemen, is the world." At last the task which has been the inspiration of all

11. *Ibid.*, 240.

of mankind's intellectual and scientific pursuits has been accomplished: that complete unification whereby we finally understand how everything fits together. This pursuit, Sartre shrewdly remarked at the end of his ominously titled work, *Being and Nothingness*, reveals our secret desire to be God, to be omniscient. We are destined, however, for frustration. Man is an unhappy, restless *dieu manqué*, a defeated god. Failing to be all, we lapse into nothing.

Sartre, of course, has profited from Hegel's re-thinking of the thought process: on Hegel's part a speculative journey through the history of philosophy that ended on an ambiguous note. How are we to interpret that final step, the Absolute? Have we reached our goal, a genuine absolute knowledge, and thus brought to a successful conclusion the efforts of our metaphysical forebears? Or has the metaphysical tradition brought us through its failure to wisdom: to an acknowledgment of the fact that not only does complete understanding elude our grasp, but even more basically, we do not even understand our own understanding. In order to think we must presuppose the validity of thought. Have we anything else besides Mind to investigate Mind? What is more, our logical construction of English sentences presupposes the entirety of our language — no one pretends to know all the words in the *Oxford English Dictionary* or to have contemplated every conceivable usage — so that any act of thinking presupposes this totality of meaning as its ground. But this ground is, in fact, ungrounded, a necessary presupposition that remains unattainable. This paradox, I believe, was the goad that compelled Heidegger "beyond" metaphysics.

Philosophy came to birth in the laudable desire to understand ourselves and our world. Knowledge was to be an achievement. It would enable us to regulate ourselves and to order our environment to our advantage. But it has not turned out that way. Centuries of "rationality" are besmirched with blood, and reason has devised increasingly effective means of destroying both our humanity and our world. What began as a servant has become our master. Philosophy has taught this lesson in its academic way, and perhaps we have missed the point because of its abstract, jargon-laden vocabulary. Since reason or thought cannot be rationalized, it remains a useful tool but a tyrannical master. Surely the redactor of *Genesis* was not just anti-intellectual when he reworked his myth to make the fruit of the tree, the knowledge of good and evil, a sin. From the viewpoint of contemporary philosophy, the point would seem to be that thought is a boon, but . . . This important "but" is an abrupt reminder of a change of perspective. Reason as a useful tool had led us to think of ourselves as capricious masters. We were creators with a powerful instrument in our hands, who were so taken by its power that we had forgotten that the tool is not completely in our control. It is regrettable that Heidegger's philosophy of Being, which makes this point, is linguistically so inaccessible. Being or Meaning, he reminds us, is not for presumptuous disposal because frankly it is not ours. Nor is it something merely given, which once again would imply that we are masters of the situation. Because meaning is expressed in us or through us, the only situation of which we are masters is that of Un- or Non-meaning: the denial of the meaning of our world in a lie. Yet even the expression of this denial is not our servant. Is it not true that language, the *logos* of Being, masters us?

> Man acts as if he were the shaper and master of language, while it is language which remains mistress of man. When this relation of dominance is inverted, man succumbs to strange contrivances. Language then becomes a means of expression. Where it is expression, language can degenerate to mere impression (to mere print). Even where the use of language is no more than this, it is good that one should still be careful in one's speech. But this alone can never extricate us from the reversal, from the confusion of the true relation of dominance as between language and man. For in fact it is language that speaks. Man begins speaking and man only speaks to the extent that he responds to, that he corresponds with language, and only in so far as he hears language addressing, concurring with him. Language is the highest and everywhere the foremost of those assents which we human beings can never articulate solely out of our own means.[12]

Like Hegel before him, Heidegger has meditated long on the

12. *Dichterisch Wohnet der Mensch*, 1954; cited in *After Babel*, x 1.

checkered metaphysical tradition. The pursuit of rationality —
embodied in the key terms: "Being," "essence," "thought,"
"reason," etc. — began within a mythical framework, the religious pattern of a shaman's mystical flight.[13] The history of
rationalism ignored this religious provenance, in particular by
directing our attention to the immanent aspect of knowledge: to
the human mind as the creator and thus sole criterion of meaning. The transcendent aspect of knowing, crystallized in our
notion that knowledge and consciousness are *of*, was no more
than an objective, going-beyond moment: what more recent
philosophers emphasize as the "othering" attendant upon assimilation. To this tradition the philosophy of Heidegger has
posed a challenging question: Given our modes of thought, of
cognition, of utterance, is a rigorously immanent, non- or post-
theological interpretation of human existence possible? What
limits do we set for an investigation of the human? Do precon-
ceived ideas of ourselves control, or even curtail, our self-
examination? Is not this the question lurking in the phrase: "It is
language that speaks"? If our genius for lying lays bare a
deep-seated longing for what is not the case, for a realm free from
the chains of finitude that hamper us, has not Heidegger, by
bringing us to the limits of the metaphysical tradition, shown us
that there is truly more to life than the modern, rationalistic
philosophy ever dreamed of? It has been the historic role of
religion to bear witness to the presence of that "truly more." And
so, because "language is the highest and everywhere the foremost
of those assents which we human beings can never articulate
solely *out of our own means*," religion has flourished in a forest of
symbols. These it has latched onto because they are suggestive.
They reveal a meaning that never casts off its hiddenness.

The critique of religious language, beginning with Sir A. J.
Ayer's declaration several decades ago that all theological statements are meaningless, has been motivated by the praiseworthy
desire for precise meanings. Philosophy, it was thought, could do
no better than rid us once and for all of the confusions brought

13. This is a theme of my *Religious Consciousness and Experience*. It is summarized in the following pages.

about by language. Operating at that time within a narrow empiricism, Ayer observed that if in other cases we can establish either clear-cut or reasonably acceptable criteria for our use of 'good' and 'wise', we must, for the sake of consistency, apply these same criteria in theological language. "God is good" functions no differently from, and therefore is subject to the same qualifications as, "John Jones is good." It is true, of course, that there have been theologians who provided Ayer with ammunition. They conveyed the impression that using terms analogously was no more than a qualified comparing, dropping from terms like 'just' and 'beautiful' the limitations inherent in their application to men and their affairs. Today, however, with our increased awareness of the importance of context in the determination of meaning, we realize that the language of analogy is the expression of the religious form of life which theology articulates. "God is good" is symbolic in that it is an expression of the believer's encounter with God. The statement always retains its mysteriousness because it reflects that participation in, or illumination by, the divine which constitutes the believer's reality as a symbol. In the past philosophers would have it otherwise. To be reputable, theology's expression of mystery had to clarify, that is, to dissipate all mystery.

How philosophers came to be of this mind is the story of modern philosophy, for us an important narrative because it comprises our philosophic-religious history. The terms I have chosen for its telling are derived from the customary label for the period, the Age of Immanence, a span of history that began with Descartes (d. 1650) and reached its zenith in the Enlightenment (Kant, frequently called the greatest of the enlightened, died in 1804). During that time Western Europeans purportedly lost their religious transcendence and became secularized. Because this philosophical rationalism is usually traced back to Plato, it is with his pattern of thought that we must begin.

Today it is acknowledged that Plato's philosophy is indebted to the shamanism with which he most probably became acquainted when he visited the Pythagoreans in Western Greece around 390 B.C. Interestingly, this religious phenomenon had moved off the Asiatic steppes, so that by the time Plato began to speculate, it appeared over the broad area that stretches from the Ganges to southern Italy. The shaman, as I noted, was a religious ecstatic, a specialist who combined the traits of the medicine man, mystic and wise man. An adept in crowd psychology, he made use of various techniques: drumming, singing, dancing, and the like, to work himself into a trance in order to climb the tree "at the center of the world" and mime the arduous journey in search of wisdom. For his audience the shaman described the perils of his quest and upon return shared with them the fruits of his labors.

How Plato transposed this religious into a metaphysical scheme has been depicted in Dodd's *The Greeks and the Irrational*:

Reincarnation survives unchanged. The shaman's trance, his deliberate detachment of the occult self from the body, has become that practice of mental withdrawal and concentration which purifies the rational soul — a practice for which Plato in fact claims the authority of a traditional *logos*. The occult knowledge which the shaman acquires in trance has become a vision of metaphysical truth; his "recollection" of past earthly lives has become a "recollection" of bodiless Forms which is made the basis of a new epistemology; while on the mystical level his "long sleep" and "underworld journey" provides a direct model for the experiences of Er the son of Armenius. Finally, we shall understand better Plato's "Guardians" if we think of them as a new kind of rationalised shamans who, like their primitive predecessors, are prepared for their high office by a special kind of discipline designed to modify the whole psychic structure; like them, must submit to a dedication that largely cuts them off from the normal satisfactions of humanity; like them, must renew their contact with the deep sources of wisdom by periodic "retreats"; and like them, will be rewarded after death by receiving a peculiar status in the spirit world. It is likely that an approximation to this highly specialised human type already existed in the Pythagorean societies; but Plato dreamed of carrying the experiment much further, putting it on a serious scientific basis, and using it as the instrument of his counter-reformation.[14]

14. E. R. Dodds, *The Greeks and the Irrational*, Berkeley and Los Angeles: The University of California Press, 1964, 210.

A careful perusal of this passage can suggest the idea that Platonic philosophy was a form of spirituality for a new type of shaman. It reserved true knowledge or wisdom to a group of ascetics. It was the fruit of a purifying effort. It entailed the transcendence of the material, sensible world. It was made possible through one's spiritual nature, the soul.

For our immediate purpose, the importance of this Platonic transposition lies in what it says about knowledge. There must be a continuity of knower and known, and Plato achieved his "like knows like" by underscoring the soul's kinship with the Forms, which, we said, was accomplished at the price of an ontological discontinuity between physical or material body and spiritual or immaterial soul. In setting the soul at odds with the body, Plato aligned himself with the religious tradition of shamanism that has been called a "drop of alien blood in the veins of the Greeks."[15] The transcendence in knowledge, therefore, was to be accounted for by a transcendent principle of divine origin. If it made one ontologically discontinuous with his corporeality, it likewise made him ontologically continuous with the Transcendent. There are ambiguities in this ontological continuity which I shall indicate in a moment, but they did not hinder the early Greek, Christian theologians from latching onto this religiously congenial aspect of Platonism.

So important, both philosophically and religiously, is this whole movement of thought regarding immanence and transcendence that I will be considering it from different angles throughout this work, hoping that my reader will not be discouraged by what can appear to be flights of philosophical fancy. In reality, we are dealing with one basic question: What is it to be human? The answer given by what, for convenience sake, I call Platonism is that we are symbols. We are spirit and matter, the meeting place of upward and downward currents, and therefore in our thought and action involved in the tension caused by immanent and transcendent forces. It was, we said, a religious myth or framework that gave rise to this picture of the true human being

15. E. Rohde, "Die Religion der Griechen," in his *Kleine Schriften*, II, 338; cited by Dodds, 139.

as a shaman. In a nutshell, the story of this book is one of philosophers attacking that myth and its picture of us: a description complicated by the fact that no one can attack anything intellectual in a wholly external fashion. The philosophers are both in and outside the framework under fire. But now the whole arsenal of weapons, should we say, employed by these attackers has been put into question. If the presuppositions of modern philosophy made a view of mankind and the religion behind it obsolete, what is to be said now that we are skeptical of the attackers' position? However convoluted, my idea is that for us to understand religion, we have to look at this perplexing history. Willy-nilly, we are part of a culture that has been shaped by the controversies we are exploring.

Having located ourselves once again, then, let us return to Platonism, for it is from this source that both the religious and secular streams of our culture have emanated.

Why do I give such stress to the soul, Plato's ontological principle of transcendence? Because the picture that it offers of ourselves is hierarchical or vertical (synchronic in the anthropologists' language). We are comprised of matter, soul and *pneuma* or spirit: ontological components that carry us beyond ourselves to the source of our being. What is greater or higher on the scale of being explains what is lower because the lower exists for the sake of the higher. Matter is vivified by soul so that we can rise above our bodily conditions to universal concepts and the spiritual life of freedom. Conversely, the horizontal or diachronic view of us, the evolutionary perspective of our time, by undercutting the hierarchic, ontological grounds of transcendence, has called for its radical revaluation. Explanation now moves in the opposite direction, from lower to higher. The movement of life is away from, not toward, the source of one's being. As a consequence, the perspective of modern philosophy has been that immanence (human knowing) explains transcendence, which is the reversal of the religious viewpoint that transcendence (God or the Sacred) explains immanence.

Undoubtedly a number of factors was responsible for this reversal. With the esteem for the methods of quantification and observation highlighted by the new science, the doctrine of the soul as a metaphysical (non-empirical), "divine" principle became increasingly problematical. Moreover, in the rules he set forth for directing the mind in his new philosophy, Descartes emphasized that since all science, all knowledge, is nothing but human wisdom, rays of light generated by the Mind, our task is simply to augment the natural light of reason. And so, although Descartes himself proposed a version of the ontological argument — our idea of the perfect could have come only from God, which would seem to indicate that in his own mind he had not completely eliminated the priority of the transcendent over the immanent — nonetheless, his successors came to regard the soul as a dispensable "myth." Knowledge could be explained without it.

In my opinion, the immanent thrust of Greek thought is exhibited in the philosophy of Plotinus, the fourth century A.D., intellectually fashionable amalgamation of Plato and Aristotle. Because of this overwhelming movement, many of the early Church Fathers rejected philosophy; those who did not, modified it considerably. For Plotinus' interest was to establish a purely rational system by showing how our world is intelligible because of its derivation from, and sharing in, an ultimate principle of intelligibility. Two problems are urgent in this kind of enterprise. First, if the principle is one of immanent intelligibility, is it in any way transcendent to the objects known? In Plotinus' terminology: does the One exhaust itself in its emanations? The other problem is freedom. If the system is one of rational determinism in which the necessary connections of cause and effect are displayed, then the world that we experience is rational because these things had to happen. From a Christian standpoint, this meant that God had to create; and that the question the system was designed to satisfy: Why world? has only the answer: it had to be. Consequently, the religious response to the Platonist continuity of knowledge, which in its emphasis upon immanence culminated in a wholly transcendent, unknowable One, was to emphasize two principles of transcendence: creation and freedom. Freedom was, above all, that of God in creating, but it was ours too. Choosing to be virtuous, the Greeks maintained, was simply a matter of knowledge. Not so, said the Christians, for what about the experience of St. Paul which Ovid succinctly phrased: "I see and approve the better things, yet I do what is worse"? That experience shattered the neatness of rational schemes and introduced that note of contingency which makes life unpredictable, surprising, and sometimes mad.

Interestingly, as the problem of immanence and transcendence has shifted down the centuries, the legacy of the Patristic period has endured as the religious bulwark against total immanence. In its medieval form, the problem was complicated by Neoplatonist interpretations of Aristotle and the philosophical-theological debates carried on within Islam. Still, creation remained the linchpin of Aquinas' thought, and like his predecessor, St. Augustine, he treated the will as a rational power, an *appetitus rationalis*: distinguished from the intellect in its movement (*ad-petere* in Latin means *to seek for, to desire*) toward its good, truth. Not for them a power of the "absurd." We shall see that a proper understanding of creation and freedom is essential if we are not to succumb to the attractions of the Age of Immanence. Indeed, it was because these concepts lost some of their pristine luster that the anti-religious drift toward immanence gained momentum and still lingers on.

If we characterize the Renaissance in the usual way as rebirth of the Latin and Greek classics, we have to recognize that it was in many ways an exercise in fantasy. I suffered through a professor of Greek who had the singular misfortune of being born too late. In kinship with his colleague, the professor of history who thought that nothing had happened since 1900, he sighed for happy, carefree Athenian days, for the heroic deeds of Thermopylæ and Marathon, for a Phidias, a Sophocles, a Demosthenes, and almost blamed the tortuous Greek of Thucydides on the disastrous expedition he chronicled. In philosophy, too, we have had this kind of nostalgia. Even though Descartes' announcement that his *Meditations* were an *eversio*, a changing about of everything he had learned, he has been interpreted as harking back to Plato, to the pure springs of philosophy before they were contaminated by medieval theology. Yet the Cartesian plunge into dualism had only the faintest Platonic ring. The soul was divorced from its mechanical counterpart; the continuity of deductive knowledge was preserved from the error-inducing discontinuity of will; the function of a transcendent God was to guarantee the immanent operations of the human mind. Surely Cartesian man bears little likeness to Plato's philosopher-shaman.

In retrospect, Descartes' philosophy can be understood as an antidote to the shattering experience of the Reformation. The religious upheaval had put an end to the old securities, notably the Bible and the Church. Even States were splintered by the principle: the religion of the land is that of the prince. If there were no Descartes, we usually say, his world would have invented one. A search for a new ground of certitude was imperative. That he should have sought one within himself seems less remarkable when we recall the Reformers' emphasis upon the gift-character of salvation: a stress that was intended to safeguard divine transcendence but inevitably resulted in an "impossible" or irrational because "wholly other" transcendent. God, Luther had insisted, decided to remain unknowable and incomprehensible outside of Christ. It is unfair to Luther that the philosophers, having forgotten about Christ, relied upon themselves. Still, we cannot read the philosophy of the Age of Immanence except as an articulation of that contention, as Nietzsche perceived. The Protestant pastor, he remarked, was the grandfather of German philosophy. Kant's God, philosophically postulated because beyond the ken of knowledge, aptly expressed hometown Königsberg pietism. Yet what kind of religion is this that exists on the other side of the abyss, totally alienated from a person's deep intellectual committals? Kant's successors, notably the seminary classmates Schelling and Hegel, tried to bridge that abyss without wholly surrendering all the premises that necessitated it. That led Nietzsche to formulate their preoccupation with the Absolute in another of his celebrated one-liners: "One need only utter the expression 'the Tübingen Seminary' to grasp what German philosophy basically is: an insidious theology."[16]

Were this accusation simply the result of pique, we could, indeed should, dismiss it. But Nietzsche's quips call attention to the ironies or perversities of our history and repay careful study

16. *Der Antichrist* in *Werke*, X, Leipzig, 1906, 367.

with insights denied us by more circumspect commentators. In this instance, I believe his remark has to be projected on a broader historical screen. As a trained classical philologist with a good grasp of things Greek, he was particularly competent to criticize a philosophy that prided itself on its classical heritage.

Descartes' ego-based philosophy was not simply a revolt against the "holy Scotists," as Erasmus had called them: the scholastic thinkers whose methods reduced vital topics to dust and ashes, but a determined effort to break up the marriage of convenience that united philosophy and theology throughout the medieval period. In a period of religious altercation, it is normal to look around for a nonsectarian common ground. Descartes, of course, believed that he had found such a ground and never ceased to believe that his secular discovery would, in fact, benefit religion. His protestations of loyalty to the Church, his finagling to get the Jesuits to use his *Principles* in their colleges, his dedication of the *Meditations* to the theological faculty of the University of Paris: all these are moves made by someone who never suspected that he had founded a new religion. Although we have been reminded by the specialists that Descartes' break with the past was not absolute — he was indebted to scholastic terminology and has pronounced Augustinian strains, probably picked up from the Oratory — it was in a very real sense absolute. By making human consciousness the Absolute or ground of knowledge and thus guaranteeing the independence of philosophy, he likewise inaugurated the trend of explaining transcendence by immanence. Either the lower explains the higher or there is no higher to explain.

It was during the period after Descartes, with Voltaire, Diderot and the group known as the *philosophes*, that a philosophy independent of religion became a philosophy against religion. Undoubtedly there were many reasons for this change of direction. In general terms, since antipathies are usually caused by specific experiences — economic, political, social, etc. — we are wont to point to a growing intellectual freedom precipitated by the Reformation and the new science. I am inclined to think that Nietzsche perceived a certain irony in the fact that the religious movement known as the Reformation played a key role in unleashing the forces which became destructive of religion. To free oneself from the old scholastic philosophy that was tied to theology and the Church was one thing; to free oneself from religion in one's thinking — Luther had sanctioned the move by calling reason the devil's harlot — was something else. This latter meant free thinking without qualification, without committals or responsibility of any kind. Freedom, that is, became the right to think, say and do whatever one pleases, which was what the new subjectivism was all about. The immanent owed nothing to the Transcendent, nor was the Transcendent any guide for the immanent. That this kind of thinking should have been developed by people who, ostensibly, were religiously committed or had made formal studies in theology — Kant, Schelling, Hegel — struck Nietzsche as perverse.

But I believe that there is more to "insidious theology" than that, whatever Nietzsche may have intended by the words. Either it means that these people who used words like "Faith," "God," "Trinity," "Absolute," etc., were in good faith: they offered a philosophy or philosophical theology which, like that of the scholastics, was compatible with their religious beliefs. Or it can mean that they talked religiously, mindful of Fichte's expulsion from the university over atheism, so as not to upset political authorities, yet in reality were intent upon offering a new "secular theology." That Hegel went down into his grave with the secret of interpreting his texts undivulged illustrates the alternatives. Were his writings not capable of discordant interpretations, we would never have had the Hegelians of the Right (religious interpreters) and the Left (irreligious or atheist interpreters). Difficult as he is to interpret, Hegel presents our problem in a peculiarly striking way, and so we shall return to his thought after we have related these developments of modern philosophy to Plato.

I return to Plato once again to examine the pedigree of modern philosophy. As we proceed in this book, we shall be looking at Plato from different angles because the attack on modern philosophy is directed at those features in Platonism which purportedly have been the mainstay of the modern conception of philosophy. Immediately, I wish to concentrate on that feature which can help us understand why Nietzsche used the word "theology."

It is significant that Aristotle called the study of first principles theology, by which he undoubtedly meant that an investigation into the ultimate principles of reality carries us into the
realm of the divine. This, I believe, was the mystery that
prompted the reflections which we call Greek philosophy. For
Plato the ecstatic journey of the shaman was the reality to be
explained. For if the search for wisdom brought the human into
the divine, then the human must have some kind of intrinsic
divine principle. Today, both philosophers and theologians,
myself included as will appear subsequently, complain about the
reliance of Greek thinkers on visual metaphors, which in this
case suggest that nothing other is required for knowledge than
"taking a look." But we have become hooked on these metaphors because we have put too much stock in the figure of the
broken line and the imagery of the Cave in the *Republic*. We
forget that their point is to illustrate different kinds and degrees
of knowing: distinctions which never belie the underlying conviction that for knowledge to be possible there must be a continuity
of knower and known. The soul, I have emphasized, is not a
dispensable "myth" but is that principle of continuity. Difficult
to understand without a doubt, for no one can read Aristotle *On
the Soul* or wade through even some of the Persian, Arabic,
Hebrew and Latin literature that little treatise provoked and still
believe that the issue is "mere knowing" and blown up out of all
proportions by faulty picturing. Heidegger, I believe, had it right
when, in his rethinking of the metaphysical tradition, he formulated the problem as the relationship of beings to Being. How
can what is finite and changing grasp, and so become part of, the
unchanging or infinite? The problem, Truth, is, as St. Augustine
recognized, that of humanity and its religion; and the Greek
thinkers who devised a philosophy in order to throw light upon
it, never, as far as I can see, tried to make it into something else,
even though some of them did their best to tidy up the thought
in which the problem was presented. They were fascinated by
the idea of the divine in the human. What is it in the experience
of our human reality that, for all of its evil and imperfection,
continues to call for the Absolute? In spite of our transitoriness,
we continue to make definitive judgments, to assert categorically
of a particular instance: "This is the case." The Greeks were

impassioned to understand themselves. Plato's journey, like the shaman's, was for wisdom, *phronesis*.

If this interpretation of Plato and Greek thought sounds strange, it is because we have been trained to read the Greeks anachronistically, that is, epistemologically. The historians of philosophy — we might say that philosophy had no history until it became an independent discipline, which involved establishing a pedigree that would justify the prejudices of the new rationalism — were joined by the editors of the Greek and Latin Classics in the work of presenting their Plato. Rhode's reference to shamanism as a "drop of alien blood in the veins of the Greeks" exemplifies the trend. The movement, to our relief, is not without its humor. That the history of modern philosophy began in a "cerebral episode" — why did Descartes have to confess that it all began in a dream which involved, among other things, a pilgrimage to the shrine of Our Lady of Loretto? — has, if mentioned at all, been properly deplored. In the new philosophy of reason, there would be nothing, of course, that smacked of mystery. If that meant cutting ourselves down to something that we can explain clearly — Descartes had said "mind"; by the time of Kant everybody was talking about "consciousness" — so be it. In the new age of specialization with so many other sciences to explain our humanity, it looked pretentious anyway for philosophers to march under the banner of seeking an understanding of our essence and that of our world. Knowledge became their specialty which, in keeping with the new independence from theology, had to be clarified without religious entanglements. That meant getting rid of Plato's "soul" — a "myth" anyway — and reconstructing — Kant called it re-grounding — metaphysics. Most of us cynics in philosophy are inclined to think that by the time Kant got finished showing what makes metaphysics possible, there was no metaphysics to be made possible. "God," "World" and "Soul" had vanished as objects of cognition. Heidegger, once again, was perceptive when he, in contrast to those who reject metaphysics on empiricist grounds, described the situation as the death of the "onto-theo-logical" tradition. It is easy, that is, to reject metaphysics if it is an *a priori* conceptualist system like that of Christian Wolff, which is what

Kant attacked. More recently, Gilbert Ryle popularized the phrase that ontology or metaphysics is ontologizing: drawing "positive existence conclusions" from "conceptual considerations."[17] Were both of these philosophers too polite or too circumspect to admit that the new philosophy, having divorced itself from theology, had no room for an Aristotelian metaphysics because as a pursuit of an ultimate, it was in his terms a theology.

By anyone's standards, Aristotle's *Metaphysics* is a teasing work. Found bound together in a volume after the *Physics* (*meta-after-physics*), the work can be understood as a speculation that grows out of physics. That is, having discussed the principles that account for the changes in the physical world, we are led on in our theorizing to talk about more comprehensive principles: those, namely, that unify all reality. This was the first philosophy Aristotle rightfully called theology; it described the human intellect in its pursuit of truth as *theion*, divine. Although he disagreed with his master concerning the theory of Forms, he did not change the direction of Greek thought, as is evident from Plotinus' synthesis of him with Plato. Mankind is a movement toward the source of its being; and the soul, even though it is the form of the body, still has a mysterious ontological continuity with the divine. Metaphysics, therefore, was inescapably theological as is evidenced by the fact that the mystery of our psychology was given perspective only later by a doctrine of creation. Thus Kant's re-grounding of metaphysics came to no more than what he called the little work that summarized his three *Critiques*: *Prolegomena to any Future Metaphysics*.

There would be less confusion, to be sure, if Kant had been more forthright and dropped the word 'metaphysics', and if the historians who followed in his wake had not been so eager to establish a pedigree for modern philosophy that they have us thinking of Greek metaphysics in the light of the projected Kantian "metaphysics." In order to show us how any metaphysics is possible, Kant would establish its grounds. His

17. The expression is Gilbert Ryle's in the "Final Discussion" of *The Nature of Metaphysics*, D. F. Pears, ed., London: Macmillan; New York: St. Martin's Press, 1957, 150.

philosophy can be summarized as an effort to show us how the structures of consciousness ground our knowledge of reality. Superficially, it is possible to envisage Plato's Good, Aristotle's Unmoved Mover or Plotinus' One as models for Kant's consciousness. Grasping them, we have laid hold of ultimate or eternal truth. The history of metaphysics, in this perspective, would be a history of the grounding model. We have simply moved from the postulate of an ultimate idea, "God," that human cognition requires. Although I have argued elsewhere[18] against the grounding model as the bane of Greek philosophy — others, too, have attacked it, together with the previously-mentioned visual metaphor[19] — and recognize that the Greek preoccupation with intellect can incline us to read them as direct ancestors of the Enlightenment. I do not believe that the platonic shamanism can so easily be bleached out. Plato regarded understanding as the prerogative of the few because it was the fruit of ascetic training, whereas Hume's distinction of the philosophical from the vulgar impresses me as an instance of intellectual snobbery. For Plato, that is, philosophy was less a knowledge than a quest. True, Aristotle, who was basically a biologist, sounds much more like a modern rationalist, yet Plotinus apparently found no difficulty in weaving his thought together with Plato's into a mysticism of the One. Thought, as described by these philosophers, is a surging upward movement toward the source of all intelligibility which, in turn, is the ultimate ground of meaning. But, as is clearest in the case of Plotinus who, I believe, caught the spirit of his predecessors, we never comprehend that ultimate font of meaning. We are drawn toward it by the whole thrust of our being, a movement that the doctrine of the soul attempts to express. The Absolute, therefore, in this Greek thought is an ultimate intellectual principle, but one that compels us to think it because it forms the milieu in which we exist. Both Plato's Good and Plotinus' One are the sun whence the light of intelligibility shines. We begin philosophizing be-

18. In *Religious Consciousness and Experience*, The Hague: Martinus Nijhoff, 1975.

19. Richard Rorty, *Philosophy and the Mirror of Nature*, Oxford: Blackwell, copyright Princeton University Press, 1980.

cause we stand in that light, so that our search for truth is an effort to understand why we are beings of this kind: beings that in the immanent act of knowing move toward a transcendent because they share in that transcendence. The language of analogy that we have alluded to fits into this perspective.

The contrast with the Absolute of modern philosophy can scarcely be less striking. When Kant postulated a wholly transcendent God as a requirement of thinking, he crystallized the modern view that philosophy is a quest for truth, but from the old standpoint an impossible task because we no longer stand *in* the truth. If the mind is the sun of the new human science so that the movement of thought is always toward truth but never within it, by what criteria are we to judge anything as true? Thus all of modern philosophy became a mad search for these criteria which, by stipulation, had to be uncovered either within a mind or by a mind that was not a transcendent principle. Kant's postulated God is indicative of the transcending movement within thought, not *of* thought, which explains why he reduced all traditional proofs for the existence of God to the "invalid" ontological argument. Because we lack an ontological principle of transcendence, these arguments attest the transcending requirement of thought. They are purely "logical" or "conceptual," because they do not carry us into the transcendent. From the ancient standpoint, philosophy could no longer grapple with the mystery of ourselves, having dissipated it.

I have already mentioned that Hegel's pondering of the Absolute, which he presented as the culmination of the history of Western philosophy, ended on an ambiguous note that propelled Heidegger beyond metaphysics. Taking his keynote from the Greeks, Hegel insisted that we begin in the Absolute. Present implicitly in the first moment of thought, it carries us along through a process of successive explications. Hegel thus distanced himself from the Cartesian-type demonstration of modern philosophy. To prove or to explain was to clarify, an *Erklärung*. Although in the past Hegel's Absolute has been interpreted as God, so that the movement of his thought has been understood as a progressive dissolution of the Sacred, we are now more willing to accept his averment that the *Phenomenology* is a study of knowledge. He must be understood in the light of the post-Kantian philosophy of his day. That, of course, is the difficulty. For Hegel was aware of the fact that the insoluble dichotomies of Kant's philosophy: of thought and freedom, of science and morality, of phenomenon and noumenon, stemmed from knowledge's requirement of an Absolute-God-Totality that remained wholly transcendent. He therefore translated the Absolute not as an ultimate but as the immanent, freeing moment of thought, as a process of ab-solving. The problem with this translation is that as much as he talks about the Whole or Totality and assures us that the truth of the system is to be apprehended at the final moment of thought, that final moment crumbles in our fingers. For if the Absolute is actually thought's movement of negation or "othering," it is obviously not a vision of things whence everything is intelligible. It is nothing less than what he declared it to be: an insight into the transcending or "othering" nature of thought. In other words, having started from the position common to both Greek and Kantian philosophy, that thought somehow engages us in or requires an Absolute, Hegel ended with the paradox that thought is itself the absolving Absolute: a transcending movement that is on the verge but falls short of eliminating transcendence. No wonder that he accentuated the "cleverness of reason" and made this paradox the puffing engine of his system. Surely it was this result that, as I say, catapulted Heidegger beyond metaphysics because the modern metaphysics, bolstered by its interpretation of the ancient metaphysics, shows us the bankruptcy of thinking transcendence as solely a moment in the immanent activity of knowing.

Hegel has, from our standpoint, provided us with a very important insight. If thought is a successive negating, it cannot, if it is to continue its transcending movement, eliminate its "other." This, I believe, was the significant aspect of the Greek analysis of thinking which modern philosophy chose to ignore. The inspiration of modern thought in thinking the Absolute has been that thought could justify itself, that we could construct some kind of closed system, whether of thought or Being or language, which was the once-and-for-all truth. This is what I meant by my earlier contention that modern philosophers would provide us with an *ersatz* religion. They had reasons for believing religion to be such a system. Yet had they been faithful to the Platonic heritage and less impressed by the truly astounding developments taking place in Western Europe which led Europeans to regard themselves as a superior and privileged people, the modern philosophers might have recognized that they were actually offering another system which was as hidebound as the religion it replaced. Were it not for the still widespread acceptance of this parody of religion, we might console ourselves with the thought that the desire to be perfectly rational which sustained the moderns was, as our contemporaries have taught us, itself irrational. Negatively, the history of modern philosophy bears witness to the limitations of thinking ourselves as minds.

The reaction of contemporary philosophers has been an emphasis upon the import of the corporeal to any analysis of thought. If by our bodies things are present to us, it follows that knowledge is rooted in presence, in the temporalizing factor of our being. In philosophical circles, Heidegger's descriptions of Being as temporalizing or historicizing are well known. Less so, regrettably, are the explorations of Elizabeth Sewell in her fascinating study, *The Orphic Voice*, a remarkable work that has received little attention from philosophers. Elsewhere I have summarized her formulation of the question posed by the myth of Orpheus as follows:

> What power and place has poetry in the living universe? or, What is the biological function of poetry in the natural history of the human organism? These questions voice another protest against the Greek and modern legacies of radical discontinuities — subject/object, nature/history, mind/body, reason/imagination, etc. — that have sundered Western man by compelling him to divorce his poetry from his prose and to ask himself how either his poetry or religion might be true. Having made the profoundly ethical decision that the ideal of knowledge is realized in detachment so that the discovery of truth is contingent upon a prolonged objectification, the Westerner was saddled with that acute discontinuity which his literature of alienation has recorded. For a literature of involvement, Sewell would have us ponder more deeply Francis Bacon, Shakespeare, Vico, Hooke, Milton,

Linnaeus, Erasmus Darwin, Swedenborg, Novalis, Goethe, Coleridge, Wordsworth, Shelley, Emerson, Hugo, Renan, Mallarmé, Rilke. They can show us that because the whole man participates, the fittest who assure the survival of culture are the artistic explorers, not the philosophical and scientific investigators, whose mentality, so often devoid of artistic fervor, has brought us to the sickness unto death of Western civilization. These creative people indicate how it is that an organism in its exploratory movements instigates further adaptations.[20]

The literature of involvement begins from the fact that we are corporeal beings and thus rooted in a specific time and place; hence we need a power of transcendence in order to realize the full meaning of our situation. It is this aspect of transcendence that Heidegger explored. Presence, he noted, is in reality a composite of our being *pre-sent*, embracing a moment of fore (pre-) and aft (sent). The realization of presence is accomplished, therefore, by the deployment of an horizon, the imaginative existential, as it has been called, which by bringing into focus the rich actuality of the present, has in religious circles fostered the development known as liberation theology. A meaningful Christian proclamation must deal with present realities: the actual functioning of church structures, the plight of the homeless and jobless, the impact of multinationals on an agrarian economy, etc.

As horizon-deploying, the act of transcendence must be seen above all as creative. There is the danger of supposing corporeality to be strictly inhibitive. We appear to be so locked into our historical situation that we cannot fully enter into other times and places, much less create something different for ourselves. But this, I would suggest, arises from our failure to be truly *present*. The pre- or past moment of our presence is composed of an actuality and any number of unrealized possibilities. Do we appreciate what has happened if we are ignorant of what might have occurred? Responsible lives are fashioned by choices, either those we ourselves have made or those in which we now acquiesce. And so, only if we have "lost the past," that is, chosen to

20. *Religious Consciousness and Experience*, 167.

ignore it or failed to realize the wealth of its possibilities, are we bound to what seems the fate of the future. To be fully present means that our grasp of the past enables us to project a future (our forward movement of consciousness or being sent) that is likewise a realm of possibilities. The act of transcendence, therefore, enables us to grasp the potentialities of our human existence. Through the creative imagination we deploy a meaningful horizon in what may be called an act of hope.

Clearly, if there is any merit in this manner of conceiving transcendence, it is that the notion has been freed from the philosophers' constriction of it to the "othering" moment of consciousness and made a constitutive activity of the integral human person. Transcendence — here it manifests itself as an essential part of our mythic activity — thus culminates in a vision of cosmic proportions. But this alone would scarcely reserve for it an exclusively religious interpretation. Marxism, to cite but one instance, is certainly a vision of this kind. It differs from the religious primarily in its account of the origin of its vision of things. When pressed to deal with origins, with the inspiration of a particular religious way of life, religious people resort to the language of theophany or hierophany. Something happened to trigger such an outlook that called for a transcendent "object": the divine, the Sacred, God, etc., as the proper way to characterize an experience. Hence it is that the transcendence we have described can receive a theistic interpretation. An implied world of meaning is disclosed in which we find ourselves situated, dependent, yet not so situated that the entire course of history is fully laid out before us. Somewhere there lurks a challenge, usually that of a person, in response to which one becomes a person. Thus in the act of religious transcendence the horizon, as I have already noted, is, in a personal sense, received. Conversely, in an atheistic or secularized interpretation, the world of meaning unfolded is one in which we are to achieve ourselves either by helping to usher in the new proletariat heaven of Marxism or by actuating our potential to be an integral person. We are, in a sense, complete, totally situated by ourselves, independent. The vision answers to the hope of a better individual, a better world: something to be achieved by solely human resources. Transcendence of this kind is ultimately reduced to immanence.

Personally, I find this description of transcendence as an act of horizon-setting rooted in our bodily condition important because it furthers our understanding of what it means to call us symbols, places of encounter. It leaves open, however, the question of our relationship to a transcendent "object." If there are psychologists who interpret the phenomenon as simply the becoming of person — Jung's self-realization, Reich's personal liberation, Laing's creation of ourselves in a meaningful community — there are others who acknowledge that this becoming requires the Transcendent for its completeness. Regrettably, the persons we need to bring us out of ourselves are themselves limited, burdened with the imperfections that grate upon us and readily turn us back upon ourselves. Hence to sustain the outward movement of becoming, we need an unfailing source of motivation, of love, the perfect "Other," whom Saint Augustine invoked as the one more intimate to him than he was to himself. Similarly, if there are philosophers who have translated transcendence as the cognitional moment of "othering" in which a totality of meaning is presupposed, there are likewise those who argue that the Being in which beings participate is analogous to what religious people call or mean by God. Because the interpretation of transcendence is thus consequent upon the kind of vision we have chosen for ourselves and our world, the theologian, even though he or she may see the deployment of an horizon as a de-conditioning, as a bursting of our temporal conditions through the act of understanding them, will resort to other features of our experience to explicate that de-conditioning which Eliade has called the core of all religions. He will have us heed Heidegger's invitation to ponder our own death, not just because it reveals our present finitude, but more so because it manifests a pervasive longing to overcome, to triumph over, death. Accordingly, the temporalizing or horizon-deploying transcendence — what characterizes us as rational beings — is, so to say, but the tip of the iceberg, revelatory of a deeper impetus to overcome all of our physical, intellectual, moral and spiritual limitations. For this reason theological transcendence has everywhere had recourse to *metanoia*, to the language of conversion, a complete change of heart.

It would be a mistake to suppose that because a change of heart necessarily implies freedom — and here we must be cautious: for even if we know that we should change and to that extent want to change, it does not follow that we will change — the choice involved in an interpretation of transcendence is not simply a matter of preferring one meaning or world view to another. You choose to be a physicist whereas I prefer to be a sociologist. Today I have chosen a red shirt to wear; tomorrow it will a blue one. For if my reading of Heidegger is correct: that like Hegel he has shown us how thought cannot be grounded or rationalized (both men emphasize its circular character), then it follows that we cannot continue in the philosophical tradition of thinking transcendence as merely the "othering," the reaching-beyond-ourselves moment in knowledge. Understandably, Marxists and other convinced atheists, by dint of their commitment, will persist in reducing transcendence to immanence. Heidegger's Being-toward (in the face of)-death thus has no further meaning than the realization of our inescapable finitude. If that is his message, then why the clarion call to rethink Being? Why the agonizing, and sometimes perverse, "retrievals" of Heraclitus, of "the Greeks," of Kant and Hegel? What purpose do the purported excursions into etymology serve if the result is nothing but a rehash of Kant's metaphysics of finitude? The "later" Heidegger has been accused of obscurantism — for instance the suggestion that language is our mistress — of dabbling in poetry, of foresaking the rational philosophical tradition in order to show that the true philosophers are the poets. They are, as the Greek root *poiesis* itself indicates, the creative people. Yes, he has abandoned the philosophical tradition of the moderns and has pointed us in the direction of a fundamental ontology. Since what I have said in this chapter about myth and symbol are pertinent to Heidegger's project, I can best clarify and summarize these strategies by relating them to the issue of transcendence and immanence that the Heideggerian philosophy enjoins.

By presenting myth as a framework in order to distinguish it from mere myth-making or fictionalizing, I drew upon religious myths, like that of *Genesis*, because these are comprehensive. Science is a myth, more restricted than religion's offering us a reason to live and a reason to die, but still general insofar as it provides us with a methodological framework: investigative techniques, modes of verification, etc. Chemistry likewise affords an outlook for the chemist but hardly one, except, perhaps, for the most dedicated of professionals, that we think of as life-encompassing. Consequently, I looked to language for an analogue. For although a language does not offer reasons for our existence, it does bring us into a world of meaning. We saw that religious myths are conveyed in stories because a story not only captures our imagination (in a significant way it influences the way we picture things) but also inculcates attitudes and community values. Stories, I said, run the risk of being just stories, amusing tales for children. But their historical and cultural features compel us to seek "the point" and thus can instigate our critical appraisal.

What probably requires greater emphasis in this account is that the kind of framework I am talking about is life-oriented or life-enhancing. I have referred to attitudes, values and ways of "seeing" or imagining because the framework, unlike one for chemistry or biology, is not simply a knowledge framework. Or perhaps we should say that it is a knowledge framework but not one understood as a patterning for a being who is thought to be only a mind. Descartes may have flattered himself that he was a mind, to which his body, its feelings, etc., were mere appurtenances. But thinkers before him who were aware that thinking always takes place within an horizon of meaning were more realistic in their approach to thought. It is the whole person who thinks, not just a mind. A philosophy reflects one's life, not just his thought. A knowledge framework, therefore, is one that encompasses the entirety of the human person. To emphasize this point I seized upon Ricoeur's use of the term '*gnosis*.' It is a label for the one-track mind which makes a mockery of reason's freedom. Myths are "open," not to be dogmatized in a single interpretation. Are we wrong in aligning Ricoeur with the Cartesian tradition? Had he acknowledged that it is the whole being who thinks, would he not have given some emphasis to the fact that thinking or interpretation does not take place in a vacuum? To propose *the* interpretation of a myth sounds less outrageous when we couple the closing-off nature of reason as determinative with its concrete operation within an historical community. Could one offer *the* interpretation to a group unresponsive to it?

I have mentioned that Lévi-Strauss would appear to agree with Ricoeur; every interpretation of a myth is equally valid. But whereas Ricoeur's '*gnosis*' suggests that anyone offering an interpretation — would anyone do so if he did not believe it to be *the* interpretation? — possesses a secret insight inaccessible to others, Lévi-Strauss' rich proliferation of details invites us to see each interpretation as valid because of the historical context in which it is offered. At the end of his four volume work, *Mythologiques*, he stated that his intention was to present a myth of mythology: a framework for understanding themes and variations (the work is structured like a symphony). "But," he noted,

> we have never dreamed of accomplishing anything else than a work of knowledge, that is to say, of becoming fully conscious (*prendre conscience*). Nonetheless, philosophy has for too long a time kept the human sciences imprisoned in a circle by not permitting them to present to consciousness any other object of study than consciousness itself.[21]

Lévi-Strauss' knowledge takes into account all of the concreteness of man's historical condition. Ricoeur, on the contrary, appears a *bona fide* member of the modern philosophical tradition, for "mind" divorced from history would have to be blessed with *gnosis* in order to offer any mythology or *the* interpretation. Perforce it takes refuge in a skeletal framework, in "myth as myth."

I introduced the notion of transcendence into the discussion of myth for two reasons. First, it is essential to knowledge because as the act of horizon-setting it allows knowledge to be. In addition, it is descriptive of the movement of knowing: as it were, the movement "beyond" in order to assimilate what is "other." We *come to know*. Second, our philosophical tradition harks back to Plato, whose use of the idea of transcendence to explain

21. *L'Homme nu*, Paris: Plon, 1971, 562–3.

human knowledge is doubly significant. By borrowing a myth or framework from the religious tradition, Plato, whatever may have been his intention, opened the door to questions regarding the role of religion in knowledge: a question exacerbated by the modern and contemporary trend of divorcing religion from either philosophy and/or knowledge. Besides, his discussion was not carried on within the confining modern categories, "mind" or "consciousness," but within the broader context of what this knowing prompts us to say about human existence. Transcendence for Plato, therefore, was not an epistemological category in the modern sense of the term. It was, of course, epistemological but in the deeper sense of being an ontology of knowing. In short, Plato spoke of knowing as the way in which a human being exists, not about knowing as the pre-eminently important part of human conduct because it is the foundation of all the sciences.

The history of symbolism, concerning the debasement of which we shall have more to say, is a record of symbols losing ontological meaning (I have said we use symbols because we *are* symbols) and achieving the status of "just symbols."[22] In our post-modern period, however, there are those who have wanted to restore the tattered dignity of symbols but by negotiating the difficult passage between the "Scylla of metaphysics" and the "Charybdis of anthropocentrism." Take, for example, the Neo-Kantian existentialist theology of Paul Tillich.

> Tillich regarded the predicates traditionally ascribed as properties to God as symbols. The utterance 'God is merciful' is not a categorical attribution but an expression of acceptance of a 'symbol'. Tillich concedes to his inhibitions about metaphysics that 'The criterion of truth of a symbol naturally cannot be the comparison of it with the reality to which it refers, just because this reality is absolutely beyond human comprehension'. Tillich draws his inspiration for an alternative account of the 'truth' of religious symblos from existentialism. The suggestion he makes is that the truth of a symbol depends on its 'inner necessity for the symbol-creating consciousness.' He is very impressed by the fact

22. This history is adumbrated in my *Religious Consciousness and Experience*.

that such symbols cannot merely be invented. Their 'inner necessity' consists in their ability to keep a hold on how people look at things. Symbols may not be adequate to new situations. Those which are 'true' are those which can retain their hold whatever new situations men are confronted with.[23]

From what I have said in this chapter, Tillich's indebtedness to the history of modern philosophy should be clear. The question of truth which agitated him will be discussed subsequently. It has not been my purpose in this chapter to point out all the factors that have contributed to the debasement of symbols, for I have said nothing as yet of the religious currents that carried it along. One of the results of the Reformation — the expression 'religious currents' is indicative of the fact that the cataclysm was not a volcanic-like explosion — was that many symbols became "just symbols". The theological argument over the presence of Christ in the sacrament turned on the meaning of "symbol," on whether or not "real" and "symbolic" are antithetical. It was the genius of modern philosophy to have given intellectual respectability to that juxtaposition to the detriment of the symbol. These philosophical developments have been perceptively traced in Rorty's book.

My contention, therefore, is that Hegel's *Phenomenology* belongs to the modern philosophical movement insofar as its goal was an insight into the knowing process. The Absolute with which that work ends is proof that the attempt of the moderns to find the unity and justification of the sciences in a philosophy of mind or epistemology was futile. As a consequence, Hegel changed the subtitle of the *Phenomenology* from "Part I" to "Introduction" (a shift that has been the source of endless scholarly dabate) which has left some of his readers wondering into what they are being introduced. For the "second part" or main work that followed was the *Logic*: a detailed study of the Kantian categories as we find them in the *Critique of Pure Reason*, but presented to us not as a formal logic but pointedly as an ontology. At least this would appear to me a sign that Hegel had not been reading the

23. Stuart C. Brown, "Religion and the Limits of Language," in *Reason and Religion*, Ithaca and London: Cornell University Press, 1977, 242–3.

Greeks in vain. Whatever we may think of his product, he worked with the conviction that a free-floating epistemology was untenable.

That Heidegger should see Hegel as the end of the metaphysical tradition is, from our standpoint, the supreme irony. The end he is insofar as he has shown us the outcome of the theory of knowledge. But to see him as the end of the line of metaphysicians commencing with Plato who were concerned with ontology as a development of the entirety, not just the cognitive dimension, of human existence, requires an imaginative leap. At the outset, of course, this was no leap for Heidegger. His fundamental ontology was, in my understanding, a rethinking of Kant after Hegel's critique of him. In other words, Heidegger staked out his own position with reference to the Hegelian ontological logic, that is, within the modern, post-Kantian, epistemological tradition. But in the later Heidegger, we have argued, we have more signposts, more "byways." The hiddenness of Being — Heidegger borrowed expressions from the mystics; he even uses "the holy" (*das Heilige*) — can suggest why religious people instinctively have recourse to symbols. At the end of his career *Transcendenz* for Heidegger apparently still meant the movement of Being-Knowing which it was in *Being and Time*. Yet he, too, employed many different strategies in his philosophy. These have brought us, I believe, to the point of seriously wondering how rational, logical or scientific is that choice which characterizes transcendence merely as a phase of knowing. If it is no longer possible for us to entertain the idea that philosophy "grounds" the sciences and all human knowledge, why do we continue to expect it to "ground" religion? Must we, because we cannot escape our modern heritage, suppose that if our immanence cannot establish the Transcendent, then a Transcendent is irrational?

CHAPTER III

The Religious Imagination

C AN you imagine Immanuel Kant, whose philosophy presents the image of a dour, humorless intellectual, although he is said to have been an engaging table companion, on the day he discovered he had a transcendental imagination? He must have kicked up his heels and run outside to spread the good news. Or perhaps, like Archimedes when he dashed from the bath with the cry, "Eureka!" he startled his neighbors. But his neighbors' joy or wonder would have as quickly disappeared had they been told what the discovery was. They, too, had a *"transcendentale Einbildungskraft."* It must have sounded like a new form of the Black Death. But, of course, Professor Kant was a philosopher, and in their ignorance, they probably thought that philosophical wonders never cease. Had he not told them, they would never have suspected the priceless treasure they harbored.

In spite of the kind of note the German word may sound in our ears, it carries nuances that I find helpful in understanding our usage of 'imagination.' Like our English word, the root, *Bild*, means a picture, an image. It is important that we hold onto this basic meaning, leaving the connotations associated with 'fiction' or 'imaginary' to one side. For how we picture the world is important. Our emphasis in the previous chapters upon framework or myth underscores the indispensable role of the imagination.

Without it, without the patterns and schemes that enable us to order our experience (think of trying to cope with the seven million colors that are said to be discriminable), we cannot think. For this reason, sociologists and physicists, among others, resort to models. These offer the scientific investigator a convenient way of going about things. A mass of materials has to become data, and the complexity of these has to be so organized that our finite minds can handle them. In this perspective, the imagination is not a separate picture-making faculty or power of fantasy. It is an essential moment of what we call the thought process: a fact we acknowledge when we say that people who enable us to see things differently are blessed with creative imagination.

Related to *Bild* is the German expression, *Bildung*, which refers to one's educational formation. An educated person is *gebildet*, formed to a mentality so that he or she "pictures" the world in the way that others do in a given society. This, we noted, is the purpose of education: to form someone so that he can communicate with others through the use of appropriate symbols. Thus if we push the German expression a bit, *Einbildung* would mean to form one in the sense of the English "acculturate." The imagination, therefore, might be described as the 'power' (*Kraft*) that acculturates us. As I have already suggested regarding the learning of languages, where considerably more is involved than memorizing vocabulary and grammatical forms, acculturation entails the taking on of all aspects of a way of life. Americans who come to Europe suddenly realize how Americanized they are, even how different they are from others whose native tongue is also English. We have, in other words, the American imagination: not only forms of expression but a whole outlook or a feel for things that is at work when we think.

Our history compels this clarification of imagination because the forces that brought about the debasement of symbols succeeded by traducing the imagination. They emanated from the philosophical tradition which we have described in the preceding chapter. Thought, it was said, was a product of "mind," and Professor Kant himself was responsible for directing philosophical energies to consciousness understood as a group of structures that made knowledge possible. He had to say something about 'will' because in the Prussian State philosophers were expected to do their part in upholding the moral order, which is to say, in maintaining the *status quo*. But why should he worry about a transcendental imagination? Knowledge, it is agreed, is an acknowledged fact but mysterious nonetheless. How is it that those biological mechanisms which delight behaviorists generate flights of fancy, philosophical speculation and theological conundrums? No one has as yet given us a wholly satisfactory way of comprehending the process. In Kant's day, in fealty to the tradition, one went about explaining the mystery by talking about the material or sensible component of knowledge and then relating this, however mysteriously, to the immaterial or spiritual (intellectual) component. It was that relation, we remarked, that Kant fudged. Something had to do the trick, and what better than the imagination? After all, the word had a philosophical pedigree, even though a not very respectable one. What indeed could be better than explaining the unknown by the equally unknown?

Bearing in mind that Kant philosophized in the heyday of rationalism, we can appreciate that it took some courage on his part to have accorded the imagination so prominent a role in thinking, even though its workings eluded him. But that mattered little. The business of philosophy was reason; and it was to safeguard reason, and reason's brilliant accomplishment, science, that Kant sought to parry the devastating thrusts of Hume. For most students of Hume, their interest is his empirical theory of knowledge, with the result that they tend to soft-pedal the significance he attached to our natural instincts. The inferences of reason, he argued, are actually carried along by natural impulses. Is not habit, the ingrained "custom" of believing that the future will be like the past, a conditioning or forming of the imagination? I wish that Hume had been less polemical in his philosophy and had developed further his interesting suggestions about the nonrational. Subsequent philosophy might then have escaped earlier from the narrow idea of reason he attacked and saved the imagination from its damnation in philosophy's hell. Hume might even have contributed his bit to Elizabeth Sewell's

literature of involvement. That, of course, is probably setting our
expectations of him too high. His criticisms are trenchant because he operated from within the system he denounced. He
was, philosophically, too much of his times to have revolutionized
them.

From what I have said in earlier chapters about frameworks,
about the nature of myths and the mythologies that concretize
them, and about the evocative power of symbols stemming from
the fact that symbolism as a language carries with it a whole
"feel of things," it is evident that our use of 'imagination' is at
odds with most of the philosophical tradition. Or perhaps I
should say with what those historians who have been mesmer-
ized by the Enlightenment and have therefore taken its accomplishment as the paradigm for philosophy would have us believe
to be the *bona fide* philosophical tradition. Obviously, I have no
quarrel with the contention that philosophy has studied thought.
The problem is, simply, that the rationalists would have us
forget that it is the concrete, historical reality, the "whole
person," who thinks. There are philosophers, needless to say,
who have rejected this heritage of rationalism. Rorty's book is
evidence of this. Yet its publication evinces the lingering vitality
of that heritage. For this reason I find myself at times apologetic,
at times polemical. As a philosopher, because I want to be
certain that a reader familiar with the discipline does not cast my
expressions into a rationalist mold, I feel that I am constantly
digging up old bones for reburial. Our history makes it difficult
for us to outgrow these time-worn epistemological battles.
Theologians, too, are caught up in the same kind of apologetic.
But, generally speaking, religious thinkers, because of the holistic nature of religion itself, are not Cartesian rationalists. In the
West, where rationalism came to birth, the major religious
traditions are historical: tied to historic personages and specific
interventions of God in human affairs. History precludes the
image of the human being as a disembodied mind contemplating
or fashioning "eternal truths." Besides, religious thinkers are
instinctively wary of rationalist philosophers. From Descartes
on, those most intent upon pulling down the temple were those
who had been nurtured in it. Regrettably, the new effort to be

"rational" was fueled by a great deal of venom and talent for obloquy. Was it necessary that religion be so invidiously contrasted with "rationality" or science? Before condemning it, ought we not take religion at its finest hour? Do we reject science as such because of our fear of a nuclear war or our disappointment with scientists who have succumbed to pressures and manufactured data? In this work, concerned as it is with the kind of thinking that goes on in religion, we can as well speak of the scientific imagination as of the religious.

Important as the idea of God may be to most religious communities, I believe creation to be the central myth of religious thought. The myth has been presented in numerous mythologies. Eliade offers a rich sampling in *From Primitives to Zen*: stories of creation by thought, by an earth diver, from nothing, through a struggle with chaos, by a division of a primordial unity, by sexual intercourse, by sacrifice. Understandably, their variety has worked against them. It led the early historians of religions to comment on the hopeless naivety of the prescientific mind and no doubt confirmed the good intentions of the colonialist powers in their civilizing mission. For a long time we have had to live with Lévy-Bruhl's "pre-logical" mentality. Only recently have we suspected that 'primitive' might harbor some prejudices that ought to be discarded. Trapped as we are in our history of scientific explanation, we can suppose that these fantastic stories were not intended as explanations but, as Paul Ricoeur has suggested, as means of "opening up and disclosure."[1] They inculcate an outlook on life but were not meant to explain. Yet this will not do, given the obvious intent of the stories.

> All through the first millennium B.C. intelligent minds in India were striving for convincing explanations of the cosmic mystery. In the latest phase of the Rg Veda poets began to wonder about creation, which was not adequately explained by the current mythology.[2]

1. *The Symbolism of Evil*, 165.
2. A. L. Basham, *The Wonder That Was India*, London: Sidgwick & Jackson, 1961, 247.

The myths studied by Lévi-Strauss were likewise clearly intended to explain such things as a society's preference for mat-
rilineal kinship or fishing. Hence, Basham continues,

> This wonderful 'Hymn of Creation,' one of the oldest surviving
> records of philosophic doubt in the history of the world, marks
> the development of a high state of abstract thinking, and it is the
> work of a very great poet, whose evocation of the mysterious
> chaos before creation, and of mighty ineffable forces working in
> the depths of the primeval void, reminds us of the cosmic phanta-
> sies of William Blake.[3]

To appreciate what is here at stake, we must keep in mind the
fact that the modern, rationalist philosophical tradition owes
much to the case of Galileo. It flourished not only because the
new science proved itself in the practical order, but also because
its propagandists, with plenty of ammunition from their antagonists, were determined to break religion's hold on people and
to humiliate the Church for persecuting Galileo. Causal reasoning, as proposed in Descartes' mathematicism, became the paradigm of thought. This discovery had become part of the
academic lore of the West with the translation of some of
Aristotle's logical works in the twelfth century. Later translations — by the thirteenth century the Latin West finally knew all
of Aristotle, even if many versions were at first slanted by their
Neoplatonist Arabic translators — shifted logic from the center
of the stage so that Descartes' method burst upon the scene as a
triumph of ingenuity. Explanation thus became a matter of
causal determination: singling out *the* factor or element which
serves as something's foundation.

For example, water — the primeval waters of *Genesis* —
features prominently in many creation accounts. We can suppose that because many "primitives" found water by digging,
they deduced that it must be the basic element. Or like the early
Greek cosmologists, they so concluded because they noted the
necessary link between water and the growth or sustenance of
living things. But why are we to assume that "primitives" were

3. *Ibid.*

or are doing our kind of science? Moreover, while acknowledging the validity of analysis, must we stipulate that we know things only by breaking them into their constituents and isolating their basic elements? We can know a person by consulting his or her medical chart and ascertaining the condition of his liver, spleen, heart, etc. But surely this is not the only mode of understanding a person and scarcely the basis for all understanding. It is this fallacy — the confusion of the grounds of a belief, the *how* I have come to it, with its justification, the validation of *what* I believe — which Rorty, following T. H. Green and Wilfrid Sellars, identifies as the original sin committed by Locke that has vitiated modern philosophy.[4] Indeed, we learn little about how water functions in creation stories by thinking solely in causal terms; and water as "the ultimate" hardly justifies most of what is said about it in these stories.

For the agriculturalists who recited the Babylonian *Genesis*, the *Enuma Elish*, water was essential to their living. It thus symbolized their dependence, and creation stories resolutely affirm man's fundamental dependency. Religious myths, I said, instill a value system: basically an attitude toward one's self, others and one's world summed up in the phrase: life, though a gift, is a mixed good. We have chosen neither to be here nor the circumstances of our being here. But like it or not, we mature as persons only by working with what has been given to us. Water, for agriculturalists, aptly symbolizes this mixed situation. It is the source of life and many of life's pleasures as well as of untold suffering. It is remarkable how many creation stories contain memories of a flood. If we are inclined to take the *Genesis* story of Noah literally, we might try building an ark according to the specifications laid out there. It is obvious that the story-teller knew little about ships and the buoyancy of water. But given an experience of the destructive power of a flood, we can understand why the ordering of the world was depicted as the rescuing of it from the waters of chaos. Since water purification rites are religious commonplaces, the world was cleansed in the flood of *Genesis* and returned to its primordial, undifferentiated unity. As

4. *Philosophy and the Mirror of Nature*, 139 ff.

the waters receded and our land appeared once more, a sign of covenant, the rainbow, was given, symbolic of the fact that our land was once more the "sacred" land, marked off from the non-human, transcendent, infinite, chaotic. I shall have more to say about this use of 'sacred', for it manifests a distinctive feature of religious symbolism.

I have displayed some of the meanings of a familiar creation myth — the story of Noah emphasizes the cosmic dimensions of human rebellion; in corrupting themselves, humans have contaminated their world — to give a clearer picture of what I mean by the religious imagination and its holistic kind of explanation. Science, we noted earlier, explains by de-anthropomorphization, by universalizing abstractions or quantifications that assure "objectivity." Conversely, a creation myth places human beings in their totality at the center of the picture, not because the world revolves around us but because nothing else is of more interest to us. We live in a world that, for all of its corruption and sickness unto death, is both ours and divine: a creative venture that is as mysterious as it is intriguing. In the course of history we have tried to picture that mystery to ourselves in both artistic and philosophical pictures that, as symbols, conceal as much of the real mystery as they reveal of ourselves. Michelangelo's famous Adam fresco in the Sistine Chapel captures a wealth of meaning in the outstretched fingers: the man's reaching out to God is likewise God's reaching out to him. It emphasizes human dignity. The relationship of dependence in creation is not enslaving. Religion is not a stultifying, addictive opium of the people. But the attitude of the painting is contemplative: the eyes of God and Adam meet in a gaze of mutual respect. It is the primordial "beatific vision" that says nothing about our role in the creative process.

The philosophical discussion of creation, by contrast, has concentrated exclusively on beginning. A generation or production model — God as a potterer; Hume's God the watchmaker — has been developed in a metaphysics of causality, with its attendant problem of clarifying our knowledge of the cause from its effect. We noted that the emanation scheme of Neoplatonism was a metaphysics of rigorous causal determinism which, among other difficulties, cancelled out the freedom that preserves the wonder of creation as a gift. Why should we expect the metaphysics of creation suggested by religious commitments to resolve the perennial problem: how does the finite come from the infinite? Philosophically, we are back to square one because we cannot agree on what kind of answer we would accept for the basic question: "Why is there something rather than nothing?"

The intention of creation stories, precisely because they were told and compiled long after the events they purportedly describe, voice the conviction that although this is our world because we live in it — one thinks here of the injunctions of *Genesis* to subdue the earth and its creatures, to increase and multiply, etc. — it is nonetheless God's world, totally his. Yet this world is unfinished. Creation was a genesis, only a beginning, so that if we are to understand ourselves, we must see ourselves as con- or co-creators, as working to accomplish something that is both ours and not ours. Religion never allows us to escape the mystery of immanence and transcendence. Work that is ours is the product of our immanent activity. Yet both ourselves and our association in this work attest a freedom that transcends us. Creation stories are assertions of that freedom, a transcendent 'Act', 'Power', 'Presence' establishes a relationship with us and makes us what we are: people who through our activity show forth the meaning of creation. Creation, therefore, is not that happening "back then" which gets us into trouble with evolutionists. It is the fundamental revelation of what we and our world are all about, so that subsequent or historical revelations are to be understood as simply other or developed manifestations of that fundamental meaning.

Because this notion is not easily grasped, let us consider some of its consequences and some further expressions of it in religious language.

First, in saying that creation is a *revelation* of *our* meaning, two things are being asserted: a) as revelation, the meaning of ourselves and our world is also transcendent. We can, and often do, offer completely "this-worldly" or immanent descriptions of human activity. The revelation of creation is that any full description of this activity implies going beyond us, for this is

"God's world." Man and world are mysteriously related to something beyond them; and b) as *our* meaning, we refer to the totality of the human: the individual cannot be divorced from his or her world. The truly cosmic vision of *Genesis* is echoed in St. Paul's remark that it is "all creation" that groans and looks for salvation. Second, it follows from this viewpoint that history is revelation and that revelation is history. As a record of the activity of human beings in developing their world, history reveals creation. And so correlatively: history is itself a revealing process, manifesting to us the meaning of ourselves and our world as a creative activity. Third, because history reveals creation and creation is above all an affirmation that this is God's world, then we are

> compelled to think of the one God and to exclude nothing. Joy and misery, slavery and freedom, belief and disbelief, polytheism and monotheism, pantheism and atheism, even good and evil: they all appear as witnesses to the meaning of God and the actual relation between Him and His creation.[5]

Throughout the history of religion, different sorts of stratagems have been called into play to avoid this unwelcome conclusion. The "problem of evil" has given us everything from a philosophically finite God to a theologically incarnate principle of evil. Undoubtedly one can think of many reasons why it became religion's Achilles' heel during the Age of Enlightenment. Yet it is significant that the philosophers held responsible for the unhappy aftermath of the debate were, in their formative years, educated in a religious tradition that salvaged the holiness of God by segregating him from our sinful world. It was inevitable, that is, that the post-Reformation theology of mankind's total corruption should eventuate in the philosophy of Deism. The picture of God as the supreme mechanic was a natural appendage to the new mechanical science of the day. But this picture, which is neatly captured in the comfortable Deist phrase: God is in his heaven and all is right with the world, was too tidy for the

5. Wilhelm Dupré, "Culture and the Meaning of God in Creation": a paper delivered at a conference on monotheism held at Rome, November 18, 1981.

grim reality of everyday experience. In his *Dialogues Concerning Natural Religion* Hume attacked the idea of an infinite, all-powerful watchmaker. Why would one who wound up the world and then let the machinery take over be content with only the best of *possible* worlds? Is not anything possible for God? The answer to this dilemma: either God is all-powerful and does not care or he is not all-powerful, has been the religiously disastrous "Who cares?" Laplace's famous retort to Napoleon: "I have dispensed with that hypothesis," was the foregone conclusion of the problem of evil. God is irrelevant to human affairs.

The secularization of Western culture is assuredly a complex phenomenon. To pinpoint *the* cause of it is not only rash but foolhardy. But it is instructive to connect the "this-worldly" meaning of secularization with the further connotation, "of this age." For it was during the Age of Enlightenment that the original meaning of creation — the statement of faith that this is God's world that we are privileged to "create" through human activity — was lost for reasons logically connected with a theological premise. To make God "wholly other" only serves to deepen the mystery of his relationship to a sinful world. If we credit the "enlightened" philosophers with the intent to overcome an "impossible transcendence" (this was, of course, the Age of Immanence, and a "wholly other" God was philosophically unknowable), we must deplore the result of a God who, as the world's mechanic, was too closely identified with his "evil" machine. Better by far to dissolve the problem, which entailed getting rid of God and leaving human perversity as an inexplicable datum. For religious people, on the contrary, creation reveals our situation, though it does not dissipate the mystery surrounding the gift of our creative activity. Indeed, it is creation which reveals that aspect of our activity which has been both scandal and stumbling-block to the "enlightened" of all ages. The relationship of God to mankind has been on our part a prolonged "ego trip." Our history reveals a continuous rebelliousness: a refusal to accept the fact that our role is one of dependency: to create *God's* world. Hence for Christians the sacrificial death of Jesus was not an act of expiation offered to a pitiless tyrant obsessed with justice. Rather, it, too, manifests our version of a creative relationship, in that we would go so far to assert our independence as to kill God. Thus the death of Jesus, as I understand it, is a lesson of love. Since love is the activity that matures us as persons, only love can restore us to the relationship that is the basis of our creative humanity.

It should be clear that I have referred to the Judaeo-Christian story both because of its familiarity and because, as Westerners, our intellectual history has been within that tradition. In addition, I have mentioned the sacrifice of Jesus because it is integral to the *Genesis* creation myth. Later in this chapter we shall see how death and its sequel, eschatology, complete the arch of which creation is the keystone. For the moment we must return to creation stories in general to detect how their meanings can be distilled in other religious terms.

I have used the word 'sacred' in connection with these stories because creation is depicted as an ordering, the formation of a cosmos by "setting it off" from chaos. In religion segregation plays an important role, for originally something was made sacred by separating it from the profane, from everyday usage. The consecration that incorporates one into a "holy" people carries with it distinctive marks: circumcision, caste signs, a special garb, etc. All religious literature deals with holy places, holy objects, holy persons, and it is in terms of these as focal points of order that a group finds its unity as a people. Eliade has made much of these centering symbols. In some tribal societies villages are laid out from a center according to a theological scheme. A tree or pole can mark the "center of the world," just as for the ancient Greeks the cave of the Delphic oracle was the world's navel. These centers — Eden's tree of knowledge of good and evil is a good illustration — are focal points of meaning. Our "lived space" is intelligible in contrast to the darkness outside. It is out there that the dead and spirits roam, and we do not know our way about. But it is not just the village layout that reflects the conviction that this is God's world. Every facet of life, political, social and economic, although from one standpoint a human creation, has a divine provenance. The idea that God or cultural heroes have given us the arts of civilization attests the depth of meaning to be attached to creation. Society, as Durkheim purportedly said, is a religious phenomenon. We create it, but its creation is part of an all-embracing relationship. Our ordering or making sacred is likewise the Sacred's ordering of us. Thus in Eliade's remark that "the world becomes apprehensible as world, as cosmos, in the measure in which it reveals itself as a sacred world,"[6] full weight has to be given to "reveal" and "sacred." Our creative activity, the fashioning of a world, reveals the Sacred, the principle of order and meaning, which has chosen this way to make itself manifest. As a consequence, order has always been a conspicuous part of religious tradition. Both East and West, each in its own way, would integrate us once again, knitting us and our world together in a comprehensive whole. Yet each of these traditions acknowledges that the order of the world, an important philosophical datum in Western thought, is perceived as ordered within limits. Yes, our world is sacred but only because the limiting chaos beyond enables us to grasp order. So from this point of view, the real sacred is not our everyday, finite world. Rather, the sacred is that on account of which we distinguish our world. From this angle, our "sacred" world is actually profane, and the profane "outside" is the genuine Sacred, the In-finite.

Why do religious terms function in this dialectical way? *Prima facie*, creation suggests a picture of God making a world. But as we have seen, if we allow the picture to captivate us, we never understand the term as revealing our role in the world. So, too, of the "sacred." Because the churches as organizations are wedded to order — one studies, for example, church "order" or "sacred canons" or "sacred theology" — a passion for identifying our way of doing things with God's blinds us to the deeper meaning of the liturgical phrase which Rudolf Otto borrowed to describe the holy: *mysterium tremendum et fascinosum*. The sacred is a mystery: a word frequently associated with "inscrutable," but which in its liturgical usage is a symbol, with all of the connotations we have already attached to that word. In fact, the two adjectives, *tremendum* and *fascinosum*, indicate its symbolic character.

6. Mircea Eliade, *The Sacred and the Profane. The Nature of Religion*, translated from the French by Willard Trask, New York: Harper & Row, 1961, 64.

Tremendum carries emotional overtones. Something is 'tremendous' because it is fearsome; it causes us to tremble with fear, and therefore, instinctively, to run away. But on the other hand, repelling as a mystery may be, it also fascinates. Like Icarus toying with the destructive flame, we are drawn, impelled by curiosity to this cause of aversion. Thus by calling something a mystery or sacred, we indicate its symbolic nature. It is a cause for us of fear and wonder. Poor Jeremiah was, as God's prophet, touched by the sacred. He belonged to the most privileged; the wonder of the holy filled him with an attitude of humble worship. Yet he was the most miserable of men, despised by his contemporaries because he filled them with dread. Therefore, the answer to the question why religious terms function dialectically is that they are symbols. Not only do they express a way of life; they involve in the root sense of so *turn us around in* it that we live through its dialogue. These root meanings are important because they show us how much we miss by imagining that we are simply shuffling terms in a deck of cards. These symbols are called dialectical because a dialogue is a give-and-take affair. We work our way through (*dia*) words or reasons (*logos*) to get into a world of meaning and share its truth. Accordingly, Heidegger's discussion of *logos* harks back to the ambiguity of its verb, *legein*, both "to speak" and "to gather." It is because we are gathered together in a language or culture that we can speak to one another or "dia-logue," and thus further our unity by an increased "gathering."

Of all the symbols used by religious people, the most important and most confusing is undoubtedly 'God'. Earlier in this work I stated that the characteristic of the religious framework is that it inculcates the attitude that the world is a gift. Religious people are challenged to become persons by an encounter with something or someone that in some sense of the term must be called a person. Deliberately I left the matter in that vague sounding way, both because one cannot say everything at once and because I knew I would have to come back to it anyway. Here, too, I shall defer discussion of religion and the human person, for my present purpose is to make clear that I see no contradiction in saying that God is a symbol and that he is a person. The sentence that I have just written illustrates the difficulty. We all know that God is not a "he." If I had not known that before women's lib, I certainly would now. And so, as misleading as our pronominal adjectives may be, I cannot write "his/her/its" every time I refer to God. Besides, none of these adjectives is germane to the way I want to talk about God as a person. It also should be noted that because I think of 'God' as a symbol, I might have used the word to define religion and ignored the objection that Theravāda Buddhism, presumably without God, is the counterexample that undermines the definition. Even Theravāda would bring us to wholeness through enlightenment and therefore has to have some symbol for its de-conditioning. Like all other religions, Buddhism is creationist in that it would reintegrate us in the divine order of things. For us, 'God' is embedded in the cultural pattern of a revelation religion. But there is no reason why we cannot prescind from our modes of conception enough to allow the term to function as a symbol of transcendence for Buddhists as well.

Our previous discussion of creation and the sacred should enable us to see the point in calling 'God' a symbol. If creation reveals the meaning of ourselves and our world, then both the 'sacred' and 'God' contribute their bit to our understanding of this meaning, either by shifting our sights back and forth between order and disorder or by concentrating attention on the quality of our relatedness or dependence. The teasing out of meaning has always been, even in philosophy, the purpose of dialectic. What we say about 'God', then, could have been said about the sacred, although the remarks with which we begin our discussion of the evolution of 'God' will provide, I hope, a deeper insight into how religious people think.

Perhaps the most striking feature of all descriptions of God is their sheer anthropomorphism. Among hunters and food gatherers, God was the "master of the animals," the "lord of the beasts"; among other peoples, the headman, leader, chief, etc. A number of different themes come together in these characterizations. They exhibit the conviction, surely, that God is the one who is concerned about our lives. He is involved in the hunt because lives depend on it, just as by pastoralists or agriculturalists he is portrayed as a shepherd or fertility deity. In Tikopia, for example, the tuber is planted in ceremonies that emphasize human solidarity with plant and vegetable life, and the prayers addressed to the tuber can lead us to suppose that it is the god. I am reminded of an incident that occurred at the end of a meal with a large Arab family. As one might expect in such a gathering, the children were playing about the table where someone had inadvertently dropped a piece of bread. When everyone had gotten up and the table was being cleared, an old man came across the bread and immediately stooped over, picked it up and kissed it. We take our bread for granted. Routine prayers over food fail to convey that deeper connection of God with life. Moreover, a puritanical strain in us can prevent us from appreciating the significance of the linga of Shiva or the bizarre sexual representations that adorn the temples at Khajurāho in India. Does anyone really believe that God is sexed or that he is an androgyne? God, as this last portrait reminds us, is the fullness of life, the completeness for which we seek in all sexual love. But for us sexual intercourse terminates in what has been called a "little bit of death." The desire to prolong pleasure unmasks the deep-seated lack behind our grasping for completion. Even in our celebration of God as life is the awareness that he is death, a darkness into which we must walk alone.

Somewhere in his *Tristes Tropiques* Lévi-Strauss has commented upon the importance of the chief to the marginally subsistent nomads living in Brazil's Amazon region. Upon his sagacity (which is why God is frequently pictured as an old man) the life of the group depends, for the right time to migrate is crucial to their existence. Reading this account, I better understood God as chief; and when I came across the fact that the chief was rewarded with additional wives, I thought of an Australian Aborigines' account in Eliade's *From Primitives to Zen* in which Bunjil (God) is said to have two wives, Black Swan and the Rainbow. God, in other words, is the source of all life, and the story reminds us that we are caught up in the cosmic web. Ecology, we noted, is "religious" because it, too, stresses our oneness with Nature.

As in creation stories, an obvious theme displayed in these

anthropomorphisms is order. Not only is God portrayed as one concerned about our specific form of life and therefore as the chief who maintains it in existence, but he is the one who provided us with the fire that is central to that life and taught us the art forms (pottery, music, iron forging, etc.) that sustain it. Significantly, the divine activity is somehow tied down to precise geographical features of a people's landscape. Just as in Hebrew history proof of God's deeds was to be found in specific locations: at Horma, at the waters of Meribah, at the pillar known as "Lot's wife," so are other accounts fitted into a particular group's order of things. The narrative in which we learn about Bunjil ends with surprising definiteness: "This was before Batman settled on the banks of the Warra river."[7]

In religion, of course, God's ordering is not just a geographical or cosmic phenomenon but moral as well. In his study of Christendom,[8] Werner Stark has noted that for people like the Jukun, the Shilluk or Ancient Egyptians, there was a close parallel between ensuring righteousness and securing sustenance. Both, indeed, depended upon bringing the social order into harmony with the cosmos. The theme, presented in terms of Ṛta and dharma, is basic to the Vedas; it assumes increasing importance in subsequent Greek religious writings; it is incarnate in the person of the Pharaoh or divine ruler. Current studies of Buddhism in Thai villages have emphasized the importance of religiously meritorious deeds, whether feeding a monk or financing a wat, in maintaining the social fabric.

Religion has correctly been called an "inherited conglomerate," for its history shows us that the concepts of God prevalent among early hunters were developed in the course of their being passed on to neolithic agriculturalists and later pastoralists. Agriculturalists live by the seasons. They are caught up in Nature's cycle of production and reproduction: an experience upon which their livelihood depends, and for that reason can readily suggest a train of thought that the life of the hunter precluded. If Nature is a continuous round of birth, death and

---

7. *From Primitives to Zen*, 3.
8. *The Sociology of Religion: A Study of Christendom*, Volume One: *Established Religion*, New York: Fordham University Press, 1966.

rebirth, are not we, as a conspicuous part of Nature, likewise caught up in its cycles? Is it not true that we must live in harmony with the cosmos? Nature has evidently adapted us, in pigmentation and in other ways; and if we want to survive, we adapt ourselves to heat and cold, to lightning and hurricane, and to natural needs for water, salt and nourishment. Here Nature takes on its literal meaning as the place of birth and origins; and our awareness of this obvious yet neglected truth opens us to the thought of our own possible immortality. The circumstances of one's life — it has been suggested that ownership of land heightens the sense of individuality that leads to reflections on personal immortality — can introduce a new cypher, a new trend of thought. The seeds that we sow in the ground are instruments of revelation. We are born to die, but in that death the hope of resurrection dawns.

The agricultural life brings with it a range of symbols unavailable to hunters. We have mentioned seeds. Fertility has associated with it the blood of life and, above all, woman. Eva (Eve) is life, the mother of all mankind. But not only in the *Genesis* story is she presented as an ambiguous symbol: as the source of the new that ends only in death. In her figure are life's attractiveness and its disappointment, its purity and its danger, that strange conjunction of proscriptive taboo and sacred prostitution. The apartness of the sacred is imaged in the idealization of woman as virgin. Its commerce with us and the risks that this entails is pictured in the virgin as mother.

There is another element of agricultural life that enters into the God symbol. As we saw in relation to the memories of floods, water can symbolize devastation as well as generation. Farmers and ranchers pray that rain will fall and that it will not fall. Weather aptly symbolizes the unpredictability of life. And so we would expect that the storm would play an important part in religion. Yahweh, the God of the Hebrews, was depicted as a storm deity, appearing to Moses in a burning bush, leading his people in a pillar of fire by night and a cloud by day, and manifesting his sacredness, his terror, and his wonder in a cloud flashing with lightning and bursting with thunder on Mt. Sinai. A storm is, for all of us, an object of fear and awe. I have been fascinated while watching one churning up Lake Michigan or resounding over its waters; been almost terrified at the approach of one when I have stood on top of a Colorado peak; and known people who have been so gripped by the "beauty" of the murderous sweepings of a tornado that they have forgotten their emergency plans and stood helplessly aghast. In Hesiod's *Theogony*, creation, the establishment of order, is an act of violence. Chronos, Time, castrates his father, the Sky (the eternal, the "beyond"). The story weaves together a double theme. On the one hand, our temporal order, brought about by a rupture of the eternal, is continuously threatened. Without constant effort, it easily reverts to the indistinctness, the chaos, from which it sprang. Yet this reversion to chaos is a natural dialectical moment. Unless our order dies — that is to say, if we forget that all of our orderings, religious, political and social, are finite, not once-and-for-all products of absolute, divine decrees — we will not rise to new life. As a consequence, orgy has always played an important role in religion. It is the time when the old laws, held in abeyance, (in Catholic Europe and European-settled lands, the 'death' of the Lenten fast is preceded by carnival, a festive throwing-off of one's inhibitions, and succeeded by new life at Easter) are called into question as life-giving regulations. On the other hand, creation is a victory of time over eternity, so that the coming to birth of ourselves and our world is a violent act, a sacrifice. Time, as we know, is the relentless master of our lives. It can hang heavy on our hands; it carries us with it in an ever swifter flowing current. Religion, accordingly, would free us from Time's tyranny and reintegrate us in the eternal movement of things. It would free us, we said, through a radical deconditioning, by removing those hampering conditions which Time appropriately symbolizes.

Yet is it not true that Time, like God and the Sacred, is a dialectical concept? Because God works "in time," we are told to redeem the time. Yet because he is beyond time, we are to be redeemed from time. And so, if, on the one hand, it symbolizes our finitude and need for overcoming, it is, on the other hand, the field of our activity, the dimension in which we work with God to bring about his creation. Like "Life" and other great religious symbols, it reveals our fundamental ambiguity: pledged to life yet doomed to death; destined for growth yet humbled by contraction; dependent upon God yet co-creators of his world. This truth of creation is manifest even in the little we have presented of the evolution of the God concept. It is the cultural, the socio-economic conditions of a people through which God is revealed to them. Thus we should see in this successive or progressive development of concepts how a group's way of life creates a world, the meaning of which is both concretized and revealed in the God symbol. History, we noted, is revelation. The mystery of the human creative process is that it unfolds before us symbols that mirror understandings of ourselves as existing in a God-Man-World relationship. In a sense, the Old Testament is a story of the conflict of symbols. The story of Cain the hunter and Abel the shepherd is a foretaste of Hebrew history. The nomadic Hebrews, coming out of the desert with an unrepresentable storm god, Yahweh, marched into Canaan whose inhabitants, as city dwellers, served other gods. As agriculturalists, their God symbols stressed fertility and their artisans found graphic ways of expressing life. For the migrating Hebrews, their way of life was at stake. To abandon the "open sky" of the nomad for the comforts of the city was not only debauchery but blasphemy. A similar conflict is to be found in the later history of the Maccabees: a story of the simple culture of monotheistic Jews in opposition to the cultural sophistications of the polytheistic Greeks.

My point, simply, is that we must grasp the revelatory truth of these dialectical oppositions. Different God symbols must not be seen as just so many exhibitions of modes of production. On the contrary, the human creative process as it forms a culture is condensed into a God symbol because we are aware of our activity as a dialogue. Through our creation we "speak to" God, and in that dialogue God reveals himself to us. That is the mysterious revelation of creation. If we blot out this mystery, as did Feuerbach, what is left is man and his modes of production. The stage is ready for Marx.

In the earlier discussion of myth, I suggested that the myth in the first chapters of *Genesis* grew out of that basic human experience of a world of transient things. Life is a beginning-middle-end affair. It was only natural that this experience should trigger speculation about the coming-to-be of everything. The form that these speculations took was manifold: a rich array of generation, production and other kinds of stories. But as we now see, creation stories, with varying emphases, are not just making or "bare bones" of construction accounts. Drawing, perhaps, from the experience of what is essential to our becoming, they cast the myth in a conspicuously revelatory form. Creation is dialogue. We have already alluded to this notion by characterizing the religious outlook as personal, as one that accepts the givenness of the world as gift. Understandably, this dialogue has been described in the frankly anthropomorphic form of a human conversation, especially in the great revelation traditions: Judaism, Christianity and Islam. We speak to God as Father, Lord or King, and "He" responds to the pleas of his children, his beloved. These imaginings, however helpful, must not mislead us, for I believe that the revelation of creation as dialogue is a salient feature of the religious imagination. That is, by explicating human activity as a creative relationship of dialogue, religious people offer us an insight into ourselves. We ourselves become integral persons by meeting the challenge of a world to be constructed. Through responding, we take upon ourselves creative responsibility.

To help us work our way out of anthropomorphic imaginings, we might reflect back on the discussion of language in the last chapter, in particular upon Heidegger's sentence: "Man acts as if he were the shaper and master of language, while it is language which remains the mistress of man." Like others in the history of philosophy both before and after him, Heidegger was concerned with the visual model of knowledge that we inherited from the Greeks. We revert to this fact because the notion is so much a part of our vocabulary that we are ordinarily blind to its limitations as a model. We say "see" when we mean "know", and thus interpret the biblical definition of religion, "to know God", in its realized, final form as a "beatific vision." The troubling aspect of this visual imagery that we have pointed out is its suggestion that knowledge is a once-and-for-all grasp of something. Either we see it or we do not; there is nothing in between. Having "seen" something and so grasped its meaning, we supposedly "have the truth" in a mathematical kind of certitude. For the Greeks, the idea that mathematics was the perfect science accompanied the notion that contemplation was our most noble activity.

The current philosophical displeasure with this model stems from the fact that, as *the* model, it fostered the idea that understanding is a search for grounds, so that philosophy, as I have mentioned, is the "grounding" of all science. No room here for dialogue. Thus when Heidegger turned from Being to Logos, or when Rorty recommends "conversation" as the matrix of truth,[9] their explicitly philosophical moves are in the direction of religion. They are, let me repeat, pointing toward a transcendence that the subjectivism of the Age of Immanence or Enlightenment tended to ignore. Heidegger's thought, I have suggested, can best be understood as taking this mode of thinking about transcendence characteristic of the classical moderns; namely, a moment in the immanent process of knowing, to be sterile. He recognized that in so doing they spelt the end of the metaphysical tradition.

The hearing model embedded in "dialogue" has always featured prominently in religion. To 'know God' consists of his 'speaking' to us and of our hearing of his 'word': recurring images because they highlight that characteristic of religion which sharply distinguishes it from old-fashioned philosophical knowing. To be engaged in religion's dialogue is a search, specifically the kind of seeking that I have stressed: one that involves the thoroughgoing *working at* which I have called creative activity. If we want to find God and carry on a dialogue with him, we do so by effecting his revelation in history. If we imagine this dynamic enterprise to be a once-and-for-all 'knowing' of God that prompts us to perform certain actions in the world, assisted by his divine providence of course, then we are, from the point of view expressed here, thinking like rationalist philoso-

9. Because this is the basic theme of *Philosophy and the Mirror of Nature*, one can find references to it in that book's index.

phers. It is regrettable, for the historical reasons I have previously mentioned, that religion became just this kind of knowing: the possession of a set of saving beliefs. Besides, theologians are human and if they turned rationalist in the Age of Rationalism, they were only exemplifying the essentially historical nature of our thought. And so, from our perspective, it may not be presumptuous to believe that it is the philosophers, through the kind of creative thinking they are doing, who are revealing to us the meaning of God's creation. The seeking of truth, as St. Augustine reminded us, involves us in a relationship to Truth, so that we can envisage philosophers as bringing us back to the challenge of listening to the word of God.

Evidently an attitude is conveyed by 'hearing' or 'listening to' which is vastly different from that of 'knowing'. There is no need to be attentive in knowing; and in many cases — those who confess to "learned ignorance" appear to be a minority — no concession is made to doubt or error. The word itself can suggest a picture of ourselves and of our task in life that is both reassuring and frightening. Our need for security and contempt for waffling cuts us off from the dialogue of persons. We are dispensing knowledge, not seeking it. The attractiveness of the creation symbol is that it dissipates the frightening aspect of *hybris*, the pride of all-knowing, by combining reassurance with humility. We are co-creators of God's world. This double or dialectical aspect of ourselves is what 'hearing', or even better, 'listening to' suggests. (For the sake of convenience I pack the nuances of 'listening to' into 'hearing', recognizing that hearing someone can be quite different from listening to him.) We hear because we are confident enough to hear, yet not so self-assured that we have nothing to learn. This is why music has a special function in religious celebration, beyond that of creating dispositions of worship. It belongs there because it has a structure suggestive of a religious quest. At any given moment we hear a sound or a succession of notes. To appreciate them as a melody we must press on to catch that series as a unity of sense. Only in the whole, of melody or symphony, are parts appreciated as parts. In religion, too, we forever press on since the meaning of our activities as parts of the work of creation is revealed only as the totality of creation, symbolized in 'God', gradually unfolds. Music thus suggests a dimension of transcendence, a necessity of going beyond to a fullness of meaning which a visual model precludes.

The religious imagination both structures and is structured by everyday experience. Early investigators of religion believed that they had discovered the origin of religion in death rituals or in the reflection stimulated by the universal experience of suffering. Admittedly, the poignant moments in life elicit our most urgent *why's* and lead us to question the meaning of life itself. And so it is possible that the myths that sustain us and the great symbols which condense their meaning originated there. These myths we have seen to be concretized in stories replete with local color, and their symbols evince a language expressing, we quoted Eliade as remarking, "the social, 'historic', and psychic condition of the symbol's wearer, and his relations with society and the cosmos."[10] How better can the function of religion in life which creation narratives are intended to display be manifested? Yet even granting the importance suffering and death enjoy in religious reflection because of their universality, we cannot, for sheer lack of proof, assert categorically that these experiences originated religion. More modestly, they, like "God" and "Time" can open a door to deeper self-awareness. Our remarks on death are intended to show how this is so.

We surmised that it was their life-experience as agriculturalists which suggested to people of a certain era the possibility of human immortality. Should not the human being as part of Nature be ruled by its periodicity? The thought has given us the myth of the phoenix, the fire rising from its own ashes, and the myth of the eternal recurrence.[11] Yet the emphasis in creation stories, that through our activities we are co-creators of a world

10. *Patterns in Comparative Religion*, 451.
11. The vitality of these myths is witnessed in the writings collected by Joseph Head and S. L. Cranston, *Reincarnation: The Phœnix Fire Mystery*, New York: Julian Press/Crown Publishers, Inc., 1977. The scope of the work is announced in its subtitle: An East-West Dialogue on Death and Rebirth from the Worlds of Religion, Science, Psychology, Philosophy, Art, and Literature, and from the Great Thinkers of the Past and Present.

that is in fact divine, carries the implication that we are more than parts of Nature. Even in Buddhism and Hinduism, where the idea of rebirth closely integrates us into Nature's cyclic pattern, the moral law of karma prevails. Because life is above all a moral venture, death's meaning exceeds its biological significance. The religious imagination has duly seized upon this insight to enhance life's meaning.

To call death a punishment, an omission, a mistake, are ways of describing our being out of sorts with the way things are. There are not many people who have overcome the fear of death — "Why me, Lord?" — and the tragic death of a loved one at an early age can convince us that not only is death undeserving, but life itself is hardly a square deal. We cannot avoid suffering nor the death that epitomizes it. So we devise answers, it is argued, to enable us to cope. The rationalization of our situation is "the escape" that permits us to live with it. We project our desire for happiness into a future, where "every tear shall be wiped away," and all wrongs shall be righted. The promise of unending bliss presumably compensates for our humble endurance of the present disorder: "Slaves, obey your masters."

It is not to our purpose to controvert psychoanalytic and Marxist insinuations of projection, since with good reason one can accuse these ideologies of being movements in the same direction. As much as any religion, they determine present action by future aspirations. Besides, we know that the escape of projection is psychologically destructive, totally at odds with the ideas of person and love at the heart of the religious enterprise. Hence it is more constructive for us to pursue the sense of the ideas to be found in the death symbol itself.

Because religion represents a whole outlook on life, it has never presented itself as merely an ethical theory. Morals are involved because we are responsible for our creative activity. But this creation, we have seen, is supported by the relationship — affirmed in the declaration that the world is divine — which gives life and meaning to this activity. And so, just as the law of karma has introduced the idea of merit into Eastern traditions, so is the notion of judgment of overriding importance to Judaism, Christianity and Islam. This notion underscores the emphasis given to religious *praxis*. Not only are we here to create; but the meaning we attach to ourselves, normally articulated in a set of propositions, is attested by our creative activity. In religion, for example, a creed or statement of belief is ordinarily associated with liturgy because the understanding of that profession is to be found in its celebration, in its community enactment. Thus beliefs that project into the future: an association or community of saints, a life everlasting, are present moral imperatives. We know little, if anything, about future arrangements. We do know, however, that the decisions of the moment define us as persons, as well as the community of relations we call a world.

The burden of life and its moral scope are captured in the images cast upon life by the shadow of death. Our days are "as nothing," to be compared to the fleeting passage of a bird from nothingness to nothingness through a dimly lit hall, because we are wayfarers, having here "no lasting city." Pilgrims have dotted the Indian landscape with sacred shrines, the places of pilgrimage that remind them of their innermost reality. Our Western traditions, with their emphasis upon death sealed by a final judgment of reward or punishment, impress upon us an almost overwhelming weight of moral obligation. Life's pilgrimage is a decisive test, freighted with eternal consequences. Contrastingly, Eastern traditions, with their idea that this pilgrimage is not only one from the cradle to the grave but stretches over millions of years that are as unimaginable as the light years of the astrophysicists, would relieve the burdens of moralism by fitting them into a broader picture. Life's goal is not the quest of a blissful, self-absorbing state of Nirvana that, for sheer monotony, might prove as hellish as any place of damnation. Rather, the idea and the philosophy of rebirth that accompanies it afford us a complementary glimpse of what a pilgrimage can mean. The spiritual life is more than law and morality; it is a challenge to continuous growth. In an infinite universe, should there not be infinite possibilities for growth in wisdom, in self-realization, and for the development of compassion and self-sacrifice?

A word of caution at this point might be in order. We must

bear in mind the truism that the religious traditions with which we are dealing have developed in different cultural circumstances. Since our concern is the general one of how religion or, as in this chapter, how the religious imagination functions, we are emphasizing common or complementary viewpoints. Islam, certainly, is in many ways as dissimilar from the other religious groups which I have cited as are the major components of the Eastern traditions — Hinduism, Jainism, Buddhism — from one another. I have not discussed the more social and less personal idea of immortality, becoming aggregated to the ancestors, which one finds in the works of anthropologists on tribal religions. The material is both extensive — in fairness, each tribe has a right to individual treatment — and complicated by formulations which in our times owe much to the impact upon a tribe of foreign missionary penetration. Death among the Igbos (a people of southeastern Nigeria), for example, fits into our perspective because the ancestors whom one joins are influential as guardians of tradition. Whatever imagery may be employed, the role of the Unseens is important in day-to-day living. At any rate, within this work's perspective of world religions, we cannot presume that the notion of punishment, which is useful to religion because of its moral implications, has the same significance in the East and West. That death is a punishment for sin is a Western concept, which has triggered the kind of speculation we find in the Book of Job. In the West, too, having become associated with a juridical mentality, the idea of death as a new beginning and thus as a paradigm for all religious acts has a nuance different from what we find in the East, where we are faced with a succession of new beginnings. This Eastern conception is hard to compose with the contention of Western critics that religion without qualification is simply a projection of "another life."

There are practical reasons why, in a humid land like India, funerary rites take place with dispatch. But in addition, the cycle of rebirths ill accords with either a mummified or prettified corpse. So, too, in the West, if we take seriously the contention that a fuller expressive meaning is to be found in ritual than in a proposition, we should expect to discover a development of the symbolism of death in liturgical celebration. To appreciate this point, some historical animadversions might prove helpful.

In a nutshell, the Reformation was conceived as an attack on man-made religion. The slogan, "sola Scriptura" (only Scripture), was an appeal to return to the simple faith depicted in the New Testament stories. The life of Jesus and his disciples was a far cry from the pomp and circumstance of the papal and episcopal courts of Luther's time. The elaborate rituals associated with the reforms of Cluniac monasticism, the endless theologizing over minutiæ by the learned scholastic doctors, and the dangerous devotionalism of the mass of the faithful — dangerous because they were incapable of making fine distinctions and the line between ritual celebration and magic is a thin one — were cast into a different light by people who were tired of ecclesiastical beggars. The preaching of the indulgence to raise money for the construction of St. Peter's in Rome was only the last straw. It made the "offering" a family had to make for a loved one's funeral — in most places, as today in the mortuary business, quality was a matter of price — a detestable buying and selling in the temple. We shall say more later about this passion to rid the world of magic. What is noteworthy here is that a special object of its zeal was funeral rites and masses for the dead.

It would be wrong to suppose that money was the sole issue. It was at least the occasion if not the cause for the whole theological reappraisal of "works," of the part played by human endeavor in the divine work of salvation. The funeral rite, as it was then performed, was a lugubrious affair. The service was stripped of any joyous element; the altar and its ministers were draped in black; both prayers and readings, though they spoke also of hope, fitted into the gloom of the surroundings. In a word, the service was commemorating the departure of a "poor soul": one who may have negotiated the pilgrimage successfully but was still in desperate need of help to assure a speedy welcome into the presence of God. Medieval iconography depicted the valiant angel, Michael, hovering over the dying "soul" to protect it from the assaults of Satan. Even up to the last breath of life, the struggle was relentless. The departing "soul" was fortified by the "last sacraments" — at one time these rites were, in imitation of Christ, an anointing unto glory, not a signal that death was imminent — and, after death, was hastened through purgatory by the masses, prayers and good works offered by the faithful. It was this meaning of death that, over and above financial considerations, was targeted as the real abuse. As a sign of its rejection, the funeral, as a result of the spirit of iconoclasm that swept through the churches and purified them of all forms of "materialism," became a memorial service: a coming together of those who had known the deceased in order to give the person a "grand send-off." In short, the symbolism of death had changed.

The funeral remained a memorial but a memory of a different sort. The new service that likewise alluded to, but did not make much of, resurrection (a sound theological emphasis more appropriate to a death-denying society) ended with the disposal of the corpse. There was really nothing to be mindful of in a week, a month or a year. In fact, the sooner forgotten, the more rapidly husband, wife or family readjusted to normal living. "Now," William Allen lamented in 1565, "there is no blessing on man's memory at all."[12] For all of the abuses the older rite may have contained, it carried a strong emphasis on the social significance of death. At times of bereavement community bonds are strengthened. One's neighbors and friends come to "pay their respects," a respect as much for the living as for the dead. A funeral service is, we sometimes say, really for the family, for in common worship we re-enforce those ties that bind us together as a group, as, in a religious context, the people united in and by God. But the old rite stressed that with burial those ties were not broken. Because the previous generation passed on the life of faith to the present one, those of the present remain responsible to them. The life of the Church, therefore, was seen as profoundly communal: a unity or vital "re-membering" of the dead with the living. The liturgy of the new way can, by comparison, exhibit only a shuffling off of responsibility for the past. The individual standing before his God was an appropriate picture of

---

12. Cited, with appropriate documentation, by Keith Thomas in *Religion and the Decline of Magic: Studies in Popular Beliefs in Sixteenth and Seventeenth Century England*, London: Weidenfeld & Nicolson, 1971, 603.

the sovereign rights of conscience. But it also portrayed the understanding that each member of society is a little atom unto himself. As the Puritans abolished holy days and placed a ban on maypoles, Sunday dancing, and all secular accouterments of religious ceremony, the function of religion as a social cement was lost. Thus, in the perspective of death's rich symbolism, we can understand the judgment: "Life ceased to look to death for its perspective."[13]

When Heidegger enjoined our looking to death as revelatory of our present meaning as a being-in-the-face-of-death (*Sein zum Tode*), he, as a philosopher, said nothing about death rituals and the eschatology that these express as further revelations of our being-in-the-world (*in-der-Welt-sein*) as a pronounced "being together" (*Mitsein*). But in his analysis of human temporality — a description of the movement of consciousness as out of a past and, as a project forward, into a future — he stressed the unity of time's moments (past and future) as functions of the present. Granted that for the philosophically innocent this language is esoteric — and my compression of his thought only adds to its density; yet the reader can grasp its meaning if he or she realizes that what Heidegger presents is a philosophical interpretation of the religious imagination. In other words, we speak of creation at one end of the spectrum and of death and its aftermath at the other because we want to understand the meaning of the life that is present before us.

Since no one, we noted, could have been present at the moment of creation, it is obvious that we are not being offered a bit of "primitive" science. A description of the origin of the world is an account of how our existence or horizon of meaning originated. We talk about the past, obviously, because we are concerned about the present. Historians do the same thing. They never supply us with a record of everything that happened. Their accounts are of "significant" events, which is to say, occurrences selected and interpreted to enable us to understand ourselves as part of a given situation. Accordingly, I have emphasized that creation tells us what we are, co-creators,

13. *Ibid.*, citing L. Febvre, *Au Cœur religieux du XVIème siècle*, Paris, 1957.

engaged in the realization of God's world. Death and its after-math afford us another perspective. Eschatology, the spelling out of a future, whether in the detailed fashion of apocalyptic (dazzling cities peopled by citizens with golden crowns; devils inflicting excruciating tortures on the damned in the midst of fire and brimstone) or in the tantalizingly schematic declaration, "All things shall be new," reminds us that our creation is a morally responsible activity. The stark unpredictability of death casts its shadow on the fragility, the brevity of life; we are "but pilgrims" in this mortal coil. Finally, to speak of death as a mistake or punishment relates it to our experience of suffering and pain. The explanation, as in *Genesis*, casts us back to common origins. We share a common dignity because we live in a world together and are all responsible for its flaws. Hence the religious pattern that Heidegger has articulated is that the future reveals to us that our *present* meaning lies in the depths of the past. It is the pattern that psychologists and psychoanalysts explore. They pry into our ideals and dreams which they project to a past which, allegedly, explains our present behavior — or misbehavior.

There is another avenue of thought, connected with the preceding, which the death symbol opens before us: a metaphysics of ourselves. Plato's *Phædo* purports to be a discussion of the meaning of death and immortality that took place on the day that Socrates drank the hemlock. After his death, we are told that his friends took him, or rather his body, away for burial, for the real Socrates, the beautiful soul that they remembered, had departed. Most religious accounts of death, clearly, have no metaphysical pretensions. They are not meant to be taken philosophically: as stipulations regarding the constitution of man that must be argued in the light of a history of disputes over the relationship of soul to body. To the contrary, the "soul" talk of religious documents is rooted in commonplace observation. At the beginning of *Genesis* we read that the spirit of God breathed over the waters to give them the "life" of a world. Man came into being through the breath of life. He ends it by ceasing to breathe. The soul or vital principle is described, therefore, as a wind, a spirit, a shadow. It is this imagery, of course, that has given rise to the myth of the soul. The "soul" then becomes an heuristic instrument, a tool for thinking about the meaning of ourselves and the human condition generally. For Plato, it enabled him to provide a satisfactory solution to the problem of knowledge we mentioned: How can changing man, existing in the flux of existence, come to truth, that is, to the unchanging or universal? The problem had its spinoff in the theory of Forms, in the soul's pre-existence in the idea of reminiscence and in the doctrine of immortality. The suggestion that the soul had fallen into the body, its prison, is less a theory of composition than a commentary on our mixed condition. All of our experience, as it were, is touched with a bit of heaven and a bit of hell. The theory of reminiscence is part of the mythology, as is clear from its demythologizing at the end of the *Meno*, that explains reasoning and the soul's grasp of truth. Finally, the departure of the soul in death not only leads to speculations about immortality. But, as we have seen, in wondering about its fate, we find ourselves pondering rewards and punishments as answers to the problem of justice (or injustice) which day-to-day existence presses upon us. Earlier in this work I mentioned the shaman's mystical journey, an escape from the body that offers us both a pattern of knowledge and a model of spirituality. Since knowledge is of the enduring, the universal, we must escape matter, the principle of change and limitation, to arrive at truth. Likewise, true wisdom requires asceticism. We must conquer the body and its passions in order to free the soul for communion with God. In summary, the soul contains in embryo a whole metaphysics of our spiritual autonomy and freedom. As a myth, it enables us to develop the basic ideas we have used to define ourselves: intellectual beings who can rise above the contingencies of time and place to formulate laws and general principles; and free beings who are determined neither by history nor by the power of our intellects to choose one thing in preference to another. If philosophers today shun the myth as dualistic, could it be that they have confused the myth with the mythologies developed by Plato and Descartes to articulate it? Or is it that philosophers cannot escape their legacy? Modern philosophers did not blunt the challenge: What is truth? They were only intent upon freeing us from the kind of experience that "the soul" had come to represent.

Were this myth not fruitful, did it not answer to deeply felt aspirations for ourselves, would it have survived all the attacks upon it? It is to be regretted that a vulnerable Cartesian imagery accompanies most thinking about the soul. If one "has" a soul, what is it like? How can it be totally in every part of the body? If it departs at death, where is it now? If the real "me" is my soul, what does it mean to say that I am dead? Faulty picturing holds us captive, with the result that a significant part of our meaning drops out of sight.

The Adam and Eve of *Genesis* may be more familiar to us, but their story is not the only one that, by having all mankind descended from them, emphasizes the unity of the human race. The story, of course, has received considerable theological development. It is the basis of St. Paul's preaching of the universal saving mission of Jesus: through a man all sinned; hence through a man all are redeemed. Yet there is something stirringly human about the story which I believe the myth of the soul touches. All of us find ourselves, because we have bodies that locate us in time and history, speaking a language that reflects a circumscribed world view. When looked at from a distance, the categories we have picked up in language-learning are recognized to be *a* way of distinguishing objects. Even within the same language family, we have to educate ourselves to grasp the world of meaning that was Chaucer's or Shakespeare's or even that of the Brontë sisters. Death, we have seen, symbolizes this experience of finitude, a limitation that, paradoxically, forces itself upon us the more we grow intellectually, physically, morally, spiritually. Thus death can take on the meaning of being born anew, different. It heralds a life that is pure and free, untrammeled by bonds that hinder us from understanding one another. The myth of the soul thus brings us to a spiritual realization. We are spirits: beings that long to be free of the obstacles that prevent us from communicating with everyone. Jesus, we are told, had to die. As a man of his times, with all of the limitations of the first century mentality, he had to die in order to become a spirit. Thus freed, he could reach out to touch all mankind. He was, in this respect, the perfect man, a model for humanity. We are all, in our innermost reality, spirits: called to sit down to drink together in harmony the wine of the kingdom.

To a degree, whatever is part of everyday living can be grist for the religious imagination, although we would expect that those experiences which loom larger than life more readily take on symbolic meaning. In the course of history, mankind's living with, and fighting against, Nature have provided a continuous resource for understanding life's meaning. From dust we are and unto dust we shall return, buried in Mother Earth — for many people, tellingly, in the fetal position — or scattered over her surface. One with Nature as a cosmos, we are also one with it as an uncontrollable chaos. Outbursts of violence are said, often enough, to manifest our "true nature." Even a perfunctory glance at its history can rid us of the prejudice that religion sentimentalizes the human condition. The forces of corruption spoil the dream of childhood innocence, and the image of life as a struggle between good and evil presents the reality we daily experience. Rather than laying an intolerable burden upon us, the concept of sin is essential for an understanding of our part in the creative process. Genghiz Khan, Joseph Stalin and Adolf Hitler cannot be passed over as exceptions. They, too, reveal our humanity and thus compound the mystery involved in creation itself. Because through their immanent activities too, a world of divine, transcendent meaning is effected, the religious imagination has been stretched in opposite directions in order to help us cope with the full reality of that situation. If it failed to do so because life's atrocities are "irrational" and less threatening if glossed over, its symbols would no longer be places of genuine encounter.

The intriguing aspect of our history is that the image of the human as a symbol (*homo symbolicus*: one who symbolizes because he is a symbol), which has been handed down to us since Neolithic times principally in the guise of *homo religiosus*, should precipitously and locally, at least in world historical terms, have come under attack during the seventeenth and eighteenth centuries in Western Europe. It resulted in what we commonly know as secularization: a phenomenon too complex, we noted, for a simple explanation. From our standpoint, the attack on certain religious symbols and then on religion itself as a symbolic system must be seen as revelatory of the creative process, for surely these would never have occurred if the symbols themselves had retained their vitality. Interestingly, most of the efforts to provide us with a new myth, that is, with a framework and accompanying set of symbols that enable us to make sense of ourselves and our world, deny the idea of *homo symbolicus*. The old concept of a meeting place of body and spirit, lower and higher, has been washed out of the Marxist *homo œconomicus*, the economic man who allegedly lives within a material horizon. I appreciate Marshall Hodgson's perception of the issues involved in *homo technicus*. Although no longer a symbol, the human being is the manipulator of symbols *par excellence*.

> Starting with Brahe and Kepler (in contrast to Copernicus), infinitesimal precision of measurement, with the aid of highly specialized technical instruments, was the keynote of the new type of investigation. I doubt that Kepler would have conceded priority to the ellipse over the geometrically 'purer' circle, despite his metaphysical justifications of it, if he were not, unawares, coming to assign priority to technical precision and manipulation over philosophical elegance. The result was to place in jeopardy any sense of a cosmic whole. The natural-science traditions had maintained also in the Occident that degree of intellectual autonomy they had early won from commitment to the intellectual predispositions of overall life-orientational traditions; this autonomy had made itself apparent on occasion among both Muslims and Christians in a relative empiricism, bound to but not overwhelmed by philosophic notions of the teleological and hierarchical nature of entities. But now, with intensive specialization, the autonomy of the natural-science traditions was pushed much further, and the accompanying empiricism became almost routine. Every major scientist found himself forced to try to work out for himself (if he cared) his own sense of the cosmic whole; and alert laymen were left with 'all coherence gone'. By 1800 the technicalistic spirit had spread from astronomy and physics to chemistry, geology, and biology. From Descartes to its culmination in Kant, the new epistemological philosophy was inspired by the new technicalistic science and by its very disengagement from ultimate questions.[14]

14. *The Venture of Islam*, Volume III: *The Gunpowder Empires and Modern Times*, 189.

Evidently, this disengagement from ultimate questions was consequent upon the loss of any sense of a cosmic whole. Hence critics of our science and others concerned about values and the quality of life are encouraged when they discern signs that indicate a felt need for a new myth. Wilfrid Mellers, for example, believes that the "new primitivism" in twentieth–century music exemplifies the search for coherence.[15] He finds in much of the later music evidence for an Eastern turn, that is, a rejection of Western values for spiritual contemplation. It manifests the anxiety to eliminate strife and to suppress the divisions of consciousness that have plagued Westerners since we lost the status of *homo symbolicus*.

It is a commonplace of religious thought that God's ways are not our ways. The purpose of this chapter has been to indicate how *homo religiosus*, rational as human yet tongue-tied in the presence of mystery, has tried to cope with the paradox that thought expresses. The religious story that has unfolded in the West during the past few centuries is our history. It, too, is a revelation of ourselves in the throes of bringing forth a world that is God's. So far, of course, there have been only faint signs of returning to older ways; or should I say, taking up the older ways into our different self-consciousness?

> For modern physics envisages a simultaneously existent past, present and future in which human consciousness may be the only moving element; and the modern physicist may have more in common with religious, medieval man, with the mystics of oriental cultures, with the alchemists and even with the magicians of primitive societies, than he has with the post-Renaissance rationalist. In considering composers from Debussy to Stockhausen, we have noted that artists have for years been intuitively aware of how radical a change this is. If most of us have failed to grasp the nature of our metamorphosis, the reason may be that the visual chronology of the Renaissance tradition has tied us to the conception of a historical past. This was irrelevant to primitive oral cultures, and may be equally so to our future.[16]

15. Cf. *Caliban Reborn: Renewal in Twentieth-century Music*, London: Gollancz, 1968. I have discussed his work in relation to themes presented here in *Religious Consciousness and Experience*.

16. *Ibid.*, 177–78.

For *homo religiosus*, as our reflections upon creation and death have made clear, the past was not a dead past: the kind of pastness that von Ranke stipulated as the object of scientific historical inquiry. To the contrary, through the ritual celebration of past events, as we shall see in the following chapter, religious people safeguarded the past from becoming passé. They retained history in its vital sense as a source of meaning, and to that extent they were out of sorts with the rebellious spirit of modern philosophy, which is partially responsible for the still prevailing notion that the old is antiquated and that change must be for the better. Our religious and political history of the sixties and seventies has stimulated some second thoughts about these stereotypes. And now that the Eastern religions have camped on our shores and the Muslim world is rocking our boat, maybe we are ready for a less biassed approach to the "religious imagination."

CHAPTER IV

Ritual Enactment

STUDENTS have usually greeted with skepticism my observation that, although professors appear to be masters of the
art of circumvention, they are not. A question, it is believed,
deserves a simple yes or no answer. Why is it, then, that professors get carried away: "Now of course this has to be taken into
consideration . . ."; "If you say this, remember that you have to
say that"; "We must distinguish several ways of looking at the
matter"? Can we wonder why, after the question has inched its
way through the academic sausage grinder and the student is
asked, "Does that answer your question?" the likely reply is:
"Well, uh, I'm not sure. What was the question?"

If religion spawns apparently circuitous answers, it is not just
because a way of life cannot be pinned down by a categorical yes
or no. Like any other complicated topic, we try to isolate its
different aspects only to find that these are interlocking: myth
with symbol, creation with eschatology, belief with ritual, etc.
There are advantages to this kind of repetition. It gives us a
broader perspective and can be effective, as I hope it will be now
in our discussion of symbolic behavior or ritual, in dissipating
old associations. Earlier we cited a national flag as an example of
a symbol because it embodies the ideals of a people. It can, of
course, be a sign when it serves as a badge of identification sewn

120

on a uniform. The tendency to confuse the two is natural, as when we talk about "symbols of authority" or, in religion, when we empty circumcision or sacraments of their symbolic quality by referring to them as signs. We do not, obviously, pledge allegiance to a sign. Our allegiance belongs to a people whom a shared meaning holds in unity. It is for this reason that I suggested that a symbol is a chit of recognition. It enables us to recognize one another by furnishing us with a place of genuine encounter. Surely all of us can, without preciosity, distinguish the everyday contacts we have with people in restaurants, on streets, in subways, from a chance encounter with an acquaintance, someone with whom we have something in common. When we hear someone speaking American English in Vienna, for example, we are likely to forget the reserve customary at home and say something to start a conversation. We make use of what are symbols — to an outsider perhaps so much gibberish — because of their context. They emerge as symbols within a world of meaning as instruments, the carriers of that meaning. It is within this perspective that we must understand Eliade's characterization of symbolism as a language. Symbols define, condense and express a world.

It is not an uncommon experience of Americans abroad who have to learn another language to lose their facility with English. This is especially so at the outset, when we are immersed in a foreign medium. We find after we have begun to make headway in that medium, that sometimes, however much we may rack our brains, we cannot at the moment find the right word in English. The experience brings home the importance of practice. Not practice in any narrow sense; for if we really want to learn French, we have to *live* it, become part of the life of which the language is the expression. In religious terminology, this is to say that we must celebrate a life in the symbolic action called ritual.

The word 'enactment' in the title of this chapter tells us something important about ritual celebration. If symbols were "just symbols," ritual would be play-acting, acting "as if." An enactment, on the contrary, is a realization: an actualizing in which participants both bring into existence, and are themselves brought into, a significant event. People who are bodily present to each other, not only in time but also bound together in the web of meaning which is their history, celebrate that meaning which illuminates themselves, others and their world. Hence ritual re-presents by making present once again the event or events that inaugurated a specific form of life. As en-actment, ritual emphasizes the primacy of action — the Fourth Gospel, it is said, might have begun: "In the beginning was the deed" — for it is through activity that we fashion ourselves and our environments into a meaningful world. The world of "make believe," of "let us play" only illustrates the point. Meaning is found in continuity with environing Nature, not in opposition to it. Therefore, whether secular or religious, elaborate or simple, ritual creates, in the fullest sense of the word, a world. The Christian's artless gesture of the "breaking of the bread" leads its participants into a world of meaning no less than do the intricacies of a Japanese tea ceremony.

Yet like so many other things in human existence, the strength of ritual includes its weakness. By borrowing its concrete detail from the world of everyday experience, ritual capitalizes on the familiar and enhances it by incorporating it into the more comprehensive meaning celebrated in a rite. Bread, for instance, takes on further meaning when it is no longer just food but is "daily bread," a token of God's unceasing care for us which culminates in the "breaking of the bread," in the act of Jesus giving his life that we may live. In this broader perspective, bread has become a symbol: a place where the Christian encounters the saving action of God. But without a sense of history, without the realization that bread is designated the "staff of life" because it is the universal food of mankind, the symbol begins to lose its appeal. Even if we appreciate its past importance, it may feature less significantly as a real need in our web of meaning. We can readily understand how various ways of picturing God: "Shepherd," "Father," "King," etc., are of limited attraction. They are both helpful and troublesome anthropomorphisms because they make God a "super-person": one like us, but . . . Hence my insistence that God is a symbol, not a picture. "He" is the place where we encounter the mystery of ourselves and our world: order and disorder, good and evil, immanence and transcendence. But more of this later.

There are reasons other than the decline into the prosaic consequent upon a changing world which account for the death of symbols. Their celebration, because of the shifting historical circumstances I have mentioned, can become routine. Besides, polemic may have so stamped them with a controversial image that they have lost some of their efficacy as means of achieving unity. For the idea, too, that they work "just in the doing" (*ex opere operato*) seems almost an invitation to perfunctory performance. Finally, it is inconceivable that someone be brought into the life of a group when its symbolic action has become an instrument of control.

Historically, segments of communities have seized upon their rituals to control meaning in order to ensure conformity to determinate, time-honored, yet unhistorical views of things. The powerful would wed a group to a symbolism of a certain age: a course of action frequently justified by threats from outside or inside, either real or imagined. Such fidelity, as we know from sad experience, can be stultifying in the long run. It substitutes security for the promotion of meaning, heedless of the fact — perhaps not heedless since lip-service is generally paid to the notion — that meaning is rooted in, and sustained by, the celebration of group life. A community's liturgy is its *life of service*. Obviously, with that life pumped out of it, service degenerates into a slogan. Having thus lost its context, a ritual becomes magic and, tragically, the whole structure of conviction which is the foundation of religious *praxis* begins to crumble. In this chapter, we shall revert to some of the historical factors that undoubtedly contributed to the emergence in the West of this kind of life-negating conservatism.

Ritual objects are material: altars, candles, foodstuffs, animals, incense, articles of clothing, etc. As such, they are open to abuse. When King David wanted to build a temple at Jerusalem, the prophet Nathan delivered an oracle reminding him that God, as lord of heaven and earth, was in no need of a permanent, earthly dwelling place. Notwithstanding, his son, Solomon, gratified what appears to be a natural religious instinct, a god near at hand, an Emmanuel ("God with us"). Yet a god near at hand or "within" readily becomes either just myself, as in Feuerbach's anthropology in which God was nothing but idealized man, or a god bereft of transcendence because subject to human manipulation. In the Luvale religion, for example, an anthropological investigator found no equivalent "to the concept of 'the sacred', and any rituals performed followed strict formulæ not because they were 'sacred' but rather essential and inescapable in order to manipulate and influence hidden forces."[1] Clearly, ritual had degenerated into magic.

"Degenerate," I believe, is the right word because in this case, even though 'magic' has lost its pejorative connotation in anthropological circles and refers more broadly to any use of material objects to produce or influence spiritual results, the emphasis is to be placed upon the word "manipulate." 'Magic' still means hocus-pocus for most people because the word suggests an unhealthy attitude toward the use of material things in religion. Either one actually supposes that "the god" is incarnate in something material and thus manipulable, or that the object has some lien on the god that coerces cooperation. Hence to dismiss a practice as magical reflects the sound judgment that religion can be neither overt nor covert control.

The idea that matter of any sort has no role to play in religion has a long history that stems both from philosophical and from polemical-theological roots. These I have discussed in somewhat greater detail in *Religious Consciousness and Experience*; yet some brief remarks are called for here that might provide perspective.

In their analysis of knowledge, the early Greek thinkers were fully conscious of limitation. We know things by defining, *vi vocis* a setting of limits, and by distinguishing one thing from another. Throughout modern and contemporary philosophy, the theme of coming to know has been emphasized: a process of successive negation or de-termination. These refinements make our knowledge of objects perspectival. We see something *as*; we understand it from a certain angle or viewpoint. This limiting factor in knowledge the Greeks called matter: a word that for us can

---

1. Mutumba Mainga, "A History of Lozi Religion to the End of the Nineteenth Century," in T. O. Ranger and Isaria Kimambo, eds., *The Historical Study of African Religion*, London: Heinemann, 1972, 98, referring to C. M. N. White, *Elements in Luvale Beliefs and Rituals*, Rhodes-Livingston Paper, no. 32 (Manchester, 1961), 35.

suggest physical or gross matter, but for them simply marked the limit of an object's meaning. We have already noted that their obsession with intellect created among the Greeks a spiritual climate that can best be characterized as anti-material. Just as the objects of the intellect were intelligible to the degree that they were divorced from the limitation of "matter," so, too, were the higher spiritual states divorced from bodily matter. Plato's scheme of knowledge, remember, was a transplanted ecstasy: a *standing outside* of the body. Judaism, as an historical religion, rejected this form of spirituality and so, too, did Christianity even more vigorously because of Jesus. His words had given matter an unprecedented role in religious worship. His body was the temple of the new law: even more, the true manna to be consumed, while his blood was the new wine, the life-blood of the kingdom. Stark doctrines such as these have to be borne in mind if one is to understand the controversies that began to plague Christians even before the end of the first century. As the Christian religion spread in the Greek world, it had to define its spirituality vis-à-vis the prevailing one. Above all, it had to come to terms with its own cardinal tenet: a truly incarnate God, neither God nor man solely in appearance.

From a certain angle, our philosophic-religious history has been a story of this coming to terms. At the risk of some repetition — we are back to issues raised at the end of Chapter II — we shall look attentively at some of its more controversial aspects insofar as these are germane to the whole question of symbols. But first we have to try to understand better the mentality that expresses itself in religious ritual. Eliade can provide us with a jumping-off place.

> There is no need to look into the teachings of myth to see that the sky itself directly reveals a transcendence, a power and a holiness. Merely contemplating the vault of heaven produces a religious experience in the primitive mind. This does not necessarily imply a 'nature-worship' of the sky. To the primitive, nature is never purely 'natural'. The phrase 'contemplating the vault of heaven' really means something when it is applied to the primitive man, receptive to the miracles of every day to an extent we find it hard to imagine. Such contemplation is the same as a revelation. The

sky shows itself as it really is: infinite, transcendent. The vault of heaven is, more than anything else, 'something quite apart' from the tiny thing that is man and his span of life. The symbolism of its transcendence derives from the simple realization of its infinite height. 'Most High' becomes quite naturally an attribute of the divinity.[2]

Eliade's 'primitive' is never a pejorative term. On the contrary, he would invite us to see ourselves differently, to entertain the possibility of an experience of ourselves in a world undivided by the epistemological dichotomies manufactured by modern philosophers, in a world, too, in which "wonder" and "mystery" express a deeply felt reality. Instead of the classical separations: inner/outer, intellect/sense, mind/world, which have turned myths into fictions and symbols into "just symbols" by divorcing reasoning from its roots in the imagination, he would have us come to terms with the mystery of ourselves. Because we are more than matter, the wonders of Nature of which we are a part — the marvels of heights and depths are revealed in a special way to the alpinist — can help us to articulate our deepest spiritual aspirations. Why did the philosophers need Heidegger's reminder of the primordial, everyday miracle: Why is there something rather than nothing? For symbolism, Eliade continues,

> is an immediate notion of the whole consciousness, of the man, that is, who realizes himself as a man, who recognizes his place in the universe; these primeval realizations are bound up so organically with his life that the same symbolism determines both the activity of his subconscious and the noblest expressions of his spiritual life. It really is important, therefore, this realization that though the symbolism and religious values are not deduced logically from a calm and objective observation of the heavens, neither are they exclusively the product of mythical activity and non-rational religious experience.[3]

The notion which for Eliade "really is important" derives its importance from the bias of modern philosophy, namely, the

---

2. *Patterns of Comparative Religion*, 38–39.
3. *Ibid.*

idea that we are thinking machines. As part of the mechanism of Nature, our thought is deductive: a logical process of inference from unassailable premises or incontrovertible observations. Consequently, if we are to understand ritual enactment, we have to learn to take another look at ourselves. Man the actor, who expresses himself in music and dance, is surely as intellectually significant as man the knower. Undoubtedly the dominant philosophy of the last two hundred years has made it difficult for us to talk about the mystery of ourselves. The "children of darkness" — if I may be permitted to return to the biblical viewpoint reversed during the Enlightenment — have been more successful in telling us what we are than the "children of light." If there is no transcendence in us to mediate, can ritual be anything else but magic?

In the beginning of Chapter II, I called attention to Aristotle's definition of man as the one having *logos*. Humans use symbolic language, we noted, because *homo symbolicus* is a symbol: the meeting place of flesh and spirit, of sensible and intellectual. Our knowing is a dialectical process: a mediation of these components that remained a mystery notwithstanding all the rationalists' efforts to penetrate it. Hence we can also look upon ourselves as *dialogues*: beings who, because collected in a group, speak and can thus be further gathered together (the twofold senses of *legein* to which I have already adverted) through entering into and sharing a world of meaning. Thus dialogue, however much its meaning has been trivialized by entering into current jargon, can aid us in discerning the essential mystery of ourselves.

It was not many years ago that a number of philosophers believed that they had found in language the key to all philosophical problems. In fact, all these problems would promptly disappear with a more careful attention to usage. Now, however, things no longer appear quite so simple. Man in or as dialogue is as mysterious as man the symbol. Our words, we now recognize, conceal as well as reveal. They are given to us, yet with them we are creative. Though they signify universally, we utilize them to express our individuality. Their meaningfulness is that of parts projected against a whole, that totality of our language which always lies beyond our ken. As dialogue, then, language is the mediation "through words" of the mystery of our being: a revealing which does not dissipate that mystery but retains it.

We have already shared Eliade's insight that symbolism is a language; it incarnates and communicates group meaning. Ritual, therefore, as the enactment of that meaning is likewise a mediation, a communication that in its way celebrates the mystery of human reality.

> To re-state what seems to be an essential feature in religious behaviour: in Buddhism, as in many other religions, there is, to use a Durkheimian phrase, a double relation and the linking up of contraries. A series of dichotomies, e.g., this world/other world, living human/ancestral spirits, body/soul, permeates religious thought. Religious action is oriented to influence the relationship between these oppositions, so that living human beings can experience prosperity and continuity of social life. Thus ideas such as a better rebirth, or union with the inaccessible pure divine, or immunization of the potency of the supernatural impinging on the human, are expressions of this desired mediation attempted through ritual action.[4]

From our perspective, of greatest import in this passage is the observation: "so that living human beings can experience prosperity and continuity of social life." The dichotomies, that is, which are the objects of ritual action are deeply embedded in human experience. So loud are the blasts of anti-religious propaganda proclaiming that other worlds, ancestral spirits and souls are simply projections, fantasies in which our troubled psyches seek refuge to find a measure of prosperity, that we are likely, in spite of what I have said previously, to engage in faulty picturing. Let me repeat: we know little, if anything, about future arrangements. The emphasis in religion upon the next life is a judgment upon this one and an exhortation to assume the responsibilities and overcome the difficulties required of the morally good life. Ancestral spirits form a significant part of the "continuity of social life." Because they were at one time the

---

4. S. J. Tambiah, "The Ideology of Merit and the Social Correlates of Buddhism in a Thai Village," in Edmund R. Leach, ed., *Dialectic in Practical Religion*, Cambridge, at the University Press, 1968, 50.

source of that life, they safeguard tradition. Contact with them serves to admonish us to be prudent, especially in those courses of action which are basic to the form of life we call our culture. We have already seen how the soul functions in the Platonic metaphysics as the principle of continuity with the Forms, with the universal, intelligible aspect of things. Because we can know the truth, the Absolute — for truth is the categorical assertion of what is — Plato theorized on the basis of the Greek principle that "like knows like" that the mystery of knowledge cannot be resolved but only made intelligible or clarified if we have a spiritual principle that is a share or participation in that truth. The soul, as we noted, was on that account "divine," the principle of mediation between the changing knower and unchanging or absolute truth. But the soul was not exclusively cognitive for it contained in embryo, we suggested earlier, a metaphysics of freedom because our experience of ourselves and of others is ambivalent. We are both noble and petty, wise and ignorant, compassionate and cruel, generous and selfish. To define us as beings-in-dialogue, that is, as beings living through (dia) because we are engaged in the communication and development of logos (meaning), is to emphasize the dialectic of our lives as a process of becoming and over-coming. For Plato, the ascent to truth was therefore a moral journey: a conquest of limitation through its understanding. Because modern philosophers would have us experience ourselves otherwise, specifically as minds or rational beings, "other-worldly" came to designate an improbable place, not the transcendent dimension of our being, and "ancestral spirits" and "souls" became ghostly entities in place of being ways of designating our cultural and spiritual characteristics. Ritual inevitably slipped into meaninglessness because there was no longer anything to mediate.

In most philosophical circles today, the picture of ourselves as minds or as calculating machines has been rejected as an oversimplification. But we have not been so prompt in abandoning that portrait's religious consequences. This anomaly, I believe, springs from the fact that modern philosophers were children of their times, living in, and hence articulating, a religiously tense climate of opinion. If we are to understand them and their bequest to us, we must try to piece together some of the facets of their situation and its historical antecedents.

In spite of some of the harsh things St. Augustine had to say about the philosophers, those Neoplatonists he called the "Platonici," the theology of ritual he formulated was deeply indebted to them. It was a theology hammered out on the anvil of controversy. Its supporting theory of grace was brought to maturity in his conflict with Pelagian naturalism; the appropriate use of sacraments in his opposition to Manichean anti-materialism; the efficacy of rites in his combat with Donatist ministerial perfectionism. As we would expect of the great commentator on the Fourth Gospel, the Saint insisted that the core of sacramental ritual was the efficacy of the word: not a magical invocation but an effective word because uttered in a context of belief. Any ritual, that is, which loses its context becomes magic. What meaning, for instance, do we attach to a Navajo rain dance if we are not Navajo and uncommitted to their values? What Neoplatonism offered Saint Augustine, then, was a pattern for ritual in a thought that was both mystical and contextual. As a Christian, he substituted God for Plato's Good or Plotinus' One: the ultimate in which we "live and move and have our being." Incomprehensible nonetheless, this God, the "father of light," sent Jesus to enlighten our world of darkness. Illumined by his Word, we live henceforth within a context of meaning in which we, as parts, are intelligible and intelligent because we are sharers in the meaning of that divine totality. It is this kind of thought that I have called symbolism. The context or totality is a "place of encounter" insofar as it allows us to grasp meanings. At the same time, as the source of intelligibility it accounts for the drive to ever more comprehensive understanding. The world of everyday experience is our springboard, not in the sense that we ignore sensible, material reality for an improbable "other world," but insofar as that reality draws its significance from the totality of meaning which we struggle to articulate. We have seen how the Platonic metaphysics which St. Augustine utilized is a "standing in" this totality, a mysterious participation which forever frustrates our reach for a final vision. The ultimate ground in this metaphysics, as in ritual, is to be celebrated, not comprehended. For this reason I have not interpreted the ancient science of "ultimate causes" as a science in the modern philosophical sense: the determination of a standpoint from which all is perfectly plain. It was a science only as knowledge (Latin: *scientia*), an enactment, for knowing brings into act the mysterious reality of our being.

When modern philosophers made knowledge into their special science, ritual, if it was to be retained at all, had to become a different kind of dialectic. Indeed, it had already begun to change its character, thanks to another one of those ironies which beleaguer religious history.

> By the later Middle Ages the general effect had been to shift the emphasis away from the communion of the faithful, and to place it upon the formal consecration of the elements by the priest. The ceremony thus acquired in the popular mind a mechanical efficacy in which the operative factor was not the participation of the congregation, who had become virtual spectators, but the special power of the priest. Hence the doctrine that the laity could benefit from being present at the celebration even though they could not understand the proceedings . . . What stood out was the magical notion that the mere pronounciation of words in a ritual manner could effect a change in the character of material objects.[5]

It is not to our purpose to try to pinpoint all the factors contributory to this development. In general, the Middle Ages witnessed an increasing clericalization of the Church. From the eighth to the tenth centuries, ritualism, given impetus by the Cluniac reform, became the focal point of religious life. The special officers required for the elaborate, time-consuming ceremonies received official status in the developing canon law. And if this were not enough to accomplish the laity's alienation, the model of the true Christian presented for universal emulation was the monk, devoted, Pope St. Gregory had written, to the "angelic life." The theological nominalism that became predominant in the later Middle Ages attributed the efficacy of the sacramental word to the sacred character of the utterer, which effectively shattered the context of faith which hitherto had

5. *Religion and the Decline of Magic*, 33.

bound clergy and laity together. Sacramental power, in fact, no longer belonged to the Church as such. The laity had to fulfill its ritual role in devotions like the veneration of relics which, if one is to judge from the still extant collections in some of the magnificent European reliquaries, appears to have been immensely popular, as well as highly imaginative and lucrative.

The outcome of this disenfranchisement was a burst of anti-sacramentalism. It was voiced as early as 1395 by the Lollards, who were as marginal politically as religiously.

> That exorcisms and hallowings, made in the Church, of wine, bread, and wax, water, salt and oil and incense, the stone of the altar, upon vestments, mitre, cross, and pilgrim's staves, be the very practice of necromancy, rather than of the holy theology. This conclusion is proved thus. For by such exorcisms creatures be charged to be of higher virtue than their own kind, and we see nothing of change in no such creature that is so charmed, but by false belief, the which is the principle of the devil's craft.'[6]

Deprived of a context of meaning, we can "see nothing of change" because in point of fact there is nothing intelligible to see or understand.

The success of the Reformation owes much to the "abuse of the material," and for a while Luther's polemic caught him up in the anti-sacramental tide. His zeal for the holiness of God led him, we have noted, to that fateful emphasis upon divine transcendence which destroyed the Augustinian sacramental theology by striking at the very root of symbolism: the immanence of God to his creation. Ritual enactment, therefore, became something else: neither overnight nor in every case the same something else. Because Protestanism displays a broad spectrum of beliefs, we can speak only of "trends," acknowledging the term's unsatisfactory vagueness. My point is that notwithstanding Luther's intentions, the emphasis upon the principle of divine transcendence separated God from the world of material things, which meant that for ritual purposes objects had to be sacralized. Because they were by nature profane, of the sinful world,

6. *Ibid.*, 51, citing H. S. Cronin, "The Twelve Conclusions of the Lollards," *English Historical Review*, XXII (1907), 298.

they had to become "of higher virtue than their own kind." Thus was the groundwork readied for the philosophical scoffers' charge.

Once the initial, polemical phase had passed, the question popped up again and had to be answered: What role does matter play in religion? The question is urgently practical, not just theoretical, for it involves us in the interaction of ritual and belief. Not only is belief expressed in ritual, but ritual in turn re-enforces, modifies and sometimes subverts belief. If the location of a pulpit and prolonged Scriptural readings, for example, can attest the theological importance of the "Word of God," can it not also be that the abolition of simple gestures: the washing of hands symbolic of purification or the kissing of an altar as a sign of reverence (altars of sacrifice symbolize God) aid in the task of demystifying God? Is our theologizing more about "the man" Jesus related to the disappearance of those gestures that at one time displayed and inculcated a sense of reverence? In the Eastern Churches, has the loss of the iconostasis and an economy in the use of incense led to a spirituality with less emphasis upon divine transcendence?

The reaction that turned the old rites of enactment into magic inaugurated new ritual celebrations which were in many instances interpreted to be purely symbolic or commemorative events. Superficially, there appears little difference between these and enactments insofar as both are social re-enforcements. But the former lack the ontological roots of the latter. An emphasis upon association, communal memory and concern risks an increasing neglect because rites understood as no more than social involvements are reserved for the convinced who are, in fact, already socialized. With no principle of life that is both immanent to, and still transcendent of, the celebrating group, the transcendent meaning of the ritual slips into the purely immanent, the social. Witness the transition from Augustine's "efficacious word," the conjunction of word and sacrament, to the Lollards' necromancy. The step to spiritual meaninglessness is short. A similar fate, as we saw earlier, awaited Platonic transcendence. Without Plato's ontology as a safeguard, transcendence was reduced to a moment in the immanence of knowing.

Although the religious reformers of the sixteenth century had been impelled by what they deemed abuses in the rituals of sacrament and sacrifice, they unwittingly opened the door to subsequent religious indifferentism. If the Protestant pastor, as Nietzsche charged, was the progenitor of modern philosophy, it was because his theology had trained him to be wary of "magical" words. How, the philosophers wondered, do subjective utterances relate to objective, empirical facts? It is folly to suppose that we can separate the religious aspects of the Reformation from their subsequent philosophical articulations. Initially, this philosophy, we said, was instigated by thinkers intent upon exalting science and humbling the Church. But it was the committals of their religiously minded successors that gave support to the idea that symbols are "just symbols," and that religious transcendence lies wholly beyond the scope of human reason or cognitional theory; whereas their secularly minded successors promoted the notion that transcendence is bogus because there are no realities "higher" than the material world around us, and that the criterion of the true idea is its empirical correlation, not its relevance within a context of meaning. The intellectual underpinning of ritual enactment was thereby obliterated.

Significantly, the contemporary attack on modern premises owes much to thinkers like Wittgenstein and Heidegger whose insistence upon the context of thought has earned them the epithet "religious." In his writing after the *Tractatus*, a work dating from the period of World War I when his interests seemed to align him with the Vienna Circle, Wittgenstein relentlessly pursued his quarry, beginning now from here, now from there. For our purposes, I find the reflections known as his *Lectures on Religious Belief* of the utmost importance because, although explicitly devoted to religious topics, they clearly manifest his perception that the real problem is the "mentality": the model of philosophy that dictates what criteria determine one's use of "belief," "explanation," "proof," etc. For example, let us suppose, he suggested, that someone has made a belief in the Last Judgment the guiding principle of his life. If we ask whether he believes it to be an event, he will probably say that he has proof.

But in reality, Wittgenstein says, "He has what you might call an unshakeable belief. It will show, not by reasoning or by appeal to ordinary grounds for belief, but rather by regulating for all in his life."[7]

"Reasoning" and "ordinary grounds for belief" are appealed to when we deal with those who share our frame of reference. The framework created by the axioms and postulates of Euclidean geometry, for instance, established a form of reasoning whose rigor recommended it to Descartes and Spinoza as the model for philosophy. Compelled by the logic of the system, we are reasonable to the extent that we are consistent. But the justification of the system itself, although it can in part be of this kind, cannot be entirely so. If we want to know the meaning of someone's belief, we have to cast our net wider. In what respect does the Last Judgment manifest itself in one's daily affairs: in business dealings, in the treatment of others, in the day-in and day-out coping with life's ups and downs? Besides, what reason would prompt a person to espouse this guiding principle? How does one, provided that he or she is convinced of its import, propose to share that conviction with us? The Christian criterion of love that we discussed earlier elicits similar questions, for when it come to a life-orientation, no single empirical fact or result will suffice to justify it. This is the point in talking about a context and of emphasizing the function of ritual in bringing us through enactment into that context. The bare bones of creedal statements, thanks to ritual, take on flesh and blood. Hence to appreciate a belief in the Last Judgment, we have to be "woven together," as 'context' implies, and thus be fitted into a world of meaning that supports us with its intellectual coherence and motivational power. Because Marxism in our times exacts this kind of theoretic-practical involvement, it is frequently denominated a religion.

For many philosophers a *prima facie* difficulty with contextual thinking is that it seems to imply a coherence theory of truth: that a system elicits our consent solely because it neatly hangs

---

7. Ludwig Wittgenstein, *Lectures and Conversations on Æsthetics, Psychology and Religious Belief*, complied from notes taken by Yorick Smythies, Rush Rhees and James Taylor, edited by Cyril Barrett, Oxford: Blackwell, 1967, 54.

together. Instead of the truth "making us free," we are shackled by the chains of our ideas. We cannot get out and others cannot get in. Religious people especially are caricatured as prisoners of this kind. No one can argue with them because they have all the answers, thanks to their all-encompassing framework. And yet we know that coherence is not enough. It suggests that truth is ultimately mere personal satisfaction. To help us understand why this is so, and how contextual thought must be seen differently, let us return again to some of the philosophers whose efforts to establish an independent philosophy forced upon them the question of truth.

Two prongs of the attack launched by some of our contemporaries against the classical modern model of philosophy are germane to the issue. First, the model features the visual metaphor of knowledge inherited from the Greeks which implies the concept of an eternal truth, that is, an absolute ground of human knowledge. We have noted that because sight suggests the stark alternatives: either you see it or you do not, knowledge is readily understood to be a taking hold of an abiding reality, a grasp, I called it, of something final, something permanent in the midst of the flux of existence. This idea of knowledge undoubtedly appealed to the moderns because they philosophized in the age of the "new science," with its heavy emphasis on observation. Observation was the key to science's objectivity. The constraints of an object control the observer's subjective vagaries, and the object itself lies open to the inspection and acceptance of all. We can understand why Descartes shared the Platonic and Augustinian enthusiasm for mathematics. In his age, nothing so well filled the bill of an exact, impersonal science. As a consequence, it was in the celebrated Cartesian stance that the distancing of the subject from the object of investigation — a step essential to objective knowledge or truth — received canonical form. For us, Descartes' writings can convey the impression that he was a mind which was somehow attached to a body in a unity pitted against its environing world.

A second feature of the model under attack is the basic position which determined the course of discussion among the moderns through Kant and even down to our own day in certain circles. Central to this discussion has been the position formulated by John Locke who, once he had distinguished the mind's ideas from its objects, was perplexed over how he might relate the two once again. True ideas, he said, must correspond to their objects, which we hear echoed in Hume's contention that ideas are copies of impressions: a stipulation which became notorious in philosophy as the correspondence theory of truth. Remarkably, however much these thinkers disagreed among themselves, they, their contemporaries and successors carried on a dialogue, which is to say that they all positioned themselves in a stance which, as we now recognize, was the underlying cause of their problems. Hume has described the basic components of this stance.

> Thus there is a direct and total opposition betwixt our reason and our senses; or more properly speaking, betwixt those conclusions we form from cause and effect, and those that persuade us of the continu'd and independent existence of body. When we reason from cause and effect, we conclude, that neither colour, sound, taste, nor smell have a continu'd and independent existence. When we exclude these sensible qualities there remains nothing in the universe, which has such an existence.[8]

From this same position also emerged what is commonly understood as the coherence theory of truth. Just as mathematical propositions are true because they form part of a system, so, too, are factual or belief statements because they cohere with the rest of our experience. The American philosopher, Brand Blanshard, explained the theory as follows:

> We may look at the growth of knowledge, individual or social, either as an attempt by our own minds to return to union with things as they are in their ordered wholeness, or the affirmation through our minds of the ordered whole itself. And if we take this view, our notion of truth is marked out for us. Truth is the approximation of thought to reality. It is thought on its way home. Its measure is the distance thought has travelled, under

8. *A Treatise of Human Nature,* Reprinted from the original edition in three volumes and edited, with an analytical index, by L.A. Selby-Bigge, M.A., Oxford at the Clarendon Press, 1955 edition, 231.

guidance of its inner compass, toward that intelligible system which unites its ultimate object with its ultimate end. Hence at any given time the degree of truth in our experience as a whole is the degree of system it has achieved. The degree of truth of a particular proposition is to be judged in the first instance by its coherence with experience as a whole, ultimately by its coherence with that further whole, all-comprehensive and fully articulated, in which thought can come to rest.[9]

The assertion that truth is an "approximation of thought to reality," that ideas and objects, in other words, are initially juxtaposed derives from the same stance that prompted the correspondence theory. Yet what appears to be the cement holding the coherence theory together, what rescues it from being only a subjective vision of things, is the assumption that universal agreement is achievable because Mind, the identical "thing" which we all possess, is a structured reality. If we follow its rules, Descartes reminded us, we shall all arrive at the same answer. The assumption that thought and experience are the same for all of us is insinuated in Blanshard's "thought on its way home," "thought can come to rest," and "coherence with experience as a whole." Even Hume, anti-Cartesian though he was, endeavored to establish a science of human nature such that native instincts and, above all, sympathy, immunized subjective factors and guaranteed objectivity. In his perspective, observation was a straightforward "taking a look," whereas the objectivity of reasoning was assured by "natural instincts" with which the Creator endowed us in view of the feebleness of our reason to warrant continuity of action.

Although the patina of the coherence and correspondence theories has worn thin, we must credit the philosophers who espoused them with the realization that whatever the subjective factors in truth may be, its objective character was paramount. Accordingly, the one group emphasized observation and the need of a transcendent referent for a true idea. The other group relied on the structures common to all human knowers to safeguard the possibility of universal verification. Thus, even though

9. *The Nature of Thought*, New York: Macmillan, 1941, Volume II, 264.

both theories may have led to relativism — knowledge structures are individual and observation is personal — they were staked out initially on the grounds of truth. In contrast, if everything is relative to the subject, there is no truth. Today's truth is tomorrow's fiction.

Even though relativism appears in the worst light when applied to morals, fostering, for example, the idea that to incinerate gypsies, homosexuals, Jews and "other misfits" is right so long as a group endorses it, philosophers returned to the problem of truth because of other developments. Kant's philosophy is a metaphysics of finitude, an effort to draw sharp lines that demarcate the limits of human knowledge and experience. Taking his cue from Hume, he expanded the distinction of reason and sense into the tripartite scheme of Reason, Understanding and Sense. Most importantly, his discussion of sense revolved around the forms of space and time, notions that the Greeks had excluded from their consideration of knowledge. The implications of this Kantian "revolution" for a theory of truth were explored by Hegel but only fully realized in our time. For so long as philosophers were wedded to the prejudice, fostered by Descartes, that it is the mind which knows, it was inconceivable that the contingent factors of our temporal/historical existence should play a significant role in cognition. Now, of course, the situation has changed. At the price of some repetition, let me make clear what exactly this means.

The mystery of human knowing that engaged the ancient and medieval philosophers was how a changing person can know the universal, truth. It is the human being who knows, not a mind, and this person's physical body locates him or her in time and place. And so the Platonic wonder, taken up again by Heidegger in his "re-thinking" of the moderns, concerns the immanent activity of a changing human who through knowing is evidently transcendent, able to escape time-bound conditions to arrive at the universal. The difference in the two viewpoints, traditional and modern, may appear subtle but is in reality far-reaching. The moderns who touted Mind as the ground of all knowing ushered in a timeless or eternal truth by divorcing Mind from body. For Descartes, therefore, the mind's native intuitions, its clear and distinct ideas, were necessarily true. For him knowledge was no mystery; the mind was an extra-temporal absolute. The traditional standpoint, conversely, in its emphasis upon the person who knows never extricates us from our time-bound condition. Albeit mysterious, knowledge was, as Plato's shaman attests, an ascetical discipline. We must rise above personal whim and free ourselves from constricting views if we are to understand other peoples and cultures. The universality of reason can never be purchased at the price of an abandonment of our bodies. When Sartre parodied man as the "frustrated god" searching in vain for the absolute, he was evidently thinking, I said, within the context of modern philosophy.

In order to appreciate how the contextual notion of truth I am recommending is not a relativism, we might first consider some of the ways philosophers in the past have spoken of truth. In everyday usage we talk of telling the truth. This the philosophers have called moral truth, the truth of action. The human interaction essential to our development is predicated on mutual understanding, an understanding that is impossible if my 'yes' really meant 'no'. Moreover, as rational beings we have to live in a coherent world, one in which the propositions we express hang together. Our language would cease to perform its task were we to jettison consistency. If I meet you in the corridor and compliment you on your attractive hairstyle and you reply: "I had an apple for breakfast," what am I supposed to think? For you there may be some sort of connection, but in the event communication has broken down. We cannot do without logical truth. Finally, philosophers have spoken of ontological or factual truth, of what is the case. If two of us are looking at the same wall and you say that it is green and I say that it is blue, then the question of who is right — What is the truth? — concerns our criteria of judgment. If we are to communicate, some norms must be applicable. The classifications of our language may be arbitrary; but without an agreed upon system, we would be without the coherence communication requires.

A word of caution regarding these distinctions of truth lest we read the mentality of modern philosophers back into medievals and ancients. Because Aquinas, for example, in discussing the truth of judgments used the Latin "*adæquatio*" ("making equal") or "*conformitas*" ("conformity"), he must not be interpreted as a modern. His discussion centers on judgments and their criteria, not on the connection of ideas with their external counterparts. Indeed, if he were bogged down in a correspondence theory of truth, how could he have equated Being (meaning) with Truth and Goodness? On the other hand, when placed in their proper contexts, these equations make sense. Are not the criteria of meaning or intelligibility, the determinants of truth, as norms of judgment expressive of values?

The thread that runs through these distinctions of truth might be called the coherence of reason necessary for communication. Truth, as Nietzsche has argued, is fundamentally a value; we prize coherence because we need to communicate. In choosing to communicate, we reject disorder or violence: an awesome decision, as Sartre reminded us, for by opting for "consciousness," we have chosen "knowledge with" others. Although Sartre developed this theme along the lines of "hell is other people" and his description of consciousness stressed its intentionality (consciousness is *of* something), I believe he intended that we ought to be critical of the conventional images we entertain of consciousness because these are self-absorption rather than knowledge-with.

The critical distinction between relativism and contextualism, between truth as relative to the individual and truth as a relation of communicating persons is reflected in our understanding of consciousness. Generally speaking, "consciousness" suggests becoming aware, that is, the self-reflection that issues in a deepened understanding. Yet the consciousness described by modern philosophers belongs rather to the armchair philosopher who spins an intricate web of self-evident intuitions, or one whose observations are subject to the reliability of sense impressions. And so, in spite of the tradition embodied in the senses of truth we have distinguished, that the quest for truth or understanding is a dialogue, our images have shifted our pursuit of it into a solitary journey. We cannot blame the Reformation for everything, even though it succeeded in stamping the word "conscience" with an individual bias. Conversely, a story is told of earlier times, St. Augustine's I believe, that he saw someone reading a book and was astonished that the person read without lip movement. A reading, as it is in poetry, is an act of communication. Through it we commune with one another. It is this perspective on truth — truth as conversation, truth as "corresponding," truth as an engagement of mutual commitment or promise — that sharply distinguishes contextualism from relativism.

Through an analysis of religion we have come to see that what we find meaningful and our criteria of judgment are given to us in the myth imbibed with our language. But that language cannot function unless we have a basic trust in people — fundamentally we are moral beings — which is to say that veracity is the primordial truth. When language is undercut — what we saw earlier regarding the Korean POW's — we fail to develop as persons, for there is more to human communication than animal signaling. Religion casts light on this truth about ourselves in its basic doctrine of creation. It presents us "in dialogue," as fundamentally *related to*, because we are co-creators of a world that does not belong to us. Is it surprising that Judaism, Christianity, and Islam have placed great emphasis upon the Word of God, a word (in Hebrew, *dabar*) that is both word and deed? Through word (*dia-logon*), indeed, we are because the mystery of our being is reflected in the dialectic of speech: a revealing that is a concealing, an immanence that is a transcendence, a truth that, as rational, is determinate or closed yet nevertheless open. Truth, obviously, is not just fact, nor simply value, but above all symbol. That dimension of it we express when we say that we are seeking the truth: that mysterious absolute which bewitched so many great intelligences of modern philosophy. They thought to replace the old Absolute of religion with a new one, science. But by showing us that science is a quest, were they not actually revealing to us religion's true nature as a pursuit of the Absolute?

If we need reassurance that the concept of truth as dialogue does not imprison us in a system of static criteria, we might recall: 1) that a criterion offers a standard of judging which, like knowing, is a human act. It is people, situated in a spatio-temporal context, who are called upon to adapt themselves to the demands of changing circumstances; 2) that we criticize the great modern philosophers because we are living off their patrimony. Had they not carried on the dialogue of their times, we would not today be positioning ourselves in relation to them; and 3) that it was within the religious context of their day that first the Lollards and then later the reformers called into question the validity of certain rituals. Their questioning set in motion a further dialogue for, among other things, it was a call to clarify meanings that centuries of use had evidently obscured. Protestants, it has been said, stand in need of that against which they protest, just as Catholics have needed protest to refine and correct their understanding. It is important from our perspective to underscore the fact that it was an attack on ritual that provoked this thoroughgoing inquiry into a community's criteria of truth.

In retrospect, the Reformation appears as the religious facet of a burgeoning movement of freedom, intellectual, political and social, that swept over Western Europe from the sixteenth to the nineteenth centuries. Luther's "Here I stand" was the catalyst of the movement: a declaration that, as we know, shifted the emphasis from con-science as a *knowledge with* to conscience as an inviolable, individual principle of right. As had occurred in other ages of history, there was a retreat to inwardness manifestive of a new spiritual atmosphere: "What is crooked cannot be made straight." (Eccl. 1.15) The encroachments of society without a doubt precipitated such an emphasis. But emphasis readily becomes over-emphasis. The group tended to be sacrificed for the individual so that ritual action lost its luster. It is an established fact that groups like the African pygmies, with little social cohesiveness, have weak ritual behavior. As a consequence, in accounting for the weakening or loss of ritual in the West, we cannot overlook the subjectivist attitude which modern philosophy captured and elevated into a theory of humanity. Today, of course, the current is running in the opposite direction. We have already cited Lévi-Strauss' remark at the end of his *Mythologiques*: a statement, expected from a social anthropologist, to the effect that for too long philosophy has been a hindrance to the social sciences by its exclusive concentration on consciousness.

It is part of the Lévi-Straussian sense of humor which spices these volumes that his argument against the modern philosophers and their contemporary epigones, among whom are to be numbered the Neo-Kantian Ernst Cassirer and the phenomenologists followers of Edmund Husserl, ends in a volume appropriately entitled *Naked Man*. He supports his contention that it is the whole person who knows, not consciousness, with the evidence of diverse, historically developed mythologies which, in response to changing circumstances, are elaborations of the same myth. It is for this reason, as I mentioned earlier, that all versions of a myth are regarded as true. They satisfy the variant requirements of understanding demanded by different times and situations.

It is clear that for Lévi-Strauss understanding is a "work of knowledge," a philosophical act. He is thus a representative of the philosophic tradition, following Plato's shaman in a quest for wisdom. The construction of myths and the development of mythologies are intellectual efforts to mediate life's perplexities. This mediation, certainly, is not a dissolution of that experience of ambivalence which called forth these dichotomous categories in the first place. Our intellectual devices "resolve" by enabling us to live with our problems through making sense out of them. Conversely, and it is noteworthy that Lévi-Strauss' collection does not feature religious mythologies, Tambiah's concern with ritual or mediating action aligns him with the shaman as embodying the explicitly religious tradition. Both traditions, we must repeat, are dealing with basic human experience. But there are two features of the religious tradition that must be mentioned. First, with its stress on action it cannot be interpreted, as can philosophy, as being simply a matter of knowing. Plato, we have seen, has been blamed for this "modern" concept of philosophy, even though the goal of the Platonic search was wisdom, (*phronesis* or prudent conduct) not mere knowledge (*episteme*). The Socrates Plato portrayed was above all a man who lived his philosophy. Second, although Tambiah's statement that "religious action is oriented to influence the relationship between these oppositions" can suggest that ritual is magic, it actually underscores the living aspect of the religious dialogue. The dichotomies expressed in religious language are rooted in one's personal experience as mysteriously both immanent and transcendent. The insight offered by religion is, we said, that this experience results from a more basic relationship, that of creation. Because transcendence is more than an act of knowledge, the "influence" exerted by ritual is not, then, an exercise of magical power, stemming from the delusion that divinity is, after all, in one's hands. Rather, the "desired mediation attempted through ritual action" is, if anything, an attempt by the human being to enter fully into the life of dialogue that immanence and transcendence imply. Religious mediation is *en-actment*, not hocus-pocus.

The mythologies of death commented on in the previous chapter highlight the religious conviction that life is a moral drama. But religion, as enactment connotes, is more than having an acceptable code by which one regulates his or her life. It is not just ethics, as we are told even by writers who, because of their different understanding of symbols, would not subscribe to the strong sense I have attached to enactment. For if religion is just ethics, would we need God, the divine, or a transcendence understood as more than the "othering" movement in knowledge? A number of issues are involved in this question. Why, for instance, would one suppose in the first place that religion is just an ethical system? Obviously, the question did not arise when the issue was whose god (or gods) was to prevail. But with the advent of atheism, particularly in the West, new ground rules for discussion were necessary and religion had to justify itself as a rational or plausible option. Since "Why religion?" is still crucial even for those with a certain amount of religious exposure, we must address the question even at the risk of some repetition. I shall do so by singling out factors germane to my idea of enactment.

When a religious becomes "higher" by passing beyond the limits of its provenance, it is systematized. Its message must be condensed into formulæ that permit easy assimilation, and its way of life rationalized so that both conversion and apologetic are feasible. The step to becoming a religion of the book is natural; and had it not occurred earlier, both Christianity and Islam would have taken it perforce when they became religions of an empire. Yet even with this systematizing, there was no need for either religion to defend itself as a religion. If conquest made the adoption of a different religion expedient, there was a base for the new religion to build upon because, in a world-historical outlook, every people had its religion. Only with the advent of the modern technical age did this situation change: initially in Christian Europe, for there the great cultural transformation took place. For the first time in human history the idea matured that religion was just a convenient system of ideas — an "ideology" — to which one was committed, with no particular relevance, save in one's personal conduct, to public social-economic-political life. The European adjustment to secularization was carried into Muslim lands on the wings of economic and political domination. But whereas Muslims came increasingly in the twentieth century to refer to Islam as a system, they meant a blueprint for a social order which could be set off against rival capitalist or communist social systems.

> Rather than a personal posture of faith or as loyalty to an historical community, it now was thought of as a complete pattern of ideal life, subsisting in itself apart from the community which might embody it, a pattern that communities (even more, perhaps, than individuals) ought to adopt . . . Many Muslims seemed to express their submission to God less by way of a direct personal act of Islâm to Him, than in the form of a submission and loyalty to Islam itself, at once the ideal 'system' and the historical manifestation, in which acceptance of God was but one element among many. An observer has noted that it can seem less dangerous now, in some Muslim lands, to say something slighting about God or even to be an atheist than to imply anything that might seem disrespectful about Islam or its Prophet.[10]

No doubt our failure to understand contemporary events in Muslim lands stems from our divergent cultural experience. Muslims still hold together in an ideal system components which for us have fallen apart. If their system is a social blueprint that appears to minimize belief, it is because Islam, in comparison to Occidental religion, has always been creedally uncomplicated and emphatically social: dedicated to the establishment of the

10. *The Venture of Islam*, Volume III, 389.

truly just society. The belief element in the Christian ideal that once dominated Europe destroyed itself in controversy. At first divisive and later too controversial for discussion, belief gradually disintegrated. The points of controversy as distinguished from slogans were too esoteric for ordinary people's comprehension, and in time they were dismissed because they made no appreciable difference in one's everyday behavior. "What is important is the golden rule, not what you believe." But as the secularist mentality became prevalent, even the importance of religion as a guide to conduct evanesced. The realization dawned that if belief has no bearing on conduct, why religion? Religion as morals became morals without religion. Or if you will, religion is just another, and so dispensable, moral system. It is all the more dispensable because other moral systems, at least, require no profession of dogma. For this reason, the community life that gives meaning to rituals and their supporting beliefs must be an ongoing dialogue, not only among its participants but also with the outsiders who are essential to its truth. This dialogue of truth is the vital guarantee of the immanence-transcendence dialectic of human existence.

Although the formative power of ritual is generally acknowledged, it is its expressive character that much of the literature emphasizes. Personally, I believe this emphasis, which has amounted to a serious neglect of ritual's formative power, must be judged by its fruits. It may be slightly exaggerated to claim that we need look no farther for a classical example of ritual destroying belief. A case in point: I am sure that many readers find my word 'enactment' unusual. Christian theologians, depending upon whether they be Protestant or Catholic, will in all likelihood understand it as indicative of denominational bias or commitment. "Enactment" suggests the stark realism of the Council of Trent vis-à-vis different Protestant positions regarding sacraments. But I am confident that theologians will perceive something more fundamental than a taste for polemics; and if the ordinary reader perceives that much, there is a solid ground for hope. At least in polemics an issue is engaged, which is not the case with the contemporary gloss, "celebration." Of course an important point was made by the insistence upon

ritual 'play.' We are animals too and cannot do without socia-
bility. But now all Christians celebrate together, oblivious, perhaps, of the fact that what we celebrate in a rite is the event that
forged the bonds of basic spiritual meaning. Celebration, indeed,
is an expression. Yet it fails to address the socially alienated who
stand in need of enactment. There is something to be said for the
injunction of the Gospel parable: "Make them come in."

If I resort once again to reflections upon our history, it is
because our culture, through "cultivating" us, has dulled us to
its impact. We are prepared to acknowledge the social, economic
and political rearrangements occasioned by the irruption of the
modern technical age. But part of our misunderstanding of
contemporary Islam is that we have limited our perspective on
Muslims to these rearrangements so that we are perplexed by
their provocation by "Muslim extremists." Believing ourselves,
perhaps, to be God-fearing people, we cannot understand what
religion has to do with politics. It never enters our minds that
maybe we have changed religion.

Theologians, I assume, are like philosophers in that they
rarely pursue all the logical consequences of their positions. The
fires of philosophical controversy have been fueled by human
finitude, not by lack of logic. Hegelians of the Right and of the
Left are only one of many instances. And so, while acknowledging the importance of the protest against "magical" or "superstitious" rituals, we must recognize that words which express an
understanding solidify its world of meaning. No one, for example, as a result of Reformation controversy suppressed the text:
"Do this in memory of me." But the context of a memorial of the
past is not the same as that of a memorial that re-enacts the past.
A world of meaning was undergoing change.

Let us, with a few broad strokes, try to sketch some outstanding features of the new context. We have seen that the movement
of reform can be regarded as a heightened concern for transcendence. Accusations of magic and superstition may be prompted
by the realization that ritual, too, is subject to the indictment:
familiarity breeds contempt. Repetition can contribute to a loss
of the wonder that is the heart of worship. The Christmas crèche
popularized by St. Francis of Assisi successfully brings God

down to our level, for good or bad. It can have the effect, shared
by relics, images, even the bread and wine of the Eucharist, of
breaking down the barriers which set the Sacred off as something
apart. Yet if God loses his "wholly otherness," the experience of
transcendence that originated and sustains religion likewise per-
ishes. In philosophical language, the Absolute is relativized away.

This switch to the language of the philosophers is important
because, as we have seen, it was the philosophers, thinking within
this context of preserving divine transcendence, who drew its
deleterious consequences. Once the fear of humanistic reduc-
tionism leads one to seal God off in his wholly transcendent
otherness, the gift-character of revelation and salvation is retained but at the price of giving up its rationality. To safeguard
the gift, one emphasizes its absolute inaccessibility to human
thought and deed. That left the philosophers with two alternatives. Either they could salvage 'God' as a concept, as Kant did,
while having to admit that its relevance to mankind and the
world was no more than a postulate. The advantage of this
option was that it kept the philosophers from being religiously
ostracized. Professors in Germany were government servants.
They were expected to assist in maintaining the *status quo*, which
meant, of course, appreciating religion's role as a powerful conservative force. Fichte's failure to live up to this expectation cost him
his post. Or, using the other alternative, the philosophers like
Feuerbach could relegate God to an "impossible transcendence," and hence conclude that man was the only absolute.
Hence the people who continue to talk about transcendence
must recognize that they are simply describing a moment in
human knowledge. We owe a debt, therefore, to modern philosophy for making clear these options presented us by prevailing
theological premises.

George Santayana once remarked that in philosophy there are
only two choices: to follow either Aquinas and, however discor-
dantly, maintain an immanent-transcendent dialectic, or Spinoza and suppress it in favor of the seemingly pantheistic
identification, *Deus sive Natura*. Although reared in a religious
tradition, Santayana delighted in wearing the outsider's critical
mantle. Understandably, theologians can find fault with his

assortment of *bons mots*; he preferred the catchiness of an apho-
rism to its accuracy. But I believe that he responded sensitively to
the religious climate of opinion of his day (1863–1953). The
irony is that if only recently theologians have boldly thrown off
the heritage of modern philosophy, it is because previous efforts
to do so were met by ecclesiastical condemnation and/or disbar-
ment.

The response to the Reformers' insistence on transcendence
(God's gift) was, as is the wont of polemics, an equally firm
emphasis upon immanence (man's work), albeit one that does
not deny transcendence. But in philosophy the roles of the
antagonists were reversed. The (Protestant) theologians of transcendence were sustained by the religious sounding alternative
of the immanentist philosophy — it was the Kantian inspired
theologians who provoked Nietzsche's diatribe against German
philosophy — whereas the (Catholic) theologians of the immanence of human work later reacted with a philosophy of "realism" against the atheistic, Feuerbachian alternative of the philosophers of immanence. As we expect in a situation of debate, the
ground rules were agreed to by both parties. No one, apparently,
questioned these ground rules which compelled a protagonist to
take hold of one horn of the immanent-transcendent, mind-
world dilemma. Or if anyone did so question, he was ignored as
irrelevant to the debate, and even looked at askance by the
ecclesiastical authorities who, instead of being aware of the
disastrous terms upon which their religious committals were
being debated, could only view the matter on identical terms.
After all, authorities, too, are human. We should not expect
them to be able to escape their educations, even though the very
life of the tradition to which they have dedicated themselves may
be at stake.

Instead of spelling out immediately some of the implications
of the terms of this theologic-philosophical debate — the reader
may feel that enough abstract terms have already been bandied
about — I will present the religious issue first. I apologize for
introducing it with a lengthy citation from Eliade. But he places
the issue in the broad perspective it deserves.

In fact, this paradoxical coming-together of sacred and profane, being and non-being, absolute and relative, the eternal and the becoming, is what every hierophany, even the most elementary, reveals. A mystic and a theologian like Locācārya is merely explaining the paradox of hierophanies to his contemporaries. . . . the paradox of the coming-together of the sacred and the profane was expressed in the concrete in the case of the idol, and by analytical description in the case of the verbal interpretation. This coming-together of sacred and profane really produces a kind of breakthrough of the various levels of existence. It is implied in every hierophany whatever, for every hierophany shows, makes manifest, the coexistence of contradictory essences: sacred and profane, spirit and matter, eternal and non-eternal, and so on. That the dialectic of hierophanies, of the manifestation of the sacred in material things, should be an object for even such complex theology as that of the Middle Ages serves to prove that it remains *the* cardinal problem of any religion. One might even say that all hierophanies are simply prefigurations of the miracle of the Incarnation, that every hierophany is an abortive attempt to reveal the mystery of the coming together of God and man . . . Leaving out for a moment the word 'God', this may be translated: the sacred may be seen under any sort of form, even the most alien. In fact, what is paradoxical, what is beyond our understanding, is not that the sacred can be manifested in stones or in trees, but that it can be manifested at all, that it can thus become limited and relative.[11]

Obviously, the debate in the West that was triggered by a concern for divine transcendence and articulated in an immanentist philosophy completely bypassed what Eliade has seen as the cardinal religious problem. His argument, supported by evidence drawn from a cross-section wide enough to justify his calling his book *Patterns*, is, precisely, that religious ritual has always been an enactment, not a "celebration." That is to say, the religious person on the street has always sought mediation with the divine, however much he or she may be warned by the professionals of the dangers inherent in his *praxis*. "A real religious experience", Eliade adds, "indistinct in form, results

11. *Patterns in Comparative Religion*, 29–30.

from this effort man makes to enter the real, the sacred, by way of the most fundamental physiological acts transformed into ceremonies."[12]

Personally, I find it questionable that the Christianity of the West has made any impact on Islam through the devotion of the common variety of religious person. If any impact has been made, it has been via our professional literature which, it would appear, has been content to paper over our domestic differences by subscribing to "celebration." *Enter in* smacks of the primitive, the superstitious; and our philosophy, which has celebrated man as the unique absolute, frightens us away from the suggestion that religion expresses a desire to exist in an absolute manner. We have tried so hard philosophically to make man God that our Christianity shouts across a vast cultural abyss to peoples who no longer discern in us a desire to become absolute. The paradox is that this philosophy which has made us absolute has been bolstered by our absolutizing of our political, economic and social arrangements. As the West took over the globe, people of every country, if they were not to be thought uncivilized, had to take on our superior ways. The religion that was carried with our secular culture offered no discernible evidence of a belief in our essential relativity. In fact, even our missionaries brought with them not only the absolute religion but likewise the requirement that the convert to it take on a whole ensemble of alien customs.

That the distinctions which have played an important role in Western theological thought: creator-creature, supernatural-natural, etc., have been drawn for significant reasons is not to be gainsaid. Careful discrimination has always been a sign of refinement of mind. Yet however much we are warned against letting distinctions fall apart into separations, at least in philosophy, one sometimes wonders whether the warning is taken sufficiently to heart. Santayana was remarkably perceptive when he juxtaposed Spinoza to Aquinas. For Spinoza used the traditional vocabulary: substance, God, nature, freedom, etc., but it was all grist for his mill. To avoid any form of pantheism, in which the problem of immanence and transcendence was disin-

---

12. *Ibid.*, 32.

tegrated, became the major theoretical aim of philosophy and theology. The more we read of modern philosophy, the more we find ourselves immersed in that single, overarching problem: How is the Absolute to be composed with the relative, the infinite with the finite? Heidegger's "Why is there something rather than nothing?" brings us back to the dilemma of Parmenides: "If there is Being, the Absolute, how can there be beings?" To deal with the problem of pantheism the separations of modern philosophy were useful, resulting in a spirituality that disdained this world for the other, that exalted the soul above the sinful body, that purified the world of nature of the slightest taint of pantheism by removing the Creator from creation. There was the foothold for Marx and for those intent upon "scientific progress" freed from religious restraint. Someone like Teilhard de Chardin who argued against the premises of this spirituality, oftentimes relying on the evident sense of biblical texts, must have thought that he was "born to blush unseen" by theologians and "waste his fragrance" on science's "desert air." It is not a misnomer to designate the mentality he was out of sorts with in the singular. It was shared premises that fashioned the "modern world."

If I am right in suggesting that this spiritual outlook has something to do with the contemporary rejection of "Western" values by Muslims, how much more so is this the case in the "East"? I invite the reader to ponder two passages manifestive of a different spiritual climate: one that we usually brand pantheistic. They were written by Sri Aurobindo, whose studies in England attuned him to the Christian European landscape.

> Nature, then, being an evolution or progressive self-manifestation of an eternal and secret existence, with three successive forms as her three steps of ascent, we have as the condition of all our activities these three mutually interdependent possibilities, the bodily life, the mental existence and the veiled spiritual being which is in the involution the cause of the others and in the evolution their result. Preserving and perfecting the physical, fulfilling the mental, it is Nature's aim and it should be ours to unveil in the perfected body and mind the transcendent activities of the Spirit. As the mental life does not abrogate but works for the elevation and better

utilisation of the bodily, so too the spiritual should not abrogate but transfigure our intellectual, emotional, æsthetic and vital activities.

For as it is the right relation of the soul with the Supreme, while it is in the universe, neither to assert egotistically its separate being nor to blot itself out in the Indefinable, but to realise its unity with the Divine and the world and unite them in the individual, so the right relation of the individual with the collectivity is neither to pursue egotistically his own material or mental progress or spiritual salvation without regard to his fellows, nor for the sake of the community to suppress or maim his proper development, but to sum up in himself all its best and completest possibilities and pour them out by thought, action and all other means on his surroundings so that the whole race may approach nearer to the attainment of its supreme personalities.[13]

I realize the danger in citing two short passages as example of Indian, *a fortiori* Eastern, spirituality. It is reckless to cut across cultures in apparent ignorance of the many factors that give to the written word its peculiar resonance. Yet if I must be accused of failing to honor my own precept, it must be recognized that an equally prominent theme of this work is the unity of mankind in its creative task. Our spiritual experience, East and West, is compounded of many elements. But because that experience is above all human, we can discern amidst a diversity of responses and techniques a search to fill a common need. The texts of Sri Aurobindo spell out in characteristically Indian terms that need to be made whole or "holy" through internal and external integration. Through many creation stories runs the refrain: we began with a *uni-verse* in which all things were "poured together" in a primordial harmony. Our spiritual task, whether solely through our own efforts or through these after being empowered by redeeming grace, is to bring what has become scattered together again. For this reason I referred at the end of the last chapter to Wilfrid Mellers' work on *renewal* in twentieth-century music. The dualities that began to appear in European music at the Renaissance:

those between harmony and counterpoint, subject and counter-subject, polyphony and homophony, tonic and dominant, content

13. *On Yoga, I, The Synthesis of Yoga*, Pondicherry: Sri Aurobindo Ashram, 1965, 15, 17.

and form, and so on — prove to be musical synonyms for wider and deeper dichotomies between thought and feeling, extroversion and introversion, individual and state, art and science.[14]

They testify to the spiritual condition given formal philosophical shape by the moderns. At that time Western man, we noted, lost his status as *homo symbolicus*. I have called Mellers' "new primitivism" in music a search for a new integrating myth, and it is significant that it has been accompanied by a turn to the East. The Beatles went looking for the Maharishi Mahesh Yogi. Whether they had found him or not, he or another would have appeared on a scene that features Zen meditation and an assortment of Yogic exercises. Who is to say whether this turn is to religion or to *homo symbolicus*? In either case, the East never lost the unity of the two. Both philosophy and religion are consecrated to a single task: "preserving and perfecting the physical, fulfilling the mental; it is Nature's aim and should be ours to unveil in the perfected body and mind the transcendent activities of the Spirit . . . For as it is the right relation of the soul with the Supreme. . . ."

For some time now in both our philosophy and our feelings we in the West have been rebelling against the dichotomies that Descartes' philosophy formulated. For once mind or soul had been divorced from the body, the idea that ritual is an enactment sounded odd. Spiritual existence became an increasingly private affair — literally, that of which others are deprived — so that religion was reduced to just another of life's categories. Its wars convinced its critics that it must be isolated, so that Western religion, unlike anything in the East, has been, as it is in the university, another department. We have what for us appears to be religion, yet in reality how alien this is to Islamic, Hindu or Buddhist concepts.

With the philosophical criticism of the grounds upon which we have stood for so long, and the Muslim reaction to our Christianity, is something once again being revealed to us about our creative activity? Perhaps we have had to go through the religion of Reason, heard the cry of "Écrasez l'infâme," and

14. *Caliban Reborn*, 32–3.

endured a religionless Christianity, the "death" of God, cults and the emptying of our churches to face once again the basic paradox of our existence. The long history from the Neolithic Age until a few centuries ago revealed us as *homo symbolicus/homo religiosus*. Will this critical experience of the West prove to be only an interlude or truly revelatory of a new self-concept?

CHAPTER V

The Revelation of Humanity

⮜⮞

UNDOUBTEDLY Auguste Comte, the reputed father of positivism, would be pleased with the title of this chapter. Although not many today are tempted to read his turgid prose, he has his niche, remote but permanent, in the history of philosophy. Outside of the professionals, most people who dip into philosophical literature are pleased with labels or catchwords that conveniently identify or summarize. The philosophers of Ionia are associated with elements: air, fire, water or "the boundless"; Plato with Forms; Descartes with his Cogito; Hegel with Spirit; Nietzsche with the Overman, etc. The diversity within movements of thought is bleached in mnemonic "-isms": empiricism, idealism, positivism, etc. It is the fate of Comte that he will be remembered less as the prophet of the religion of humanity than as the herald of the new age of positive science. The superstition of theology and the obscurantism of metaphysics he declared dead; with him we entered the era of unbounded progress. Happily he never lived to see that blessed state. The triumphs of the scientific method are now acknowledged to be of limited scope, and the horrors of its inventions are recognized to be the price we pay for its benefactions. We cannot, obviously, accept "humanity" within the narrow bounds Comte set for it, much less his travesty of religion. His thinking owes too much to the thought patterns of modern philosophy for it to be congenial to the viewpoint of this work. Why introduce him? In case we need a reminder to attend to context.

Both "revelation" and "humanity" are weighted with the baggage of history. To the dismay of those who are convinced that we must begin with definitions, I must apologize. It is true, of course, that we have to be playing in the same ballpark, but the world and all that is contained therein cannot always be neatly defined, that is, clearly "marked off from" at the very outset. The emphasis upon history in this book is dictated by the conviction that, caught up in a web of meaning, we come only gradually to an understanding of the terms we use. What gives them meaning is a whole way of life: something which cannot be assimilated overnight or swallowed in a single dose. Since life is nothing less than a meeting of present demands with accumulated resources, we are forever trying to make our words resonate to meet changed and novel situations. Heidegger, for instance, was on the cutting edge of the movement for truth as dialogue. To dispel the overtones of coherence and correspondence theories, he called truth a revelation and noted that its Greek form, *aletheia*, suggests in its root the notion of manifestation or unconcealedness. The etymology is secondary; the trick of pouring new wine into old bottles requires mastery.

In this chapter, we shall be dealing with other ways in which religion casts light upon what it is to be human. Creation, we saw, revealed life's meaning as fundamentally a dialogue. Can we not expect that other aspects of that conversation would also contribute their mite to an ever expanding self-consciousness?

My remarks about death at the end of Chapter III left an aspect of the topic undeveloped. There we suggested two notions that can profitably be related. As an entrance into new life, death is a paradigm of all religious acts. As an expiration, it has triggered speculation about a detachable, occult self or soul. I have already indicated in my earlier discussion of spirit one way of relating these notions. Death is the religious act *par excellence* because it is a de-conditioning. Through it we enter the new life of freedom or spirit, liberated from the body, the symbol of the bonds of finitude which have held us captive. This religious insight into death can be carried further. For if death frees us, two things follow from its definitive character: 1) what defines us is freedom; and 2) death itself must be free. At one time this latter suggestion sounded preposterous. Since no one has returned to enlighten us, the idea smacked of the worst kind of metaphysics: because something ought to be the case, it is. Besides, who wants to die? Yet it is the people whom we used to think of as exceptions that have compelled us to acknowledge a right to die and thus shifted the parameters within which we think freedom. In this way death can reveal to us what being free really means.

When Sartre proclaimed that man *is*, not has freedom, there were those who observed that existentialism was the logical consequence of anthropocentrism, the absolutizing of the human characteristic of modern philosophy. They did not read him in the light of Hegel's concept of consciousness as a freeing activity, nor did they bring some of his more extreme statements into better focus by projecting them against the background of the Resistance. The rugged individualism suggested by the declaration that "only freedom can account for a person in his totality"[1] is tempered by social responsibility.

> Yet, in the depth of their solitude, it was the others that they were protecting, all the others, all their comrades in the Resistance. Total responsibility in total solitude — is this not the very definition of freedom? This being stripped of all, this solitude, this tremendous danger, were the same for all . . . Each of them, standing against the oppressors, undertook to be himself, freely and irrevocably. And by choosing for himself in freedom, he chose the freedom of all.[2]

It is true that in his existentialist phase Sartre popularized the notion that freedom is the right to do what one pleases, not the right to do what one ought to do. But he moved away from this absolutist idea of freedom in his flirtations with Marxism, and in

1. *Saint Genêt: Comédien et martyr*, Paris: Gallimard, 1952, 536.

2. *The Republic of Silence*, English translation by Ramon Guthrie, compiled and edited by A. J. Liebling, New York: Harcourt, Brace and World, 1947, 498–500.

the work on Genêt emphasized its contextual character. The phrase quoted above continues:

> to let us see this freedom grappling with destiny, at first crushed by its fatalities, then turning back upon them in order that gradually it might direct them, to prove that genius is not a gift but the solution which is invented in desperate circumstances, to recover the choice which a writer has made of himself, of his life, and of the meaning of the universe — a choice which he reveals even in the formal characteristics of his style and composition, in the structure of his imagery, and in his own particular tastes — to retrace in detail the story of a liberation.[3]

That our much vaunted freedom is a charge, a responsibility to achieve personal liberation, is revealed by death. We have always recognized that the most ennobling of our free acts, love, is a commitment: a taking on of burdens in order to realize fulfillment. (Kant, we might note in passing, defined the Enlightenment as a freeing from the burdens we have placed upon ourselves.) Is not the powerful impact of prison literature its celebration of a liberation in the midst of hellish circumstances? The decision to maintain personal dignity in the face of every kind of assault upon it reveals the true mettle of the human spirit.

Dr. Kübler-Ross' popular book presents death as a similar challenge.[4] She has formalized the rejection and acceptance of their disease by cancer patients in a work that not only breaks a cardinal taboo of our so-called death-denying society but helps us understand an experience that we may have had but have not been able to articulate. Several times I have thought to myself when watching people die: they are ready now; they will go quickly. They have "chosen" death, it would seem, just as I have known others who have refused to die until a loved one arrived. Kübler-Ross' data has been dramatized in *The Shadow Box*,[5] the popularity of which expresses the felt need for a new mythology of death. Just as *Everyman* presented such a mythology for the

3. Jean-Paul Sartre, *Saint Genêt*, 536.
4. E. Kübler-Ross, *On Death and Dying*, New York: Macmillan, 1969.
5. Michael Cristofer, *The Shadow Box*, New York: S. French, 1977.

religious culture of the late medieval period, so is our "secular" culture trying to understand a situation created by modern medicine. Religious mythology has always presented death as a human act, which may explain why we consider accidental death a tragedy. Now, however, machines can keep us "alive," and to describe as human dying in a hospital ward in a comatose state induced by narcotics is surely a travesty: more so when we recall that the promise of the "new science" was that it would free us from tyranny, at the time understood, of course, to be religion. B. Clark's *Whose Life Is It Anyway?*[6] is a powerful dramatic appeal for the patient's right to die taking precedence over the doctor's commitment to life. We cannot circumvent death but we can refuse to be overcome by it. Death, therefore, brings us back again to the mystery of our existence. Like creation, it also reveals us as dependent and independent: in this instance bound to animal nature yet capable of transcending it by a humanizing act of choice. Such is the way in which death defines us as free.

We have all heard, or heard of, fire and brimstone sermons. They are of a piece with the kind of hagiography that capitalizes on a conversion from a dissolute life to one of austerity at the sight of a corpse, or with Ignatius Loyola's *Spiritual Exercises* that would have us think of ourselves in hell or imagine ourselves on our deathbeds. Clearly, this religious focus on death goes beyond its being a rite of passage, a birth to new life. It has us look to death in order to be converted. The new secular mythology of death is moving, then, in a religious direction. Life looks to death, as we have said, for perspective. Religion, therefore, is neither morbid nor futuristic. *Pace* Marx, it does not stupefy us with an opiate, a "pie in the sky" beyond: a charge to which his "dictatorship of the proletariat" or stateless, classless society is certainly open. In fact, religion is preoccupied with how we make use of our freedom now, as a glance into some of its history will confirm.

Because religion presents life as a drama — we said at the outset that it offers us a myth, a beginning-middle-end story as a

6. New York: Dodd, Mead & Co., 1979.

framework for life's meaning — it has, in the West, come into conflict with a philosophy that claims to supplant it. The longer one looks at this conflict, the more it appears to be another phase of the problem of immanence and transcendence. At one stage philosophy claimed reason for itself, the knowledge that, as a closed system of rational determination, leaves to religion the openness and unpredictability of freedom. Yet at another stage philosophy regarded itself as the force liberating us from the narrow, confining world of religious dogma, from an immanent system that refers to a transcendent but is itself never transcended. Obviously, religion was painted into a no-win situation. Yet if we have to choose between the two horns of this dilemma, we would have to choose freedom, openness over closure, for the very purpose of religion is to de-condition: to have us transcend the conditions that mark the finite operations of reason. Hence that preference for the language of conversion; that frequent reference to freedom (*mukti* or *moksha*) in Indian works; that message of freedom from sin and St. Paul's reminder to his Galatian converts that the Christian heritage is freedom.

These varying religious uses of the term emphasize once again the importance of understanding freedom within a context, for a freedom *to* is conditioned by the circumstances that distinguish it as a freedom *from*. Philosophically, our thought about freedom originated with the Greeks whose understanding of the notion was political. Freedom was the prerogative of the citizen who, by definition, was free to assist in carrying out the business of the city. Within that context freedom was susceptible to a kind of either-or rational analysis. A was selected in preference to B for palpable or calculable reasons. Rational choice precludes the selection of what is known to be worse. As a consequence, there was no discussion in Greek psychology of a faculty of free will. The title of St. Augustine's treatise, *Concerning Free Choice* (*De Libero Arbitrio*) reflects this emphasis.

In Chapter II we noted some of the consequences resulting from this way of thinking about freedom. Here we might observe that it was the thinkers whose religion included the concept of sin that found the distinction of intellect from free will useful. Unlike the Greeks, they not only stressed the finitude of intellect in itself, but they also accentuated this finitude by underlining its countertendency: that inclination to do the worse which our intellect tells us is such. But, as we noted earlier regarding Aquinas, religious thinkers could not permit a distinction to become a separation. As the fruit of conversion, religion was basically a free commitment; the divorce of will from intellect was tantamount to making that commitment irrational. Philosophically, it was not until Descartes that such a radical separation was tolerated. Its way had been paved, to be sure, by the rejection of the philosophy and theology of the scholastics during the Renaissance and the Reformation. In their exaltation of divine transcendence, the Reformers placed God out of the reach of human intellect. By stressing faith as a gift from God and an adherence of will, they made it philosophically irrational. The point of view was confirmed by the challenge of Galileo's science. In the face of so much that was novel and plausible, how could anyone pretend to be rational and hold onto the past? If one did, of course, it was with the recognition that the methods of knowing hailed by the new science offered no justification for a personal commitment.

The epitome of this intellect-will dilemma is to be found in the philosophy of Kant, which we would expect because his thought is redolent of the pietism prevalent in Koenigsberg. On the one hand he elaborated a system of knowledge or science with its causal determinisms, for reasoning is the process of making necessary connections. On the other hand, as an inveterate moralist he postulated the freedom of moral choice. This dualism was congenial to the anti-religious thinkers of the Enlightenment. On the basis of rationality no one would choose religion; on the evidence of religious wars, no one could possibly do so. If the "enlightened" continued to espouse it, they did so out of expediency: either to maintain the good order of the State or to keep discontented workers in line or, perhaps, simply to satisfy some personal quirk.

It has often been noted how perfectly the thinkers of the modern period translated the reformers' insistence upon the rights of individual conscience — a generalization, I maintained, of Luther's "Here I stand" — into a philosophic position. Yet this kind of individualism can account for a revolt but can never make a revolution. Luther's revolt would never have turned into a revolution had he not touched an exposed nerve in the body politic. The same must be said of the "events" associated with 1789. "Liberté, Égalité, Fraternité" were sentiments powerful enough to start a revolution but not strong enough to sustain it. The individualism enshrined in modern philosophy prevailed, for what else could brake the movement and allow the old autocracy to be restored within a remarkably few years?

Yet this setback was only temporary, for the movement it embodied was something too deeply human to be suppressed. Perhaps it was the self-consciousness of modern philosophy that stimulated once again that desire for freedom which is the essence of the human spirit. Hegel, it has been said, spent his life celebrating the French Revolution. In what better way than by making freedom the touchstone of political rationality? We may disagree with his theory of history; his hopes for Napoleon were disappointed and, dying of cholera in 1831, he never lived to see how those French principles, which bore such splendid fruit in America, were eventually to change the life of Europe. But whatever we may think of his academic philosophy, Hegel's thought vibrates with that spirit of freedom which the Reformation and Galileo's science had unleashed.

That spirit was not to be extinguished by the fact that Kant was unable to rationalize it. Indeed, his failure to do so turned philosophical attention from the *First Critique* to the *Second*, from the structures of consciousness to freedom's domain of morals or *praxis*. Thus the consciousness of Hegel's *Phenomenology*, although still the element of knowing, is a movement of distinguishing so that in his philosophy the part distinguished is essentially related to the totality from which it has been distinguished. The "wholeness" characteristic of the new age of Romanticism was thus reflected in philosophy. Kant's emphasis upon analysis was balanced by a new attention to synthesis so that the juxtapositions of the past: individual and universal, person and society, knowledge and freedom, even philosophy and religion, were to be overcome. This last 'overcoming' would prove the most difficult. When knowledge became the preserve of philosophers, echoed, we noted, in Hume's cheerful contrast of the philosophical with the vulgar, in Hegel's distinction of how things are in themselves and the philosopher's comprehension of them "in and for themselves," religion obviously lost its title to justify itself. If philosophy alone is comprehensive and determinative of the criteria of knowledge, then we must accept the moderns' reductionist understanding of Plato. He allegedly reduced a religious quest to its reality, simply a knowledge scheme. The philosopher, therefore, was the veritable shaman, albeit one who no longer seeks wisdom but dispenses truth. This was the outcome of Kant's battle to turn metaphysics into science. The metaphysical disease he set out to cure was its endless bickering. If scientists build on solid "facts," why should metaphysicians, in order to arrive at truth, have to grope through the underbrush of outmoded theories?

There are two reasons why the juxtaposition of philosophy to religion has proved difficult, if not impossible, to overcome. First, we have not gotten over the idea that our demand for the "facts" that will justify religion is a philosophical position. Because they have proved themselves, we no longer require other disciplines — history, biology, oceanography — to justify themselves by external criteria. They are useful. Besides, unlike religion, they make no personal demands upon us. Since they are not comprehensive schemes of life, we can take them or leave them, enjoying their benefits without commitment.

Second, however much it is extolled, wisdom is difficult to define, and that has led to an acceptance of the philosophers' suggestion that it is to be equated with their "science of knowledge." But that is not the only reason why the philosophers became the modern day shamans. Wisdom has always meant the prudent use of one's factual knowledge, the sage handling of practical affairs. Unlike the proverbial expression: "Smart outside, dumb in school," it presupposed knowledge. Solomon's request for wisdom was born of the recognition that governing his people required more than an accumulation of facts.

And so, if we look for either signs or manifestations of religious wisdom, at least in places where philosophers would be inclined to look, we are likely to be disappointed. The period when philosophy declared itself the arbiter of all the sciences was, we said, the Age of Rationalism or Enlightenment. Naturally, when the world turned rationalist, so did the theologians, who exercised themselves constructing proofs for God to convince hardened atheists. One can appreciate Hume, for example, only against the background of Bishop Butler and the writings of the other divines who drew Butler into the fray. Where was religious wisdom to be found in all this? Was it not just philosophy? Or if we turn to the conduct of affairs in the expectation that perhaps religious wisdom has had its impact there, do we find anything significant? Religious wars and hatreds; worldly, power hungry prelates. Pious, "little" people ordinarily do not instigate earth-shaking events, nor do they write books of interest to philosophers. As a consequence, as justified as the observation may be that a judgment on religious wisdom may reflect the impossible demand that religion justify itself on empirical, philosophical grounds, we can understand why philosophers arrogated to themselves the shamanic role. Pragmatically, religion had not done its job. Besides, the growing movement of freedom, especially manifest in the political realm, was taking place outside of, and in opposition to, religion. Was this not enough to justify the reversal of roles? If formerly religion gave birth to Platonic philosophy, was it not now philosophy's turn to give birth to religion: humanist, Marxist or whatever?

If de-conditioning is the purpose of religion, how did religion surrender its heritage of freedom to philosophy, which claimed for itself the slogan: "The truth shall make you free"? Both Christianity and Islam, we noted, became religious systems in response to apologetic and missionary needs. Although faith remained fundamentally an act of submission or personal commitment, it tended to be identified with the set of truths which articulated that allegiance and formed its intellectual content. This tendency hardened during the Reformation; one's beliefs became the touchstone of faith. This move was fateful not only because it made religion into "another" system of knowledge, subject to exclusively cognitive criteria, but it thus relegated de-conditioning to a secondary role. That "God's ways are not our ways" applies as much, if not more, to human thought as to any other aspect of our finitude. But with the importance that both Islam and Christianity attached to fidelity to their primitive revelations, that intellectual component which was "the faith" hardened into tradition. Deprived of challenge, the believer could be satisfied with his possession of the truth. Freed by it once and for all, he had no further need of de-conditioning.

The movement of freedom that commenced with the Reformation was, of course, against a form of religion. Further impetus was furnished by the celebrated case of Galileo: more celebrated, as we know now, for the picture that subsequent anti-clericals painted of a lonely hero in single combat with ignorant, yet powerful, prelates. The nasty quarrel was exacerbated by religion's claim to be *the* system of truth, so that the movement which in its origin was actually anti-ecclesiastical soon became anti-religious. Voltaire's first enemy was the Church; for him later and for his followers it was religion. In seeking to account for this broader hostility, we have to remember that Christianity had become Christendom. The Church had become an empire, so that in the divisions of the Reformation, more was involved than religious principles. The politics of the princes were as influential, if not more so, in the Wars of Religion as their religion. Rulers have a stake in good order. Because their control is tied to the *status quo*, they have never been above using the conservative forces of religion for their own ends. Clerics, too, are rarely so unworldly that they spurn access to the circles of power. In this cozy relationship, the alleged good of all is secured by orthodoxy, humility and obedience. It was the preaching of these virtues by the Danish Lutheran Church that provoked Kierkegaard's ire. Why is becoming a Christian so much more difficult than being one?

It was inevitable that in the course of history the Christian Church would not always remain a community of outcasts. The ministry of Jesus had been principally to the poor, sick, disabled, "sinners." But Paul's exhortation to slaves to obey their masters had to sound a slightly discordant note to slave-owning masters of Christendom. Surely they were aware that theirs was a community in which there was neither Jew nor Greek, neither slave nor master, neither male nor female. It is regrettable that the providential relationship of religion and civil power — kings, like bishops, were "by the grace of God" — could be invoked to sanction whatever might be the case socially or economically, unjust or not, as the will of God. Pius IX construed every criticism of his mismanagement of the Papal States as an attack upon religion. Few were the clerical voices raised against the deplorable conditions caused by the Industrial Revolution. My point is not to make hay of the sins of the clergy. Rather, it is obvious that those with power in the Church had vested interests, so that when the movement for freedom extended into the social, economic and political orders, religion, as represented by the clerical establishment, found itself not only apart from, but in opposition to, the trend. Poor Pio Nono has become a sort of model of intransigence. There were numerous errors to be condemned during his long pontificate (1846–78). But when these were published together in a syllabus comprised of pithy statements taken out of their contexts, he quickly became the epitome of everything anti-intellectual, anti-modern, anti-democratic. Probably his own gravest error was his determination to hold onto the "patrimony of St. Peter" at any price, even though he was strengthened in his resolve by the blatantly anti-religious and anti-clerical attitudes of his opponents. Today we can look back on these events with regret but also with understanding. With regret because the failure to respond to the desire for political freedom was, in reality, a refusal to recognize an essential aspect of the religious tradition. With understanding because the freedom extolled was described in the irrational and individualistic terms of the immanentist modern philosophy. The new myth of freedom, forming since the Reformation, had finally taken shape. It was that of Prometheus.

Were I to assert that the movement of freedom has now gone full circle, I am sure that most readers would simply deplore the mixing of metaphors, movement with myth, and go on. More seriously, have I failed to appreciate the irony of the situation: that a movement of freedom which began *in* religion has culminated in freedom *from* religion? Because our intellectual patterns have been shaped or profoundly altered by the Enlightenment, we have come to accept its image of Prometheus: the one bold enough to steal the fire of our humanity from gods intent upon depriving us of it. Promethean man, indeed, is a product of the modern philosophy which established the independence of human science by eliminating religion. But since the purpose of this work is to help the reader understand those intellectual patterns, we have to go beyond the pictures that hold us captive. Our culture, there is no doubt about it, is modern. But the philosophical attacks upon it are evidence of the fact that we have accepted a truncated view as our heritage. Not only are we dissatisfied with the kind of world which our option for science has produced, but we are prepared to admit or hope that some of the things suppressed by that modern refashioning might now be advantageous. In brief, there is more to us than a Promethean defiance which destins us to be torn apart by our inflated independence. We shall, therefore, in rounding out the myth of Prometheus be evaluating the way in which we think about freedom.

If Prometheus defied the gods, he was in a position to do so. Would the gods have felt challenged or defiled by simply another example of human *hybris?* The popular image makes no reference to the fact that Prometheus was the brother of world-supporting Atlas, that he was, as Aeschylus says, the teacher of all the arts of mankind, that in art he is connected with "the tree of life and a pillar and in literature both with a pillar and with a mountain that towers above an abyss, in other words, with the navel of the world."[7] Moreover,

> The eagle which tore at Prometheus' liver was no doubt always associated with him: enough is known of the disciplines of the ecstatic and other spiritual ascetics to justify our thinking that the sufferings symbolized by this image are those of the *askesis* itself, in which the novice offers his body to be devoured by what appears to him to be demoniac powers, until he learns their true nature.[8]

Prometheus, in other words, was the shaman who alone possessed the secret knowledge of the fate of Zeus. His story is that of the beneficent religious ascetic, not of the defiant rebel.

7. E. A. S. Butterworth, *The Tree at the Navel of the Earth*, Berlin: Walter de Gruyter & Co., 1970, 189.
8. *Ibid.*, 202.

Shamans are particularly associated with poetry, and have a special connection with fire and with smiths, as also, of course, with the healing of diseases. There is no doubt of the close connection of the arts, skills and varieties of knowledge with the shaman in early times. In the case of the Greek myth of Prometheus it seems clear that it is derived directly from Asia. Even the traditional settings of the mountain to which the hero or demi-god was chained lie outside Greece, and in so far as the myth has an origin in shamanism or another spiritual asceticism, it appears to be that which lies behind Akkadian tradition. There seems to be ground for seeing in Prometheus a figure of the spiritual hero who found his inspiration in Ea (Enki), and thereby, at some stage of history, perhaps incurred the hostility of the celestial power. In this way the eagle of ascetic agony was, presumably, changed into the punitive emissary of Zeus.[9]

We have already noted in our discussion of death how the myth of the soul triggered speculation about what it is to be human. The shaman's mystical flight is part of the metaphysics of freedom: representative, that is, of our fundamental transcendence. Neither in knowledge nor in conduct are we wholly determined by the conditions of our existence. Their contact with our limits have made ecstatics like Prometheus an essential feature of the religious tradition. For by their breaking of the normal bonds, they present us with an insight into ourselves that has also nurtured the philosophical tradition. We are born to be free in circumstances that demand a continuous exertion.

From the Greeks we have inherited other difficulties with freedom than the problem of rationalizing it. For reasons that I will present later in this chapter as plausible, they came to reject shamanic ecstasy as paradigmatic of the human condition. Freedom, that is, was no longer to be achieved in a religious quest but in a religious rebellion.

When we turn from Homer to the fragmentary literature of the Archaic Age, and to those writers of the Classical Age who still preserve the archaic outlook — as do Pindar and Sophocles, and to a great extent Herodotus — one of the first things that strikes

9. *Ibid.*, 206–7. Ea, the Sumerian Enki, was the teacher of mankind.

us is the deepened awareness of human insecurity and human helplessness, which has its religious correlate in the feeling of divine hostility — not in the sense that Deity is thought of as evil, but in the sense that an overmastering Power and Wisdom forever holds man down, keeps him from arising above his station. It is the feeling which Herodotus expresses by saying that Deity is always . . . 'Jealous and interfering', we translate it; but the translation is not very good — how should that overmastering Power be jealous of so poor a thing as Man? The thought is rather that the gods resent any success, any happiness, which might for a moment lift our mortality above its mortal status, and so encroach on their prerogative.[10]

The upshot of this was that Olympianism in its moralized form tended to become a religion of fear. There is no word "god-fearing" in the *Iliad*. But in the *Odyssey* it became an important virtue and thereafter remained a term of praise right down to Aristotle's time. For anyone to have claimed that he loved Zeus would have been preposterous. Obviously, this kind of religious situation called for rationalization and the philosophers responded to it. Thus was the groundwork prepared for the modern myth of Prometheus.

When I studied world history, we packaged events as did Hegel in his *Philosophy of History*: the times of Egypt, Mesopotamia, Greece, Rome, on into the ages called Renaissance and Reformation. The Renaissance, we were told, was a period of the rebirth of the Latin and Greek classics: a cultural high noon after the "Dark Ages" and their lingering medieval dawn. The classical rebirth heralded a religious rebirth which featured, as we know, a wholly transcendent God, gracious, to be sure, with his saving gifts, but always a threat to man the sinner. It is evident that the idea of achieving one's freedom through mystical union thereby became problematical; the rejection of ritual action as enactment made it altogether impossible. Obedience thus became the hallmark of the believer: an unmistakable sign that specifically Christian themes, like love, were lost in an Olympian revival.

10. *The Greeks and the Irrational*, 29.

I do not mean to imply that, once again, the responsibility for our "religionless" Christianity lies wholly in the Reformation. Although the churches are officially tolerant of their ecstatic members, these generally are a source of embarrassment. Wholehearted approval is usually posthumous, for ecclesiastical organization places a premium on order. A similar situation is to be found in Islam. Sûfî mystics have suffered much at the hands of the Sharî'ah legalists. Within Christianity, St. Paul's injunction that those speaking in tongues at Corinth not be allowed to interrupt services — glossalalia was a charism for the community — has been cited as a precedent for banning ecstatic behavior. The history of this ban is interesting, not the least because it is the bizarre narrative of a gift of God being transformed into a sign of the evil one.

The apostles and disciples of Jesus carried their message into a Græco-Roman world, to people, we said, whose form of spirituality was at loggerheads with an historical and material or sacramental minded Christianity. We saw that the early Christological Councils, beginning with that of Nicæa in 325 A.D., were summoned to repress ideas that appeared to owe more to the prevailing spiritual temper than to Christian revelation. The Middle East was a hotbed of spirit movements, so that when Montanus and his companions burst out of Phrygia speaking in tongues and declaring that he was the Holy Spirit, the charism became especially suspect. It was, then, a growing sense of order and a fear of heresy that contributed to the formulation of a theology that justified the absence of charismatic gifts. The gifts and signs of the Christian which the Scriptures had detailed were, it was said, necessary for the upbuilding of an infant church. Indeed, had not Jesus himself excoriated his contemporaries for looking for signs and wonders? And so, as Christianity in time developed into Christendom, the Roman law was gradually shaped into a system of canon law. Ecstasy had no significant place in a religion that prided itself on its legalism. The triumph of this movement is recorded in the Roman Ritual which lists speaking in "strange" tongues as a possible sign of diabolic possession. Remember *The Exorcist*? If we are living at a time when order is sacred, then, in terms of our earlier dialectic of sacred and profane, we can only await the moment when we see this sacred as profane, and ecstatic disorder as the real sacred.

If modern philosophers became the new shamans by freeing us from the shackles of religion, we have come to see that the new philosophy they concocted has failed as a religion. It has been the caricature of a liberation: apprizing us of our sense of duty yet leaving us to act "as if"; answering our need for a holistic vision of things by postulating a God who allegedly harmonizes the moral and material orders. One of its greatest achievements, a philosophy that offers both a doctrine of salvation and a moralistic view of history, has, in the practical order in which it specializes, proved an economic and human disaster. Marxism-Leninism-Stalinism makes generous use of the term "freedom." But the means it has taken to insure this boon have been an affront to human dignity. Yet the system itself still has its intellectual attraction for many, precisely because it offers itself as the replacement for an ineffectual Christianity.

> I think that Marxist atheism deprives man only of the illusion of certainty, and that the Marxist dialectic, when lived in its fullness, is ultimately richer in the infinite and more demanding still than the Christian transcendence. To be sure, it is undoubtedly such only because it bears within itself the extraordinary Christian heritage, which it must investigate still more. Living Marxism, which has proven its fruitfulness and its effectiveness in history, in political economy, in revolutionary struggle and in the building of socialism, owes it to itself in philosophy to work out a more profound theory of subjectivity, one which is not subjectivist, and a more profound theory of transcendence, one which is not alienated.[11]

Only a religious development of the kind we have traced in this chapter rescues this passage from sheer parody. There is no denying that Marxism has been effective in history and revolutionary struggle. It has also effectively changed some arrangements

11. Roger Garaudy, *From Anathema to Dialogue: A Marxist Challenge to the Christian Churches*, translated by Luke O'Neill, New York: Herder & Herder, 1966, 96.

of political economy, with increasing ineffectiveness in many areas. The incentive to produce has been taken away by collectivization. Any assessment of the building up of socialism depends upon one's definitions. Philosophically, Marxism is collectivist, with a corresponding de-emphasis of the individual or the subjective. Its transcendence, its engagement in otherness, leaves much to be desired. It does not engage in rational exchange with other systems; and its final goal, the outcome of history, in spite of the efforts to realize it, takes on progressively more of the aspects of an impossible transcendence. Will we ever achieve that blessed state, the dictatorship of the proletariat?

In this chapter I have indicated another way in which I believe that religion has contributed to its own demise. *Vi vocis*, ecstasy is a standing-out-of. When the emphasis in religion is placed upon the belief system — a normal construction, to be sure, since we are reflective beings — adherence to the truths professed becomes more important than going beyond them. Yet our propositions cannot be permitted to stand in the way of total de-conditioning. In its own way philosophy runs a similar risk. The doctrines of the master are much more easily appropriated than his art of philosophizing.

We have seen, too, how the efforts to safeguard divine transcendence have opened the door to Garaudy's criticism. If God is indeed Wholly Other, if what is important in religion is to underscore the "absolute qualitative difference" between God and his creatures, is not the challenge of transcendence lost? God reaches down to us in his gift, but what of our attempts to enter into the sacred? Earlier we referred to Tambiah's article on Buddhism in which, having listed some of the dichotomies that permeate religious thought: this world/other world, body/soul, living humans/ancestral spirits, he noted that "religious action is oriented to influence the relationship between these oppositions."[12] Religion is a mediating activity, a living relationship of God/sacred/divine and humanity. In the Christian perspective, the richness of the Infinite cannot be its wholly otherness. If anything, Christians celebrate God's impoverishment, his emptying of him-

12. *Dialectic in Practical Religion*, 50.

self in order to take on our nature, so that we might be enriched. Clearly, the overemphasis on the gift was a toehold for Marx' critique. If all is God's work, Christians bear no responsibility for the world.

The truly remarkable assertion of Garaudy's paragraph is, to my mind, that Marxism "bears within itself the extraordinary Christian heritage." It is true that Marxism has focussed attention on the poor. Notwithstanding its performance, it has continued to offer hope to the downtrodden of the world: the aspect of it that has appealed to the proponents of a "theology of liberation." Yet, given its provenance, I envisage that extraordinary heritage to be the one proclaimed to the Galatians by St. Paul: freedom. Although for many people the name Marx is associated with the cause of international socialism, it is crucial that we recognize that his contribution, certainly in his own mind, was in the field of political economy, with equal emphasis on noun and adjective. For the socialist, revolutionary thrust of contemporary Marxism grows out of the well-nigh omnipotence of the State, and Marx's career was marked by clashes with authorities and irruptions in the political order.

Marx has been the subject of psycho-historical study. We need not be partisan to the genre to surmise that his father's conversion from Judaism to Christianity, necessitated by his political job, could scarcely have failed to make a deep impression on him. Later, of course, Marx was *persona non grata* in Prussia, where the Friedrich Wilhelms III and IV were notorious for using religion for reasons of State. Harrassment by the French authorities compelled him to flee to Belgium. Finally he found refuge in England. He lived through tumultuous times: the social and economic unrest of the burgeoning Industrial Revolution and the consequent political upheavals that led to 1848, to the war of 1870, to the Paris Commune. The articles written for Americans should be read against a background of increasing violence over labor unionism. No wonder that the theme of alienation plays a conspicuous role in Marxist thought. Its entire inspiration was to free us from the economic alienation that makes our lives miserable. To accomplish this, the political, social and religious powers that supported that alienation had to be destroyed. In a sense, Marx preached a crusade for the realization of the still-born ideals — liberty, equality, fraternity — of the French Revolution. In more ways than one he followed in Hegel's footsteps. How he would have reacted to the results of his crusade makes for interesting speculation. Probably he would have thrown up his hands at fate. Were there ever revolutionaries who remained such once they were in control?

My concern in this chapter has been to emphasize trends of thought or theological tendencies, not to convey the impression that the entire lived reality of religion eddied in these currents. There are no problems, as Wittgenstein pointed out, when language is doing its work. It is only when we stop it to examine these workings that difficulties proliferate. In religion too, orthopraxy has always been the bedrock and touchstone of orthodoxy. In religious scriptures, knowing God is practical, not speculative. We are engaged in the work of salvation, not in the construction of theories. For this reason the religious vocabulary is rich in operational terms. Its doctrines are like a leaven, a seed; we follow a way, embark on a journey or pilgrimage. In Zen Buddhism, extensive use is made of the koan: a question posed in such a way that an answer to it is clearly impossible. And yet in Zen one is compelled to think the question, for only then does the nature of thinking become clear. We know by establishing limits, for distinction is, in reality, a process of cutting things down to our size. We make answers as well as find them, and both are indications that it is our desire for a solution that prompted the initial question. If thought is finite, indeed a finitizing or limiting activity, can we expect it to liberate us from our constrictions? Religious writers, accordingly, can sound hopelessly anti-intellectual. Or perhaps they only resonate thus for us who are involved in academia, especially when we read authors whose formation has been solidly Western. Writers in the Eastern traditions strike a different chord: a difference important for the understanding of both our religion and ourselves.

When Plato adopted the shamanistic pattern of thought, its influence, we noted earlier, stretched from the Ganges to Southern Italy. Its spirituality, specifically the idea that the world of appearances and material things must be transcended if one is to come to reality, is enshrined in the Vedas, and thus in the East continues to be a source of life in Hinduism, Jainism and Buddhism. Were Plato solely an Eastern phenomenon, he would take his place with the great sages. His philosophy, with its suggestion of metempsychosis, would have formed part of that religious stream which over the centuries has given shape to Indian culture and continues to nourish Indian life. Socrates, undoubtedly, would have been at home in India. We would think of him, perhaps, as a great yogin: one who was not just a man of integrity in our moral sense but whose life was a whole. Why, in contrast, has our experience been so different? Why do I refer to Plato's religious ambiguity? To the danger of reducing religion to philosophy? Is it simply that we Westerners can never outgrow the heritage which I have described? Are we destined to live out our lives aware of our Cartesianism and the secularism instilled in us by modern philosophy, yet never quite capable of bringing our knowledge and freedom together? The problem, I would like to suggest, runs deeper than our philosophy. It lies at the very heart of our Judæo-Christian tradition.

The extraordinary heritage that Garaudy discerned within Marxism is not simply Christian. Understandably we would call it such because of our historical context. But its foundation, creation, I have called the fundamental religious insight. Without it, one could not speak of the *history* of religions. If I have called the thinkers who have shaped modern philosophy "anti-religious," it is because their artillery was trained upon certain forms or images of Christianity. If I persist in maintaining that their thought was religious or that they offered a substitute religion, it is because their thinking was based upon that fundamental religious insight. The deist God of the age of mechanics was a fit subject for Hume's satire. But neither he nor the thinkers whose contrivances he ridiculed ever cut out from under themselves the religious ground upon which they stood. In writing "ground" I intended no pun, for the word is singularly appropriate. Our humanity, we are sometimes reminded, is rooted in the earth. We are "humus," a part of Nature's soil, and our basic human intuitions have their origins there. Nature has a rhythm: day and night, moisture and dryness, winter and summer. We live in a cosmos, in an ordered world, subject to its cycles, most poignantly that of life and death. If our humanity begins with this perception of law and order, so does our religion. Creation stories, running through all religions, are narratives that, however imaginatively, exhibit this fundamental law of human life. The insight, therefore, that this is God's or a divine world and that we are a significant part of it is, in the terms of this chapter, a revelation of our humanity. Hence the perennial philosophical, because human, problem has been how we are to weigh the immanent and transcendent aspects of our nature.

Today the expression comes naturally, "genetic history." We recognize that we live through an inherited structure, biologically as well as culturally. From a certain standpoint it is one of the great accidents of history that our culture has been shaped by the speculations of a particular Semitic tribe, by people whose experience of the law of human existence brought them to the realization that life is, in a much broader sense of the term, a Law. It was a concept written into their creation story: the misery and evil of life is the result of transgression. Sin is more than human imperfection. It is a personal affront, a lie, an act of treachery or rebellion. Here, we are told, are the roots of our Western guilt culture, and more besides.

> This notion of God's 'power' as the only absolute reality is the jumping-off point for all later mystical thought and speculation on the freedom of man, and his possibility of achieving salvation by obedience to the Law and rigorous moral conduct. No one is 'innocent' before God. Yahweh made a "covenant" with his people, but his sovereignty meant that it was quite possible for him to annul it at any moment. That he did not was due not to the 'covenant' itself — for nothing can 'bind' God — but to his infinite goodness. Throughout the religious history of Israel, Yahweh shows himself a sky god and a storm god, creator and omnipotent, absolute sovereign and 'Lord of Hosts', support of the kings of David's line, author of all the norms and laws that make it possible for life on earth to go on. The 'Law', in every form, finds its basis and justification in a revelation from Yahweh. But unlike other supreme gods, who cannot contravene their

own laws (Zeus could not save Sarpedon from death), Yahweh maintains his absolute freedom.[13]

How are we to read Eliade's commentary? I do not suggest through "Enlightenment" glasses. An absolute Yahweh tyrannizing over guilty mankind may answer to some people's concept, but it would produce only a caricature of "mystical thought" and rather bizarre "speculation on the freedom of man." The relationship of creation, mysterious as it is, is rightly expressed as a Law or dharma because of its base in human experience. We could not talk about chance or accidents, assuredly, were not our experience of order as well. If in their subsequent history the Jews were led to characterize that Law by rigidity and exclusivism in order to preserve that relationship, we cannot suppose that they did so to the permanent loss of the less legalistic aspects of that relationship. The condemnation of Genesis was countermanded in a promise of redemption; the threats, inspired by love, of the prophets renewed that message of hope; even the rebellion of Adam and Eve attests, in a perverse way, to human freedom and dignity. Legally minded Jews might wonder about the inclusion of wisdom literature into the canon of scripture; when one has the Law, is wisdom necessary? Yet even this literature adds to our understanding of the Law-creation relationship. We cannot resolve the mystery of evil and suffering; the world is God's. Still, we have to live in an imperfect world for which we, as humans, are responsible. The insight, that is, that translated human existence into law was, indeed, a revelation that loses its potency when it degenerates into legalism. The relationship of God to humanity revealed to us in Hebrew-Jewish history is one of free response and refusal. Can any other notion than law reveal so powerfully either a strangely impotent or beautifully loving God that would tolerate a dialogue with his creatures?

Life's paradoxes are legion, yet I am compelled to single out one that bears heavily on the concepts of sin and guilt. Surely no one has made us more conscious of our "guilt culture" than Sigmund Freud, himself a product of the tradition that we have

---

13. *Patterns in Comparative Religion*, 95–6.

been describing. I do not believe in psychoanalyzing the dead. But apart from what he learned from his patients, I wonder what Freud understood by sin. *Genesis* mentions shame in connection with nudity, but I can detect no trace of guilt in the conduct of Adam and Eve after their escapade. In fact, the curses of death and work and birth pangs are followed by Adam's triumphal announcement that the woman shall be called Eve because she is the mother of all the living. The story, of course, is rich in allusions and symbolism that connect it with a vast network of mythological lore. But certainly it is no accident that its author has connected sin with life. I understand this not only as an explanation of the situation in which we all find ourselves — we are all cracked and we live in a cracked world — but more profoundly as an underscoring of that responsibility for the world which is an important facet of the creation mystery. Perhaps we should say that our responsibility in creating the world is a greater challenge because our response has been sin.

When it is said that Eastern religions are other-worldly, it should be emphasized that they are such in comparison with the Christianity of the West. If the mystery of creation is its fundamental insight, then religion — sensitive to cultural differences, Eliade uses the singular in referring to the "religious feeling of mankind" or the "religious life of mankind"[14] — cannot extricate us from a human world. It is the ecstatic aspect of religion that would take us out of our material conditions, but no religion can be wholly ecstatic. Platonism, as we have seen, is congenial to the ecstatic temper, which it bolstered by its theory of knowledge. The conviction that truth is eternal, beyond the changing conditions of the material world, can foster the desire for a permanent ecstasy, for a spirituality at odds with the commitment of creation. Carried off into the divine, mankind is no longer in dialogue. If God is all in all, is there room for anything else?

Aside from his utilization of the shamanic, ecstatic pattern, Plato, it would appear, turned away from the idea of humanity as a relation of beings-in-dialogue because of his mission to reform Greek theology. We have remarked that fear of the gods'

14. *Ibid.*, 30.

insidious jealousy became an outstanding virtue in the *Odyssey*. Ultimately, the Homeric world was governed by Fate: an inexorable law to which no appeal, divine or human, was possible. That is to say, unlike creation, there is no final order or meaning to things. The gods, therefore, were in the last analysis no different from men, and so Homer depicted them as glorified humans, with all the passions and pettiness that trouble our existence. Their dealings with us were more often than not unseemly: a dialogue that Plato was determined to bring to an end. He would, as we know, expurgate the works of Homer lest children be corrupted by them. But from our viewpoint he did more. If he instituted an ultimate order of things — the Good or Order replaced Fate — that source of meaning or truth was not a dialogue but an object of contemplation. Similarly, the creation of the world in the *Timæus* was the work of a demi-urge, not God. The spiritual outlook is important, for it meant that God is alien from the world of matter — the incarnation of Jesus was, as St. Paul said, a scandal to the Greeks — and that our work in the world is not a divinely creative process. In the Greek world, manual work was done by slaves.

Let me repeat: it is a matter of emphasis, but Eastern spirituality has retained more of the Platonic, shamanic pattern than has the Western. The yogic, meditative techniques employed to achieve *satori* or *nirvana* are aimed at personal liberation: a transcendence of one's imperfections and desires that brings integrity. Although this emphasis has given currency to the canard that the goal is self-absorption to the detriment of social action, it clearly runs this risk, whereas Western religion runs the opposite one of becoming just concerted social action. The idea of a divine incarnation is not alien to Eastern thought. Rama, Krishna and Buddha are only some of the avatars of Vishnu. But there is not that strong commitment to the world's redemption — St. Paul's all creation groaning for deliverance — that the idea of transgression inculcates. Both Christianity and Islam have taken the idea from Judaism that religion is formative of a people. To this the concept of sin adds the idea of communal responsibility.

Because of these differences in emphases, the common religious vocabulary takes on variant shades of meaning. In Eastern thought creation, like Plotinus' One, is an emanative process: the Divine incarnating itself in myriad shapes and forms so that man's spiritual task is one of coming to the realization of God in all things. The movement is starkly immanent, as is that of the mystic or ecstatic. In the West, as in *Genesis*, God creates a world which is good; it bears the divine likeness. But sin causes a rupture between God and his creation. He remains *in* the world as its creator but not *of* the world. The divine transcendence is magnified, and our spiritual task becomes one of bringing the divine light into a world darkened by sin. We have already indicated some of the consequences of these diverging viewpoints. Western mystics often find a better reception in the East, for their immanent thrust is apt to bring down upon them the charge of pantheism. Moreover, if ritual is the kind of enactment we have described, an effort on our part to enter into the sacred, then its fulfillment in the East is relatively easy. Worship can be brought to life in little things: in a flower, in butter, in water, in fire. For Westerners in the Christian tradition its fulfillment can never be wholly theirs. The object of worship remains always a transcendent sacred. The central mystery celebrated is God's entry into the material so that the world may be transformed. The bugbear of Western religion, we said, has always been pantheism, the dissolution of the divine transcendence. To compensate for this tendency, hard and fast lines have been drawn between sacred and profane, God and world, even at the risk of making God irrelevant to the world and of opening Westerners, for the first time in the history of the human race, to a life unencumbered by the Sacred and its mystery.

In an earlier chapter we suggested that we use symbolic language because we are ourselves symbols, places of encounter where body and soul, matter and spirit, earth and heaven, meet. Religion opens us to a further dimension of thought by concentrating our attention on creation. As symbols, we are likewise beings-in-relation with a creative power, so that the symbols with which we communicate culminate in a dialogue with and in the Sacred, a communion with God. As a human activity, speech is immanent; as communication, it is transcendent. It reminds us not only that we speak in a certain way because our bodies locate us geographically and temporally, but also that we are members of a community who share a culture and through our communal action enhance it. This dialogue of humanity has perdured throughout our history — many have been the efforts to silence one of the partners — because we are fascinated by, as well as have to live with, the mystery of ourselves. The macrocosmic altercation of philosophy and religion reflects the microcosmic tension of intellect and will, of reason or rational determination and spontaneity, passion, creativity. On every level of our thought and being we are brought back to immanence and transcendence. Lévi-Strauss has been criticized for making bipolar opposition the centerpiece of his study of myths, and for the suggestion that the two hemispheres of the brain may account for the phenomenon. His work is social-anthropological. Had he turned to religion, he, too, might have been captivated by immanence and transcendence.

If in this work I have lingered on the contradictions of the philosophy-religion dialogue, it is only because our philosophy of the last three centuries has claimed a monopoly of reason. It has worked within a field which is not the whole of experience, and thus has taken the part for the whole, and inevitably imposed arbitrary limits on its own working. My concern is not that philosophy should surrender its gains; that in a gesture of reconciliation it should sweep aside what it rightfully regards as the progress it has made for the sake of peace: the peace, perhaps, of medieval days which lasted so long as philosophers were content to be the handmaids of theology. Rather, because the period of adversary relationship has for many led to open hostility, which, in fact, is a refusal to dialogue, and not to the death of religion, my interest is to reassess the situation to see what contributions each partner to the dialogue has made or can make to the other, in spite of the pretense of ignoring one another.

In Platonic philosophy religion gave birth to an angry child. We have attempted no elaborate sketch of Greek religion; but from what little we have seen, we can understand Plato's determination to rationalize it. The idea of creation as a dialogue was beyond his purview. Had it been within his ken, he might have settled for a less constricting rationalism, since of its nature a dialogue has its ups and downs, its moments of coherence and incoherence, a continuity of understanding and a discontinuity of misunderstanding. But given his circumstances, he probably regarded the shamanic flight as a welcome opportunity to get away from the incongruous world of Greek mystery religion while remaining wary of ecstasy as a movement of freedom. After all, was not the Platonic rationalism, as the early dialogues make clear, inspired by a desire to restore Athenian political virtue? The task entailed that rationalization of religion which has endeared Plato to later generations of rationalists, most of whom had lost the Platonic sense of our kinship with the divine.

> This rationalist psychology and ethic was matched by a rational-ised religion. For the philosopher, the essential part of religion lay no longer in acts of cult, but in a silent contemplation of the divine and in a realisation of man's kinship with it. The stoic contemplated the starry heavens, and read there the expression of the same rational and moral purpose which he discovered in his own breast; the Epicurean, in some ways the more spiritual of the two, contemplated the unseen gods who dwell remote in the *intermundia* and thereby found strength to approximate his life to theirs. For both schools, deity has ceased to be synonymous with arbitrary Power, and has become instead the embodiment of a rational ideal; the transformation was the work of the classical Greek thinkers, especially Plato. As Festugière has rightly in-sisted, the Stoic religion is a direct inheritance from the *Timæus* and the *Laws*, and even Epicurus is at times closer in spirit to Plato than he would have cared to acknowledge.[15]

The idea of deity as simply "arbitrary Power" is inconsonant with that order which is essential to the basic insight of creation. The abiding mystery, expressed in the phrase that we are co-creators of God's world, is precisely that this order, perceived and constituted, somehow transcends us. Accordingly, the im-pulse to rationalize deity is natural. Even the most rudimentary acts of worship, prayers of petition, are founded on a presump-

---

15. *The Greeks and the Irrational*, 240.

tion of rationality. Arbitrariness precludes communication. The difficulty is that the kind of rationalization we seek in knowledge is exhaustive. When Moses, for example, purportedly asked the voice in the burning bush for an identifying name, he was given a circumlocution. In the ancient world, a person was his name. Were Moses to have named God, he would have grasped his person, that is, controlled him. Even for us, knowledge is power. And so, when the Greek philosophers sought to make sense out of the gods and their religious milieu, they were seeking a kind of control that was nothing less than impious. It is true that the indictments brought against Anaxagoras, Diagoras, Socrates and others were political insofar as their apparent disbelief was thought to be a threat to the community. Athens relied upon the tutelage of Pallas Athene. Whoever impugned the goddess was *ipso facto* undermining the city. But there is more to the whole business than that. I am inclined to think that we fail to appreciate that more because for us the idea that knowledge is independence has lost its luster. "The truth shall make us free." Yes, but we no longer hear that declaration as a battle cry. We have to shuffle our concepts around even to begin to understand why the forbidden tree in the middle of Eden was "of knowledge."

The problem lies in the nature of knowledge as an immanent activity. It is conceived to be an individual possession, a personal appropriation, significantly portrayed in Dodds' phrase in the passage just cited as a "silent contemplation." So regarded, knowledge is absolute: literally, we are ab-solved or "freed from" exterior preoccupations and absorbed in luminous truth. The transcendent, contextual aspect of knowledge is forgotten. Rationalism has always carried with it the pride of independence, a sense of belonging to that privileged, enlightened group which upholds the truth against the onslaughts of the ignorant *hoi polloi*. Philosophical impiety, therefore, is not to be limited to its description of the object known. Even more, it consists in its pretense of absolutism. The truth that shall make us free is paid for at the price of freeing oneself from dialogue and entering into a closed system. Even the great rationalist, Plato, sensed the importance of balancing the absolutizing tendency of immanence with the othering, contextual pull of transcendence. In his own reformed version of traditional religious beliefs, he proposed incredible sanctions for these "truths" because of their impact on society.

> Plato in fact wishes to revive the fifth-century heresy trials (he makes it plain that he would condemn Anaxagoras unless he mended his opinions); all that is new is the proposed psychological treatment of the guilty. That the fate of Socrates did not warn Plato of the danger inherent in such measures seems strange indeed. But he apparently felt that freedom of thought in religious matters involved so grave a *threat to society* that the measures had to be taken.[16]

I am convinced that more is involved here than just freedom of thought; the passage voices the usual canard that religion inhibits free thinking. Can we not suppose that religion gave birth to a philosophy that would respond to the deep human need for rationality and so save religion itself from a mindless absolutism or authoritarianism just as the societal nature of religion and its transcendent reference saves philosophy from an absolute mind? Was this not really the problem of modern philosophy? Once the human being had been defined as a mind, *à la* Descartes, he lost his humanity and became a secular god. Feuerbach was right: theology was anthropology because anthropology was theology. If this suggestion sounds farfetched, we need only consider the philosophy of Immanuel Kant, the epitome of the enlightened. To close off the system of knowledge, Kant postulated, as we know, a wholly transcendent God. Religion or transcendence, that is, makes immanent, systematic knowledge possible and in a certain way, though Kant himself did not — indeed, could not, explore the conundrum — keeps it open or transcending precisely because God is unknowable. Philosophy obviously needs religion. The closest Kant could come to thinking religion, since God was ruled out of thought, was by equating it with morals. There, too, God functions as the ultimate unifying concept: the ever transcendent object that makes reasonable or moral action possible. Moreover, the free-

---

16. *Ibid.*, 223–4.

dom required to observe the moral imperative likewise transcends thought. It, too, is a postulate, which inclines one to interpret Kant as suggesting that freedom is the limit of thought. The irony in all of this is that modern philosophy, we said, began from the premise that we needed freeing from religion, from the constraint of a God who inhibits thought. Kant ended on the note that the philosopher can neither think nor act without at least a transcendent "religious" thought. Philosophical rationalism made deity into a "rational ideal" in order to save us from "arbitrary Power." Now we recognize that we were delivered over to an unresponsive postulate, an absolute requirement with which at least in *bona fide* religion we might enter into dialogue.

If Kant, as we noted previously, thought of himself as reviving the metaphysical tradition, then Hegel, as Heidegger saw, was its culmination because he made explicit what Kant, for whatever reason, left implicit. This is not to state, of course, that Hegel has been explicit about his intentions, but what he appears to have accomplished can be adjusted to our perspective. The identification of thought or truth with freedom in the Preface of the *Phenomenology*, written, as we know, after the work was completed and therefore from the standpoint of its result, is an assertion that the immanent closing off of knowledge is, paradoxically, a transcendent opening up. This may mean that philosophy is religion, and therefore Hegel at least had the courage to be blunt about what modern philosophers often only insinuated. But if this is how he is to be interpreted — the matter is disputed — it is significant that he called this final moment that of *Geist* ("spirit"), a notion owed, he said, to "modern religion." Strange that he would confess his indebtedness to religion at the moment he was, presumably, getting rid of it. Yet not so strange because the fact that our history can be regarded as a tale of philosophic-religious battles, with the tide of battle now turning one way, now another, indicates their mutual complementarity. If religion did not run the risk of an impossible transcendence, would it have given birth to a philosophy that brings us back to ourselves and a world to be created? Conversely, if philosophy were not in danger of falling into the absolute immanence of a fixated self-consciousness, it should have given up struggling with religion on the grounds that the only transcendence is that of knowledge.

The current attack on the premises or framework of modern philosophy has, expectedly, ruffled a few philosophical feathers and inaugurated a discussion among philosophers whose divergent allegiances have in the past prevented them from speaking to, much less comprehending, one another. Will this attack have further repercussions? Since the temper of modern philosophy, as we have indicated, was initially anti-ecclesiastical and subsequently anti-religious, is it not possible that an attack on its premises may instigate a new philosophy-religion debate? Those who believe that the announcement of God's death a few years back was only a belated notice have, if religious practice be a reliable guide, reason enough to be skeptical. Yet I find the idea enticing that perhaps philosophers plead the death of religion as an excuse for their unwillingness to enter into debate. Having given religion its quietus in the name of freedom, philosophers can find any number of pretexts for staving off a reincarnation or resurrection that might challenge their position as the new shamans. Presumably there is no challenge because ordinary people no longer believe; no one wants to bring back priests who control through "mummery and superstition." Face it, religion is dead. Perhaps religion is at fault because it has failed to present itself as the challenge it should be. But I find this reluctance to grasp the fact that basic human concerns are at issue — would religion have survived at all were it not vital to humanity? — at the very least disturbing. The debates of the past are no less appalling. We cannot expect thinkers to rise about their milieus. But the fact remains that Hume's supercilious reference to "superstition" and the arguments of his *Dialogues* attest his enthrallment to the picture of a mechanical god and his inability to argue with anyone who did not share his epistemology. He saw no need to defend his division of the "perceptions of the mind" into ideas and impressions. My point is not to enter into a discussion of Hume's epistemology — he is only an example — nor to engage those who continue to believe that he (and Kant) have sounded the death knell of religion for the rationally enlightened. Freud could have served as an example equally as well. For the fact is that neither was able to detect a serious challenge in religion, and that, certainly, seems to be the root of the problem.

The final chapter of E. R. Dodds' *The Greeks and the Irrational* is entitled "The Fear of Freedom." In its position, the chapter is evidently the climax of a book that was written to explain the breakdown of Greek rationalism. Yet the work, in its original form the Sather Lectures delivered at the University of California in 1949, was clearly meant to carry a message to its listeners. By hearing a bit of their history, would they escape the condemnation of reliving it? Needless to say, this breakdown has been the object of much speculation.

> But behind such immediate causes we may perhaps suspect something deeper and less conscious: for a century or more the individual had been face to face with his own intellectual freedom, and now he turned tail and bolted from the horrid prospect — better the rigid determinism of the astrological Fate than that terrifying burden of daily responsibility. Rational men like Panætius and Cicero tried to check the retreat by argument, as Plotinus was to do later, but without perceptible effect; certain motives are beyond the reach of argument.[17]

The point is made more forcibly in a summary passage.

> If future historians are to reach a more complete explanation of what happened, I think that, without ignoring either the intellectual or the economic factor, they will have to take account of another sort of motive, less conscious and less tidily rational. I have already suggested that behind the acceptance of astral determinism lay, among other things, the fear of freedom — the unconscious flight from the heavy burden of individual choice which an open society lays upon its members. If such a motive is accepted as a *vera causa* (and there is pretty strong evidence that it is a *vera causa* to-day), we may suspect its operation in a good many places. We may suspect it in the hardening of philosophical speculation into quasi-religious dogma which provided the individual with an unchanging rule of life; in the dread of inconvenient research expressed even by a Cleanthes or an Epicurus;

17. *Ibid.*, 246

later, and on a more popular level, in the demand for a prophet or a scripture; and more generally, in the pathetic reverence for the written word characteristic of the late Roman and mediæval times — a readiness as Nock puts it, "to accept statements because they were in books, or even because they were said to be in books.[18]

Although no circumstances are identical, humans have changed little over the centuries. The natural response to a storm is the search for a port. We have noted that Descartes' inquiry into certitude was inspired by the religious, intellectual and political upheavals — Montaigne's skepticism reflects the general rootlessness — caused by the Reformation. The debacle in religion heralded a period of increased conservatism: the doctrinal rigidity of the Council of Trent precipitated an equally firm Protestant reaction. The opponents knew clearly where they stood; their authorities had staked out their positions for them. Was it for the purpose of liberating us from these uncompromising adversary positions that modern philosophy delivered us over first to absolute Mind, then to unequivocal fact, and finally to the mechanical workings of a "transcendental unity of apperception" which, in the practical order, was weighted down by an irrepressible sense of duty? In contrast to the belief of "the vulgar," the philosophical or the enlightened had the security of their knowledge. In the political order, the teachings of the savants failed to bring about liberty, equality and fraternity. They did, however, produce "enlightened despotism."

Although often carried on with acrimony and, even more tragically, not carried on at all, I believe that the philosophical-religious warfare has been beneficial. In spelling out my reasons for this, I shall evoke once again some themes that have already claimed our attention.

By making the question of truth central, the philosophic-religious debate has highlighted our various usages of "true" and made us critical of the way we go about establishing its criteria. No one any longer pretends to be wholly objective. Already-out-there-now truths or those simply handed to us

18. *Ibid.*, 252.

never quite merit the ultimate human accolade: *known* as true. There is an objective or transcendent moment of truth, which philosophical empiricism recognized but exaggerated, because there is more to something's being true than the mere immanent knowing of it. Plato's soul safeguarded that moment without slipping into a multiplicity of subjective observational standpoints. But when philosophy was reduced to mere knowing and the old metaphysics was jettisoned because it was theological, the ties to a mysterious, ontological Absolute were cut. Above all, modern philosophy was intolerant of mystery. How can we be "in" truth without clearly comprehending it? The Absolute that knowledge requires is only an ideal, a postulate of intelligibility: something that in any case we determine which will provide us with norms for our truth. Obviously, the immanent had won out.

In contrast, in the last chapter I emphasized the contextual or dialogical nature of truth. Because we require different norms for different kinds of judgments, we have to be aware of the kind of communication or level of dialogue in play. But even there, the threat of conventionalism cannot, I believe, be satisfactorily rebuffed without a dialogue with religion. For it is the religious insight that it is human beings whose knowing attests that we are movements toward the Absolute: an insight that metaphysics kept alive until the day that our humanity and existence were stripped of mystery. Now that it has been acknowledged, at least by Heidegger, that language is the highest and everywhere the foremost of those assents which we human beings can never articulate out of our own means, we may be ready to resume that dialogue which, for all of its failures, nourished the human spirit continuously down the centuries.

From an historical standpoint, it seems more accurate to say that the struggles between philosophy and religion ended in a standoff that, in reality, was a put-off. Hence it has been the disputes within philosophy itself regarding basic human questions of knowledge and morals that have, on the rebound, clarified religion's role in the humanizing process. Philosophy has moved, it is commonly said, from a metaphysics of Being to one of Becoming, which I interpret to mean that we have gone from Being as absolute to Being as relational. It is not to our purpose here to rehearse all the problems of Greek philosophy and its Christian adaptations which underlie my rewording. I have already indicated my preference for translating Being as meaning. The absolute aspect of Being consists in a certain fixity of meaning. Words do change, but not overnight. Its relational aspect in that meaning is contextual. We fix meanings by our placements in different contexts. Consequently, the contribution of philosophy to the debate regarding truth can be summarized in the notion that, as relational, truth is a matter of Becoming. Even the important religious distinction of 'knowing' from 'believing' as contextual has likewise to be considered in the broader philosophy of Becoming.

The interesting feature of the work of contemporary philosophers in "going beyond" their modern forebears is that just as the moderns constructed a metaphysics of finitude out of our partial, phenomenal knowing, so our contemporaries view the becoming of meaning, of knowledge, of truth, as signs of our becoming. Although the word lacks currency, this new slant is a "metaphysics" of person. It emphasizes the dynamic, not the static. We are born with human nature; we become persons.

If the fear of freedom turned modern philosophy from a liberating quest to a doctrinaire and complacent Absolute Knowledge, it had the example of religion before it. We have seen that the basic religious insight, creation, is a revelation of awesome responsibility: one that poses a constant challenge because, although the world is God's, we are given no explicit instructions on how to go about creating it. Therefore religion is a drama of freedom and responsibility, of the tensions of independence and dependence, of a relationship in which one's self-understanding turns into that of being understood. Creation, in a word, reveals our personhood. This is a characteristic, as psychology tells us, that is developed only in response to others as persons and, as religion would teach us, only in a promise back to the one who is, in St. Augustine's words, more intimate to us than we are to ourselves. If the adepts in speculative religion have meandered through the corridors of the Absolute together with their philosophical brethren, fearful of the freedom that is their heritage and convinced that an apodictic moral imperative is to be found in Nature (which we share with the animals!) so that we are freed from the vagueness that surrounds the becoming of person, so be it. Only at this point let us hope that they will hear the philosophers recalling them to their transcendent, freeing role, and not shut their ears to what may appear the tempting Siren's voice.

CHAPTER VI

Religion's Challenge

... I have put forward the hypothesis that the proliferation of mutually incomprehensible tongues stems from an absolutely fundamental impulse in language itself. I believe that the communication of information, of ostensive and verifiable 'facts', constitutes only one part, and perhaps a secondary part, of human discourse. The potentials of fiction, of counterfactuality, of undecidable futurity profoundly characterize both the origins and nature of speech. They differentiate it ontologically from the many signal systems available to the animal world. They determine the unique, often ambiguous tenor of human consciousness and make the relations of that consciousness to 'reality' creative. Through language, so much of which is focused inward to our private selves, we reject the empirical inevitability of the world. Through language, we construct what I have called 'alternities of being'. To the extent that every individual speaker uses an idiolect, the problem of Babel, is quite simply, that of human individuation. But different tongues give to the mechanism of 'alternity' a dynamic, transferable enactment. They realise needs of privacy and territoriality vital to our identity. To a greater or lesser degree, every language offers its own reading of life. To move between languages, to translate, even within the restrictions of totality, is to experience the most bewildering bias of the human spirit towards freedom. If we were lodged inside a single 'language-skin' or amid very few languages, the inevitability of our organic subjection to death might well prove more suffocating than it is.[1]

IT should be apparent to the reader why I have chosen language as the model for religion. Steiner's theory describes the activity constitutive of *homo symbolicus*. When looked at in the round, language is not the simple thing it first appears to be. It bespeaks our mystery. Why is it that we refuse or go beyond communication as well as communicate? That we repose in silent immanence as well as reach out in verbal transcendence? That we live in a world that we prefer to be familiar yet construct others that shake off prosaic everydayness? That we hanker after an *esperanto*, an Absolute Knowledge of language, knowing that it would smother us in a stifling uniformity? Because we ourselves *are* symbols: a meeting place of contradictories that turn our lives, when lived to the full, into a dialectic of opposites. It is the tensions of our being that erupt in creativity. For most of our history the mystery of ourselves was explained and concealed in the expression *homo religiosus*. "Explained," because our world, the universe, was the product of divine creation; yet actually concealed because it defined us as beings-in-dialogue, engaged in creating a world not our own. Religion casts its spell of wonder on Steiner's words: "a dynamic, transferable enactment." By en-acting — entering into the Sacred — we effect the dialogue that constitutes us. Such, indeed, was the human self-concept for most of our history. The conviction of this book is that we must know that history, especially if we are to understand ourselves — particularly the relatively few of us who might be called Western Europeans — whose history, when measured in world-historical terms from the Neolithic Age until the present, is rather insignificant.

The intriguing feature of this history is the radical change in mankind's self-image: a change, we noted, effected in large part by thinkers who translated into philosophical form new religious attitudes. If the older philosophy represented an effort to make

---

1. *After Babel*, 473.

sense of the mysterious transcendence embodied in the notion of *homo religiosus*, the new, "modern" philosophy would rationalize the human experience of being in a world separated by sin from a holy, transcendent God. That is, in order for us and our world to become philosophically secular, they had first to become religiously profane. Like any other revolutionary change, this shift of perspective created an impressive array of slogans: "Rationalism," "Enlightenment," "Science," "The Progress of Human Nature," etc. No one could afford to resist the new trend without being branded a "despiser of the human race."

Since the suggestion that it was religion which gave impetus to the new "secularism" may touch a sensitive nerve, we shall explore the matter further, drawing on some of the themes we have already emphasized.

Because the Absolute, the Truth, which had formed the context for people's experience was disrupted by the Reformation, Descartes began his search for certitude within a fragmented part of his personal experience. His Cogito translated Luther's "Here I stand." It asserted the rights of an individual conscience over against the totality of world and others. The part no longer had meaning in relation to the whole because it was itself determinative of the whole. In the first of Descartes' *Regulæ*, we noted, it is the human mind that is the sun, the light or source of intelligibility. Methodologically, the stress was analytic, as we would expect from the founder of the analytic geometry. But this mode of procedure exposed Descartes to the criticism that his experience of the Cogito precluded him from giving a satisfactory account of his experience as a human being. Like his philosophical predecessors, Descartes spoke of body and soul, of intellect and will. But unlike them who could make these distinctions because they stood in a totality of experience, he could make only separations. Without an Absolute or whole that enables one to *dis-tinguish*, distinctions are juxtapositions. Thus the new philosophical approach was faithful to the new religious mentality. The Infinite is wholly other than, or in total "qualitative difference" from, the finite.

Descartes' starting point, though it highlighted the mind's critical role in the determination of truth, has had two fateful consequences. First, because its inspiration was the idea that we do not think "within" but in search of truth, he became the patron saint of the anti-religionists who sought to replace the ways of the old "superstition" with those of the new science. Tradition, accordingly, was degraded for today's truths are tomorrow's fictions. As a result, it has taken years of philosophical effort to restore the reputation of culture. To some degree, at least, culture has been rescued from the intellectual garbage heap and recognized for the positive contribution it makes. It educates by cultivating, that is, by providing us with tools for development, not by locking us up in a stifling prison. Second, because we had been freed from the truth of tradition, we could no longer be sure about the truth-instruments which that tradition had prized. And so philosophy became epistemology, an endless search for criteria that would guarantee our ideas and objects until it was realized that if the mind cannot be trusted, no other criterion will satisfy. Only mind can determine the supports that will bolster a faulty mind. And so, after a long detour, we are at length back to the position, common to religionist and secularist alike, that the world is worth investigating because there is something called truth. Our judgments as assertions of what we believe or know to be the case are definitive: not once-and-for-all "final" but stipulations made on the basis of rational criteria.

When we consider the ramifications of Descartes' attitude toward the body and his individualism, we can understand better why, despite all of his protestations of loyalty, the Catholic Church rejected his work as incompatible with its religious doctrine. By the time we get to Hume and Kant — for Hume, "our holy religion is founded on faith, not on reason" — the religious *animus* had abated somewhat. What we consider to be philosophy is the work of thinkers educated in the new trend of religion. With Kant we are back to the acknowledgment that thinking requires an Absolute. But because thought itself is a finite process, it is only a movement toward the Infinite which it never attains.[2] Hegel, we noted, was the last of the old

2. It is in this light that we should understand Kant's criticisms of the traditional arguments for God. Because he never *stood in* the Absolute, he could never appreciate being drawn to it by the dynamics of one's being. He could only understand the need for a whole if we are to *think* a part.

metaphysical tradition insofar as he rooted us in the Absolute. His dialectical moments are *moments*, distinctions that are not separations, because they are in and of the Absolute. But he was also an adherent of the new metaphysics: like the old insofar as the Absolute is the beginning and end of thought, but new insofar as the Absolute is not to be understood as an encompassing truth but as the freeing movement of thought. That is, the new metaphysics inaugurated by Descartes which described its task as a thinking "with a view to" and not "beginning from" truth ended on the note that truth was an endless quest and philosophy the *élan* of the chase. The attitude was captured a number of years ago by Sidney Hook in his collection, *American Philosophers at Work*. It implied that the old religion-philosophy debate was *passé*; the period formative of our intellectual era had been quietly put to rest.

> American philosophers, with some notable exceptions, no longer practice philosophy in the grand *tradition*, essaying wholesale views about the nature of man, existence, and eternity. Inspired by the results won in the sciences, they do not even practice philosophy in the grand *manner* but concentrate on the patient analysis of specific problems aiming at results which although piecemeal are more likely to withstand criticism.[3]

By a stretch of the imagination, and with the help of the modern reading of ancient philosophy, we are to conceive of ourselves as heirs exclusively of the Socratic, maieutic tradition.

In contrast, when we look at Plato in the round, we can lay claim to him as the instigator within our philosophical tradition of the religion-philosophy dialogue. His proposals for stabilizing and reforming religion, set forth in his last work, the *Laws*, have been summarized by Dodds as follows:

1. He would provide religious faith with a logical foundation by *proving* certain basic propositions.
2. He would give it a legal foundation by incorporating these propositions in an unalterable legal code, and imposing legal penalties on any person propagating disbelief in them.

3. New York: Criterion Books, 1956, 12.

3. He would give it an educational foundation by making the basic propositions a compulsory subject of instruction for all children.
4. He would give it a social foundation by promoting an intimate union of religious and civic life at all levels — as we should phrase it, a union of Church and State.[4]

Indeed, to catch the authentic voice of Plato, it appears as if we, too, must take the Eastern turn and be attentive to the Siren song, the "new primitivism" in music spoken of by Mellers.

> The whole problem of life resolves itself into this one question, "What are we to do with this soul and nature set face to face with each other, this Nature, this personal and cosmic activity, which tries to impress itself upon the soul, to possess, control, determine it, and this soul which feels that in some mysterious way it has a freedom, a control over itself, a responsibility for what it is and does, and tries therefore to turn upon Nature, its own and the world's, and to control, possess, enjoy, or even, it may be, reject and escape from her?" In order to answer that question we have to know, — to know what the soul can do, to know what it can do with itself, to know too what it can do with Nature and the world. The whole of human philosophy, religion, science is really nothing but an attempt to get at the right data upon which it will be possible to answer the question and solve, as satisfactorily as our knowledge will allow, the problem of our existence.[5]

Were the question of our nature and existence not relentless, we would never have experienced the philosophical and literary criticism of "alienation" that began with Marx and reached its climax in the "existentialist" years following World War II. The sharpest cultural critique of recent years has been fomented by the "results won in the sciences," which, as we know, have proved noxious because scientists, and apparently American philosophers imitating them, no longer "essayed wholesale views about the nature of man, existence, and eternity." "Humanity" went out because "specialties" were in; it was perilous to be a generalizer. But there were philosophical reasons that permitted

---

4. *The Greeks and the Irrational*, 219.
5. *The Synthesis of Yoga*, 397.

the thesis that we live in the midst of parallel, non-communicating cultures, scientific and humanist, to achieve notoriety. Kant popularized the notion that what we call the world is merely a collection of sense data which the mind organizes into objects. Knowledge, that is, begins in the passivity of reception and is effected through the creative or spontaneous activity of human intelligence. What an individual perceives, therefore, depends upon his or her formation, which means that tolerance is to be cherished above all virtues. Some people experience the world religiously, others do not: a situation that we are to envisage as similar to my preferring oceanography and your preferring the visual arts. Truth, accordingly, is an issue only within one's area of preference, for the truths of chemistry are irrelevant to the truths of music. Since we share no common experience, a uniformity of opinion can be effectuated only by persistent propaganda or by early indoctrination.

From our perspective, the importance of this epistemology is that it is based on the idea that there is nothing mysterious about us as human. The wonder, we said, that instigated Greek philosophical reflection was the fact that a finite, material being in its knowing has a spiritual experience. The Greek philosophers — nor would anyone else lacking the bias of empiricism — would never have understood Kant's starting point: the idea that perception is at bottom a passive reception of assorted sense data. What we perceive in a spiritual act is a thing whose unity enables us to distinguish its various sense components.[6] This was the point emphasized by Hegel in his re-working of Kant. Knowledge is the process of *Geist*, a spiritual movement, and perception is what the German word for it, *Wahrnehmung*, suggests: a taking hold of truth. This "taking hold" is the nub of the problem for it highlights the mystery of ourselves which the concept of *homo religiosus* had through the ages presented for

6. An interesting discussion of this matter is to be found in Gerhard Krüger's little book: *Religiöse und profane Welterfahrung*, Frankfurt/Main: Klostermann, 1973. At the end of the work (p. 93) he concludes: "*Geschichte is daher im Kerne immer Religionsgeschichte.*" ("History, accordingly, is always in its core the history of religion.") If, that is, we study history because we are interested in ourselves, we cannot avoid a decision concerning the kind of being we are.

reflection. But the whole impetus of the new religious movement was that we cannot take hold of the Absolute or Truth. The theologians would say that it was vouchsafed us in a gift, whereas the philosophers concluded that it was something we ourselves contrive. The new "metaphysics" was all efficient causality, not finality, which is another way of saying that we were not understood from the transcendent Truth that constitutes us and animates our activities but solely from our immanent character as makers of truth. This was the reversal of roles in explanation accomplished by the new philosophy. Kant spoke of teleology because human action requires purpose. He rejected the metaphysical notion of finality because that would have required him to think of us as symbols, as people whose spiritual nature both accounts for and transcends their material activity.

In a previous chapter we spoke of spirit as a liberating force, that power of transcending the limitations imposed on us by our bodies which enables us to become truly universal: a one in communion with others. For Kant, because we were no longer symbols, we had ceased to be spirits. Our ties to humanity were cut, for in the new currency of the Reformation, we were concretized individual consciences. Religion, a life "within the limits of Reason alone," was not a spiritual experience but a zealous observance of the precepts of the moral law. For many this transformation was not odd. Did not Luther's summons to the obedience of faith echo the legalistic preachments of the traditional clergy? Looked at from the pulpit, the spiritual life lacks the crispness of thundering do's and don'ts. Contemplated by the enlightened philosopher, it can only be a pattern for rational living.

I do not wish to imply that Luther himself would have conceived of a human being in any but spiritual terms. My point is that his message of reform transfigured a milieu. The detailing of religious abuses fed the fires of religious animosity. His insistence upon the rights of conscience heralded the new mood of individualism. Finally, when religion was conceived of as law, it shifted the relationship away from a spiritual emphasis upon "God and we" to the more legalistically accountable "God and me." Hence there were but two ways left to think "humanity":

either as Man written large or as a biological concept. It was this
latter notion that, regrettably, colored many people's thought
about the so-called Natural Law.

I have introduced Natural Law because the period of modern
philosophy, thanks to the individualism that stemmed from
heralding the rights of conscience and Descartes' Cogito, unleashed the forces of freedom — economic, political and social —
to which I have previously adverted. The era might fairly be
described as one of the rights of man, which naturally expressed
itself in the social and political philosophy that still forms the
mainstay of present day legal theory. *Taking Rights Seriously*[7] is, as
I shall indicate, an important issue both philosophically and
religiously. A brief discussion of it can serve to underline the
import of the new concept of what it is to be human. In a
nutshell, my argument is that when we ceased to be spiritual
beings, the mysterious unity that I have called a symbol, *humanity* lost its wonder. Wonder, of course, is basic to the attitude of
worship. Without it, talk about the dignity of man degenerates
into the empty rhetoric of causes. It is significant that during the
modern period humanity was not the issue. It was the rights of
man. The importance of this issue is evidenced in the following
commentary on the events that inaugurated the revolutionary
situation in Iran.

> We should not be surprised to find, therefore, that 'human rights'
> tend to become a cause of action only in the minds of people who
> have the historical consciousness through which to understand
> their local meaning. In the absence of that consciousness, the
> doctrine is felt merely as a kind of generalized anti-authoritar-
> ianism, a license to the individual to take no notice of obligations
> towards the state, and to ascribe legitimacy to almost any gesture
> of rebellion. The children of the Iranian middle classes who
> were sent to America for their education absorbed from the idea
> of 'human rights' only the ability to foreswear allegiance to es-
> tablished power. The influence of their 'education' spread

7. The title of a work by Ronald Dworkin (Cambridge Mass., Harvard
University Press, 1977) which represents a position on the nature of law critical
of the sophisticated positivism of H. L. A. Hart, exhibited, for example, in *The
Concept of Law.*

to their contemporaries at home, and was easily incorporated into old habits of vengeance. Young Iranians, having learnt how to disguise barbarity behind the Western dignity of 'student', proceeded to invade the 'natural rights' of the only American citizens weak enough to fall victim to them. And there is no arguing with them. Islamic law has always vested the exercise of criminal justice in the sovereign and so dispenses quite easily with a doctrine with what is 'natural' irrespective of place and time. It need make no room for the 'human rights' which, propagated by American liberalism, served merely to instruct the violators of right in the arts of injustice. Rebellion which has vengeance and not natural justice as its aim is a local affair, indifferent to the large metaphysical questions of the rights of man.[8]

So the Iranians are not part of our context. They have not grown up in a milieu in which one's strong sense of justice is nourished by constitutional guarantees that protect us against arbitrary State or mob power. Their history affords them no experience of American liberalism. But would their behavior have been the same had any exposure they might have had to the "large metaphysical questions of the rights of man" been to those in the old tradition of metaphysics and not in the new? Because this question returns us to the theme I have been developing, I shall try to clarify it without delving into the whole history of natural law theories.[9]

In contrast to what developed in the modern period, medieval natural rights theories were rooted in the ecclesiastical, Canon Law. The setting was Christendom, so that any discussion of rights did not prescind from evangelical precepts.

Ecclesiastical law was of course greatly concerned with general questions of welfare: in the Church, Europe had an institution unprecedented in the Roman world in that it was actually designed (at least in part) for charitable purposes. It is not surprising

8. Roger Scruton, "Viewpoint," *Times Literary Supplement*, March 14, 1980, 291.

9. The reader interested in a rather dry but informative study might consult Richard Tuck's *Natural Rights Theories: Their Origin and Development*, Cambridge: Cambridge University Press, 1979.

that a theory about rights as claims should have evolved from within an institution which was so concerned with the claims made on other men by the needy or deserving.[10]

Until the time of Aquinas, the philosophy in Western Europe energizing theological thinking was, thanks to St. Augustine, principally Platonic. That philosophy revolved around the lofty ideals of Truth, Justice and Good: abstractions, perhaps, but noble ideals which lend a philosophy its particular tonus. In the new age of the individual, Aristotle became preponderant. As the great expositor of the syllogism, he was interested in the interplay of universal and particular, so that his discussion of justice, defined as a proportionate giving to each his due, was largely taken up with equity. His late Renaissance revival — in an "authentic" Aristotelianism that was anti-Aristotle in terms of the Scholastic use of him — accompanied the challenge to the Roman ecclesiastical institution made in the name of the rights of conscience: a challenge which inevitably spilled over into the political realm.

> Much more could be said about the relationship between Protestant resistance theories of the period 1540–80, and the humanist legal theories of the period 1510–30; but it is enough for my purposes to stress that the Calvinists were not putting forth a theory of natural rights, and indeed were not particularly concerned with the notion of right at all. Like the humanists, specific constitutional remedies were at the focus of their concern. If we are to understand the developments in rights theories during the sixteenth and early seventeenth centuries, then we must group the Calvinist theorists with such men as Alciato, and see them all as engaged in a retreat from the position where the natural law and natural rights enjoyed primacy to one where the major concern was human law designed by men for common utility either under their own initiative or under the command of God.[11]

This retreat from the natural to the positive or human law was, in our perspective, inevitable. It was in keeping with the individualistic spirit of the times that the concept of humanity

10. *Ibid.*, 15.
11. *Ibid.*, 43–4.

should recede into the background, with the result that "natural" took on a different meaning in 'the new metaphysics. "Natural" was what was opposed to the spiritual. It emphasized that the force binding mankind together was neither an experience of the Sacred nor a community of thought or understanding. Along with the new mechanical science in which Nature was the concatenation of laws that regulate us, the natural law became basically a biological concept. Its prescriptions were either ordinances read off our bodily members: lying is wrong because the tongue is made for communication, or such regulations as were necessitated by the fact that, like most of the higher animals, we live in a herd. In one case the "large metaphysical questions of the rights of man" were trivialized into an assignment of bodily functions — the "natural law theory" I was taught entailed a whole treatise on sexual morality derived from the reproductive purpose of sex organs[12] — and in the other the common good that was supposedly promoted was reduced to a series of enactments to prohibit us from scratching one another's eyes out. Obviously, I do not believe that the separation of law from morality which characterizes our society springs from the need to be tolerant in a pluralistic situation. On the contrary, when we were no longer symbols, our spiritual achievements lay beyond the scope of natural, "human" legislation. Our proscriptions of murder, theft and the like are based on animal togetherness, not on considerations of humanity.

I may be wrong, but I suspect that for many people "human dignity" has more to do with inviolability, the right to be left alone to "do one's own thing," than with "large metaphysical questions." Given the character of human beings, we can detect the *religious* premise that underlay Jimmy Carter's campaign for human rights. We can understand, too, why that campaign

12. Although I have no idea what he actually means because his statement is unexplicated, I can understand what John Ladd ("Law and Morality: Internalism vs. Externalism," in *Law and Philosophy: A Symposium*, Sidney Hook, ed., New York: New York University Press, 1964, 63) may mean because of this caricature of the natural law: "Like many other philosophers, I find the natural law theory objectionable on metaphysical and epistemological grounds." I would suspect that his "epistemological" tells us what we must understand by "metaphysical."

fizzled. The rhetoric of rights is everywhere a political asset. The large metaphysical, and thus religious, questions that save it from vanity await the day when the philosophers have finished demolishing the premises of modern philosophy and the philosophy-religion dialogue has recommenced. For the unabated irony is that all of us know — the history of East and West is too much a part of us — that we cannot rely on human benevolence, the State or any kind of human legislation to guarantee our rights. For this reason, legal theorists like Dworkin are casting about for new foundations. But having rejected legal positivism, they are not quite ready for "metaphysics." Their ideas of that field are "modern," and they are still convinced that the repute of the law stands or falls with its being a science. Perhaps the problem of "judicial activism," — are judges legislating instead of interpreting the law? — will open some eyes to the concept of the human presupposed in contemporary jurisprudence.

Because we are involved, as Sri Aurobindo clearly saw, with the problem of our existence which transcends any immediate ideological battle over rights, the point at issue merits some repetition. The question of rights is important not merely because of contemporary relevance. It brings into focus the basic question: What does it mean to be human?

Legal positivism is the creation of modern philosophy. Those who espouse it deny one of the following claims: "(1) there is a natural moral order, (2) that natural moral order is accessible to human understanding, and (3) the concept of law must be understood by reference to a natural moral order."[13] Everything, obviously, hinges on the idea of "natural." What I have suggested is that during the period when the religious trend was to exalt divine transcendence in order to stress the gift-character of salvation, the natural came to mean the unregenerate or sinful. Because our spiritual existence was of the order of grace, we were "naturally" physical beings, parts of Nature. In short, because we were no longer "by nature" symbols, the complex of ideas that underpinned the old idea of natural law crumbled.

13. Thomas Morawetz, *The Philosophy of Law: An Introduction*, New York: Macmillan Publishing Company, 1980, 38–9.

The doctrine that there are "human" (which is to say "universal") rights has its antecedents in medieval theories of natural law, according to which there are principles of justice which preside over the affairs of men independently of the local practises which have achieved the status of law. Authority is useless without power, but the Church gave enactment to the authority of natural law, by exerting international influence. Right and might did not diverge; moreover, each seemed to stem from a single divine origin, so that the first neither concealed nor distorted the second. The question whose interest was advanced by the observance of natural law did arise, but it never led to the rejection of the doctrine. When sovereigns were able to break from Rome it was because they had acquired national churches, and a common law which enshrined those principles of natural justice that had formerly been the property of an international Church. Such sovereigns appeared to be constrained, not by an external power, but by the conditions of their legitimacy. And still the same "natural law" was used to denote the authority which interceded between sovereign and subject.[14]

Although the natural law did not die with the Reformation — for religion itself did not succumb, and the idea that society is conditioned by universal principles of justice or morality is a religious concept — its life line had been cut. When God became wholly transcendent, alien from a sinful world except through a condescending gift, the door for philosophy's "natural" consideration of the world was opened. It was opened wider by the wars of religion, which convinced the hostile *philosophes* of the need to separate right from might. Obviously the conditions of society had changed because we as human beings no longer stood in the Truth, the Absolute. If we were symbols, spiritual as well as material, it was by choice, not by nature.

By design I use the word "choice" because the new mentality proclaimed itself to be a liberation from the old. Henceforth freedom was to be the condition of rationality, whereas formerly people had considered themselves free because they were rational. I have called this latter the traditional rather than the old view because 'old' can connote outmoded or antedeluvian. In

14. "Viewpoint," 291.

that event, a dialogue of contrasting viewpoints is doomed to failure aforehand. Moreover, 'traditional,' suggesting involvement in a history and the 'handing on' that is essential to cultural formation, is more consonant with the comparison of religion's mythic functioning to language. In language learning we take on a group's logic, a system of coherence that enables us to understand ourselves and our world and to develop that understanding through communication. Were this learning mere reception, then rationality would preclude freedom. But because reception is also a spiritual undertaking, a spontaneous act that is creative of meaning, we open ourselves to new and untried dimensions of thought and action. Thus our self-awareness is an act of unification accomplished through community.

We have seen that this insistence on the tradition that we stand in the Truth, the Absolute or the Sacred expresses a religious conviction, the mystery of creating a world about us that belongs to God. The standpoint, which is the basis of the "contextual" discussion of truth in Chapter IV, was productive of great achievements through countless ages of human history. In the past we found it convenient to ignore or dismiss other civilizations, prehistoric and historic, Eastern (Chinese) and Western (Mayan). Was it because we preferred to think that everything great in the modern world stems from Western Europe? Or was it because we have been led to believe that religion has inhibited scientific development? The more our archæologists uncover, the less complacent can we be. What is the meaning of Stonehenge? Of the monuments on Eastern Island? Not only do we stand in awe of the minds that conceived and the artisans who executed the intricacies of the cathedral of Chartres, but we now know that neither our natural science nor mathematics was a seventeenth century creation. Our modal logic was a late discovery because we ignored the medievals. The great literary renaissance of the fifteenth century is now recognized to be a continuation of the classical revival of the twelfth.

It is religion, I am convinced, that in the West brought about the change in mentality and thus contributed to its own demise. How could the protagonists of the Reformation stand in the Truth when they proceeded to divide the world on the basis of who possessed the truth? Philosophically, the great mistake was to have so emphasized divine transcendence that the philosophers could lay claim to the world as the exclusive domain of *knowledge*. But in doing so, they were, willy-nilly, living off their religious heritage: a fact that Kant made explicit by calling the final goal of thought "God." This, of course, is the irony of the whole philosophy-religion debacle.

> But one will have understood what I am driving at: our faith in science still rests upon a metaphysical belief. We, the godless and anti-metaphysical scholars of today, even we, I say, draw our flame from the fire which the belief of a thousand years has enkindled — from that Christian faith which was Plato's too, the belief that God is the truth and that the truth is divine.[15]

I fear that many philosophical readers of Nietzsche may interpret this passage as no more than a theological statement that the final word belongs to religion. But I am inclined to think that Nietzsche had more perspicuity than that. He acknowledged the spiritual character of our knowledge: that perception, as I have indicated above, quâ unifying activity, transcends the material conditions of sensation. We are, therefore, basically spiritual beings. Our pursuit of truth indicates what we are because of what truth is. This, I said, has been the point of departure for Western philosophy and inspired its metaphysics. It is the fundamental fact about ourselves that cannot be ignored.

> The essential element of our proposal is to show that the *problem of atheism* is actually the *problem of philosophy* itself. There is, of course, the question whether one affirms or not the existence of God. But prior to that judgment is the far more questionable issue of *philosophy's understanding of itself*. Moreover, one can add immediately that the problem as posed is that of man's understanding of himself.[16]

15. *Die Fröhliche Wissenschaft*, para. 344. A readily accessible translation of "The Gay Science" (now "The Happy Science") can be found in Walter Kaufmann's *The Portable Nietzsche*, selected and translated with an introduction, prefaces and notes, New York: The Viking Press, 1954.

16. Jean-Yves Jolif, "Remarques sur la signification philosophique de l'athéisme" in *l'Existence de Dieu*, Tournai: Casterman, 1961, 13.

To picture our standing within the Truth or Absolute as a positioning of ourselves within a once-and-for-all system of truths is a travesty. Perhaps it was this image or something like it that roused Voltaire's Gallic temper, for the cataclysm of the Reformation had made *statements* of belief the touchstone of orthodoxy. Regrettably, too, many religious people confirm the parody. But the fact that the imagination can, to wrench Auden's striking figure out of context, commit "promiscuous fornication with its own images"[17] need not lead us to suppose that we are intellectually committed at the outset to any more than an honest investigation into the meaning of being a spirit.

For us, two things of significance follow from that starting point. First, "spirit," as I have characterized it previously, is an impulse to the universal: the force within us that compels us to overcome those temporal and geographical limitations imposed upon us by our bodies. Accordingly, to begin with it is not a setting out from a Cartesian Cogito. It is, precisely, a beginning within the realm of spirit: the standpoint of the universal that circumscribes the particular, of the individual that is truly *in-dividuum*, undivided from others. Interestingly, contemporary biology has made this starting point again intellectually respectable. What is important biologically is the race, the gene pool, not the truncated or deviant individual. In biological terms, it is my genetic inheritance that is determinative of my individuality.

Second, since we are not just spirits but also symbols, there is an unbroken continuity between the highest forms of our æsthetic activity and our biological inheritance, "between art," as Schiller observed, "at its most sophisticated and . . . 'material' play."[18] Can it be that those who criticize the symbolization of religion as inspired by magic and conducive to idolatry fail to see its parallel with the visual arts and music?

> The religious symbol is not a sign that merely indicates the divine
> being to the believer. Rather, the deity is directly present *in the*

17. W. H. Auden, "For the Time Being," in *Collected Longer Poems*, New York: Random House, 1969, 182–3.

18. Elizabeth M. Wilkinson and L. A. Willoughby, *Friedrich Schiller: On the Æsthetic Education of Man*, in a series of letters. Edited and Translated with an Introduction, Commentary and Glossary of Terms, Oxford: at the Clarendon Press, 1967, clxxxvi–vii.

symbol, is one with it and is also directly beheld in the symbol by the believer. The believer in the presence of the symbol does not *think* of his god; he does not associate religious *feelings* with the image — association does not enter in at all, otherwise religious experience would be learnable — he apprehends his god in the symbol in a direct perception. He cannot but see him there. Great as the difference between musical tone and religious symbol may be, in this one essential point they are alike: in both, a force that transcends the material is immediately manifested in a material datum. In this very special sense, then, we can speak of the tones of music as dynamic symbols. We hear forces in them as the believer sees the divine being in the symbol.[19]

"See," is open to misinterpretation. But the important point is that we understand the dynamism of religious symbols: what Eliade called the paradox of the coming-together of the sacred and the profane which "remains *the* cardinal problem of any religion."[20] We have already described these comings-together as enactments, for through them the human spirit experiences its reality. It enters into the fullness of spiritual existence.

The underlying conviction of this book is that because spirit is universal, the achievement of the fullness of human existence, which for religious people is the mandate of creation, cannot be realized without dialogue. Dialogue, of course, is predicated on the idea that truth is one, that it cannot be philosophically, religiously, politically and socially compartmentalized. Hence the two great religious traditions that have developed in the West must enrich each other for they exhibit complementary aspects of the message of the Hebrew prophets: in Christianity, God's enduring love for mankind witnessed in its redemption by Jesus; in Islam, the continuation of divine salvation through the establishment of a just and honorable society. Is it not obvious that either faith without the other produces a monster? Indeed, now more than ever the upholders of the monotheistic tradition are in urgent need of dialogue. Is that God's message of love and justice to be drowned out by the screeching of bombers and the

19. Victor Zuckerkandl, *Sound and Symbol. Music and the External World*, translated from the German by Willard R. Trask, Bollingen Series XLIV, New York: Pantheon Books, 1956, 69.

20. *Patterns in Comparative Religion*, 29.

explosions of mines and mortars in the troubled land of these great prophets?

Throughout this work I have noted that the different emphases within Christianity are the results of controversy. Nothing religious in the West since the time of Jesus has had more repercussions than the Reformation. We have returned many times to the significance of its stress on divine transcendence: a laudable effort to highlight the gift-character of salvation by juxtaposing an all-holy God to a sinful world. But as I have frequently reiterated, that effort has had undoubtedly fateful consequences. The myth of Genesis, the story of the mystery of creation, offered believers a God-Man-World pattern: a framework for an understanding of our place in the general scheme of things. That account and others like it attest how human beings for ages experienced themselves. Suddenly, however, God became "wholly other," separated from us and our world, and the door swung open to a thoroughgoing secular philosophy. What had previously been experienced as a movement of religious transcendence became a moment in the philosophical explanation of cognition. Henceforth mankind was to live a life devoid of mystery, and mystical experience. The reaction within Roman Catholicism was to draw hard-and-fast lines that would keep the faithful from being swallowed up in the tide of immanence. Pantheism, as represented by Spinoza's *Deus sive Natura*, was targeted as the principal snare for the unwary intellectual. Naturally, the pantheistic sounding language of ecstatics put them under a cloud. The touchstone of orthodoxy seemingly became the ability to maintain clearcut distinctions between real and symbolic, myth and reality, nature and supernature, reason and revelation. Surely one could be excused for entertaining the doubt whether anything of the mystery of creation was left.

Today finally, in some circles at any rate, we have moved away from our highly touted rationalism. The turn to the East betrays a hankering for the ecstatic element of religion. Or perhaps it manifests the need to balance Western transcendence with Eastern immanence: an appreciation of God's holiness with an insight into his continuous working throughout creation. In the West we were hitherto ordered to choose between God and

Reason. The East, by contrast, would ˙counsel us to choose Reason in God.

But even if, under the pressure of wars and other inanities, we have forsaken philosophical rationalism, are we still clinging to the image of ourselves the rationalists contrived: that of a Mind standing over against the world?

> Your moderate attempts to construct a moderate nihilism do not seem destined to long life . . . What awareness can you have of this universe, on which you have based your unanimity, and which you call reality? . . . The history of the psychological life of Europeans, of the new Europe, is a record of the invasion of the mind by emotions which are made chaotic by their conflicting intensities. The image of all these men dedicated to maintaining an idea of Man which allows them to overcome their thought and live, while the world over which this Man reigns becomes each day more foreign to them, is doubtless the final vision I shall take away from the West.[21]

Malraux' vision is crucial. What idea of Man are we maintaining, that of the old metaphysics or of the new? One in which we are part of the larger mystery of God and world or in which we are the be-all and the end-all?

For Christians, the central question of the Gospels is still: Who do you say that I am? If Jesus was the stumbling-block to the Jews and scandal to the Gentiles that Paul described, was not the mystery of his person foreshadowed in creation itself? "One might even say," with Eliade, "that all hierophanies are simply prefigurations of the miracle of the Incarnation, that every hierophany is an abortive attempt to reveal the mystery of the coming together of God and Man."[22] That first coming together has in almost all religions been narrated in creation stories; its memory has been the task of religion to preserve. Religion has accomplished this throughout our history by presenting *homo religiosus* as *homo symbolicus*: man the symbol because he is himself the place of encounter. The purpose of this work has been to

---

21. *The Temptation of the West*, Eng. Trans. Robert Hollander, New York: Random House, 1961, 97–8.

22. *Patterns in Comparative Religion*, 29.

present some of the difficulties of its task that have confronted religion in the West. Our religion gave birth to an angry child, modern philosophy: a philosophy that now appears willing to smother its anger and, in its newfound maturity, even pry into the grounds of its hostility. For if the Enlightenment call to Reason has become faint because of the kind of world it produced, it is heartening that the heirs of the enlightened seem willing to concede that the call itself was shrill. We no longer expect the immanent to justify the transcendent. As knowledge, it cannot even justify itself. Hegel started us thinking in that direction; more recently, Heidegger has encouraged us to persevere. Indeed, is not the mystery of our creating and shaping a world that is God's evidenced in the fact that once more we can *think* the possibility that perhaps it is the Transcendent that justifies the immanent?

Epilogue

Having completed the writing of this book, I picked up my friend Karl F. Morrison's recently published *The Mimetic Tradition of Reform in the West.*[1] Understandably, I read his book in the light of my own preoccupations and thus welcomed its historical focus upon an important strategy of organization that corroborates my philosophic-religious concentration. "Conversely," we read in his Appendix,

> there are non-mimetic and anti-mimetic habits of thinking about history, and the first point I must register here is that the place that mimetic theories of history played in the evolution of Western culture may well have been obscured in recent times by a widespread hostility to integrative theories of human experience.[2]

Prof. Morrison's book pays more attention than mine to cultural continuities. As an historian, he emphasizes the reform aspect of revolutionary movements: their indebtedness to the very patterns of thought that they seek to undermine. We all stand, it has been said, on the shoulders of the giants who have preceded us. To the contrary, while not ignoring these continuities which are imbedded in the traditional philosophical vocabulary — my reference, accordingly, to the "old" and "new" metaphysics — I have been at pains to stress the discontinuity that comes to light in the "widespread hostility to integrative theories of human experience." We are dealing, I have maintained, with how we perceive ourselves as human. Does

1. Princeton: Princeton University Press, 1982.
2. *Ibid.*, 400.

human life stand in need of commanding images that guide and direct thought and action? Ancients and medievals so experienced themselves, and their reflective, philosophical thought abounds in terms like "form," "unity" and "order," as well as those terms expressive of order: "number," "hierarchy" and "measure." Prof. Morrison has provided us with a summary view of the idea of Reason that these terms encapsulate.

(1) The first was that the visible world reflected an invisible, rational order. It existed as a whole composed of many parts that, left to themselves, would have been mutually antagonistic. An archetypal reason drew the parts into a harmony of beauty and goodness, a vast continuum in which dissimilars were reconciled in a deep and universal similitude. (2) The formal disciplines of speculative knowledge recapitulated the order of nature and, therefore, the invisible order that it manifested. The continuity among things matched the continuum of knowledge. Man was the image of God in his reason. Imprinted in his mind were natural dispositions towards the archetypal virtues of beauty and goodness that informed the world and that were transcendent above it in the divine intellect. Thus, the formal disciplines for studying the material world were rooted in the very principles of cosmic order, and, by applying them, man could pass from the material world to its immaterial order, and beyond, from visible creatures to the invisible things of God. (3) Each person, and each generation, formed a link in the chain of knowledge by recapitulating and criticizing the received tradition. The continuum in things and knowledge also pervaded time. By this mimetic criticism of criticism, progress ensued in the arts and in sacred doctrine, a collective advance made up of the reflections of countless individual persons.[3]

In this work I have been concerned with the contrasting view presented to us by the classical modern philosophers, notably by Descartes and Kant. I have singled out these two thinkers because their works mirror in philosophical form the intellectual ferment of their times. Descartes stood at the cutting edge of post-Reformation thought; Kant rationalized the commitment

3. *Ibid.*, 240–41.

to the new science. Because both men were sensitive to religious issues, they compel us to re-think religion in the light of a changing world view. But since we, I believe, no longer share the religious animosity that developed during this period, we have likewise become increasingly skeptical of some of the premises relied on by the moderns, as well as of the lineage they constructed for the new metaphysics. Perhaps we are ready to experience ourselves afresh, that is, to question the criteria we use both to uncover our inmost selves and to describe and evaluate the world in which we find ourselves.

Bibliography

Only the principal works cited in the text have been included in this bibliography. Generally speaking, the readily available editions have been preferred.

Auden, W. H., *Collected Longer Poems*, New York: Random House, 1969.

Aurobindo, Sri, *On Yoga, I, The Synthesis of Yoga*, Pondicherry: Sri Aurobindo Ashram, 1965.

Basham, A. L., *The Wonder That Was India. A Survey of the Culture of the Indian Sub-continent Before the Coming of the Muslims*, New York: Grove Press, Inc., 1954 (1959).

Blanshard, Brand, *The Nature of Thought*, New York: Macmillan, 1941, Two Volumes.

Brown, Stuart C., ed., *Reason and Religion*, Ithaca & London: Cornell University Press, 1977.

Butterworth, E. A. S., *The Tree at the Navel of the Earth*, Berlin: Walter de Gruyter & Co., 1970.

Clark, B., *Whose Life Is It Anyway?* New York: Dodd, Mead & Co., 1979.

Cristofer, Michael, *The Shadow Box*, New York: S. French, 1977.

Dodds, E. R., *The Greeks and the Irrational*, Berkeley & Los Angeles: University of California Press, 1964. Copyright, 1951.

Dupré, Wilhelm, "Culture and the Meaning of God in Creation": a paper delivered at a conference on monotheism at Rome, November 18, 1981.

Eliade, Mircea, *From Primitives to Zen: A Thematic Sourcebook of the History of Religion*, New York: Harper & Row, 1967.

———, *Patterns in Comparative Religion*, Translated by Rosemary Sheed, Cleveland & New York: The World Publishing Co., A Meridian Book, 1963.

———, *The Sacred and the Profane. The Nature of Religion*, New York: Harper & Row, 1961. Copyright: Harcourt, Brace & World, 1959.

Garaudy, Roger, *From Anathema to Dialogue: A Marxist Challenge to the Christian Churches*, translated by Luke O'Neill, New York: Herder & Herder, 1966.

Head, Joseph & Cranston, S. L., eds. *Reincarnation: The Phoenix Fire Mystery.* An East-West Dialogue on Death and Rebirth from the Worlds of Religion, Science, Psychology, Philosophy, Art, and Literature, and from the Great Thinkers of the Past and Present, New York: Julian Press/Crown Publishers, Inc., 1977.

Hodgson, Marshall G. S., *The Venture of Islam. Conscience and History in a World Civilization*, Vol. I: *The Classical Age of Islam*; Vol. III, *The Gunpowder Empires and Modern Times*, Chicago & London: The University of Chicago Press, 1974.

Hook, Sidney, ed., *Law and Philosophy: A Symposium*, New York: New York University Press, 1964.

Hume, David, *A Treatise of Human Nature*, Reprinted from the original edition in three volumes and edited, with an analytical index, by L.A. Selby-Bigge, M.A., Oxford: at the Clarendon Press, 1955 edition.

Jensen, Adolf E., *Myth and Cult among Primitive Peoples*, translated by Marianna Tax Choldin and Wolfgang Weissleder, Chicago & London: The University of Chicago Press, 1963.

Jolif, Jean-Yves, "Remarques sur la signification philosophique de l'athéisme," in *L'Existence de Dieu*, Cahiers de L'Actualité Religieuse, no. 16, Tournai: Casterman, 1961.

Krüger, Gerhard, *Religiöse und profane Welterfahrung*, Frankfurt/Main: Klostermann, 1973.

Kübler-Ross, Elizabeth, *On Death and Dying*, New York: Macmillan & Co., 1969.

Leach, Edmund R., ed., *Dialectic in Practical Religion*, Cambridge: at the University Press, 1968.

Lévi-Strauss, Claude, *Mythologiques IV: L'Homme Nu*, Paris: Plon, 1971.
———, *Tristes Tropiques: An Anthropological Study of Primitive Societies in Brazil*, translated by John Russell, New York: Atheneum, 1964.

Lienhardt, Godfrey, *Divinity and Experience: The Religion of the Dinka*, Oxford: at the Clarendon Press, 1961.

Malraux, André, *The Temptation of the West*, Eng. trans., Robert Hollander, New York: Random House, 1961.

Mellers, Wilfrid, *Caliban Reborn. Renewal in Twentieth-Century Music*, London: Victor Gollancz, 1968.

Morawetz, Thomas, *The Philosophy of Law: An Introduction*, New York: Macmillan Publishing Company, 1980.

Morrison, Karl F., *The Mimetic Tradition of Reform in the West*, Princeton: Princeton University Press, 1982.

Munson, Thomas N., *Religious Consciousness and Experience*, The Hague: Martinus Nijhoff, 1975.

Nietzsche, Friedrich, *Gesammelte Werke* (Grossoktav Ausgabe), 2nd edit., Leipzig: Kroner, 1901–13. Readily accessible translations of *The Antichrist* and sections of *The Gay Science* in *The Portable Nietzsche*, selected and translated with an introduction, prefaces and notes by Walter Kaufmann, New York: The Viking Press, 1954.

Pears, D. F., ed., *The Nature of Metaphysics*, London: Macmillan, 1957.

Polanyi, Michael, *Personal Knowledge: Toward a Post-Critical Philosophy*, London: Routledge & Kegan Paul, Ltd., 1973. Copyright, 1958.

Ranger, T. O., and Kimambo, Isaria, eds., *The Historical Study of African Religion*, with special reference to East and Central Africa, London, Nairobi, Ibadan: Heinemann, 1972.

Index